Practical Usage of TSO REXX

T0184093

Springer
London
Berlin
Heidelberg
New York
Barcelona
Hong Kong
Milan
Paris
Singapore
Tokyo

Anthony S. Rudd

Practical Usage of TSO REXX

3rd revised edition

Springer

Anthony S. Rudd, BSc, MSc (Hons)

ISBN-13: 978-1-85233-261-7   e-ISBN-13: 978-1-4471-0755-2
DOI: 10.1007/978-1-4471-0755-2

British Library Cataloguing in Publication Data
Rudd, Anthony S.
  Practical usage of TSO REXX. - 3rd ed.
  1. REXX (Computer program language)
  I. Title II. Practical usage of MVS REXX
  005.2'62
ISBN 1852332611

Library of Congress Cataloging-in-Publication Data
Rudd, Anthony S., 1945-
  Practical usage of TSO REXX / Anthony S. Rudd. - - 3rd ed.
    p. cm.

    1. REXX (Computer program language) 2. Time-sharing computer systems I. Title
  QA 76.73.R24 R84 2000
  005.2'28—dc21   00-020844

Apart from any fair dealing for the purposes of research or private study, or criticism or review, as permitted under the Copyright, Designs and Patents Act 1988, this publication may only be reproduced, stored or transmitted, in any form or by any means, with the prior permission in writing of the publishers, or in the case of reprographic reproduction in accordance with the terms of licences issued by the Copyright Licensing Agency. Enquiries concerning reproduction outside those terms should be sent to the publishers.

© Springer-Verlag London Limited 2000

Softcover reprint of the hardcover 3rd edition 2000

The use of registered names, trademarks etc. in this publication does not imply, even in the absence of a specific statement, that such names are exempt from the relevant laws and regulations and therefore free for general use.

The publisher makes no representation, express or implied, with regard to the accuracy of the information contained in this book and cannot accept any legal responsibility or liability for any errors or omissions that may be made.

Typesetting: Camera ready by author

34/3830-543210 Printed on acid-free paper SPIN 10754897

Preface

The aim of *PRACTICAL USAGE OF TSO REXX* is to show the practical use of REXX in the OS/390 TSO/E environment. The book covers not only the basic language elements but particularly emphasises the expansibility of REXX. In addition to its use as a procedures language, one of the major uses of REXX is interfacing to and from other components. Consequently, the major part of this book is devoted to the interfacing aspects of REXX. The chapter on the programming interfaces includes a wide range of examples in Assembler, C (C++), COBOL, and PL/I.

This third edition of the book, previously titled *PRACTICAL USAGE OF MVS REXX*, has been revised to discuss the new REXX features introduced for the OS/390 TSO/E environment. It also includes two new chapters that cover the REXX compiler and provide a general discussion of the implementation aspects of using REXX as a programming language.

For historical reasons, the TSO/E REXX implementation uses the term MVS as synonym for the host operating system environment (e.g. OS/390 in this case).

At this point I would like to thank Detlef Insel for his help.

Table of Contents

1

Introduction

Please allow me to introduce myself ...

Sympathy for the Devil

Mick Jagger and Keith Richards

1.1 REXX BACKGROUND

REXX is IBM's Systems Application Architecture (SAA) procedural language. The name REXX is the acronym derived from **R**estructured **E**xtended E**x**ecutor.

A procedural language is a language used to create **procedures**. In simple terms, a procedure is a series of operating system commands together with any necessary control logic. REXX procedures are usually called **execs**, which are synonymous with **programs**. In this book, however, I use the term **REXX program** to refer to a program written in a conventional programming language (e.g. Assembler) that uses REXX services; such REXX programs provide language extensions for REXX execs.

Most operating systems have a simple language that can be used to write procedures; in OS/390 TSO/E (subsequently referred to just as TSO), this is the CLIST (command list) language.

Not only can REXX be used as a replacement for such a basic procedure language, but its powerful built-in functions allow it to be used for many general programming tasks (this is particularly true when the optional REXX compiler is used). Furthermore, with its expandability and its interfacing capabilities with other system components, REXX can be used as interface between components. For example, a REXX exec can use TSO facilities to allocate files and ISPF (Dialog Manager) to display panels. This can be compared to the use of JCL (job control language) statements in batch mode.

1.2 REXX CHARACTERISTICS

REXX is primarily an interpretive language, although a REXX compiler is now available for OS/390. The basic REXX language has a small number of **instructions** that are used to create executable procedures. These instructions can use REXX basic elements (expressions, etc.) and **functions**. OS/390 REXX provides two function libraries: the standard SAA functions (common to all platforms that support SAA) and functions particular to OS/390 TSO/E. Many of the standard SAA functions are concerned with string processing. These functions can be augmented with user-written (or third-party) functions that can be written in REXX or in a conventional programming language. Any statement that is not recognised as a REXX instruction is a **command** that is passed to the current host environment. Some host environment handlers are supplied as part of TSO/E REXX (e.g. TSO), whereas others are supplied with program products (e.g. ISPEXEC (Dialog Manager), DSQCIX (QMF Callable Interface)). Other host environment handlers may be supplied with third-party products or be user-written.

The REXX language has several features that enhance programming:
· REXX has a small number of instructions that have simple syntax.
· REXX has a full range of structured programming constructions.
· REXX has only a single data type. All REXX data items (including numeric values) are strings. REXX data items are not declared.
· REXX is an interpretive language, although an optional compiler is available. Compared with compiled languages, interpreted languages are generally easier to write and debug.
· The powerful PARSE instruction and many built-in functions make REXX well-suited for text and word processing applications.

The expansibility of REXX and the availability of open interfaces may it eminently suitable for use as scripting language for applications. Many IBM products use REXX as their script language.
One of the basic design criteria of REXX was to make it an easy language to use, even though this did not always simplify the implementation.

1.3 REXX APPLICATIONS

Because REXX implementations exist on most hardware and software platforms, it is easy to port applications. Similarly, the absence of machine-related dependencies (precision of numeric values, etc.) eliminates many unexpected porting problems.

REXX is especially useful for tasks such as:
· a CLIST replacement
· the procedural logic to make an application from individual components
· prototype creation
· test data generation
· data manipulation (file reformatting, etc.)
· the integration of existing programs

· an interface to program products and applications (database access routines, application-specific file storage, etc.)
· a replacement for logic-based batch JCL (Job Control Language) procedures.

However, it is by no means limited to such tasks. REXX is not restricted to being used for small programming tasks, one organisation has over six million lines of REXX program code.

1.4 REXX'S FUTURE

The ANSI X3J18 committee was founded in 1991 to create a standard for the REXX language. Although even without a formal standard (other than that of M.J. Cowlishaw's book: *The REXX Language, A Practical Approach to Programming*, commonly known as *TRL*), the existing implementations generally have a high degree of compatibility, the presence of a standard should enhance the importance of the REXX language. An increasing number of products either use REXX as their command language or offer interfaces to REXX.

With regard to REXX, there have been two major recent developments in the OS/390 environment: the availability of a REXX compiler and REXX for CICS. In accordance with the trend to object-oriented application development, an object-oriented version of REXX (Object REXX) has been released, although not yet for OS/390.

2

REXX Facilities
The fatal facility of the octosyllabic verse.

The Corsair
Lord Byron

2.1 INTRODUCTION

To give the reader a feel for REXX, I will show a simple REXX procedure which I will extend to illustrate typical REXX features. The various concepts will be explained when they are first used.

The ubiquitous "hello world" C program in REXX is a single line:

```
SAY hello world;
```

The verb SAY is the instruction: write to display output. The two following operands (hello and world) are actually **variables** that have their (uppercase) name as default contents. The semicolon terminates the statement. So this statement would actually display HELLO WORLD. To display hello world, the text would have to be specified as a literal ('hello world') or a function used to convert the uppercase to lowercase.

Variables are not declared in REXX; they are implicitly defined with their first use. Variables are not only not defined, but they do not have any explicit type or length. REXX has a single data type: string. A variable can contain a string of any length (subject to main-storage restrictions). Numeric data have a maximum precision, by default 9, but can be set as large as required. This inherent use of variables as literals is bad programming practice that can lead to unexpected problems if a (literal) variable is inadvertently changed somewhere in the procedure. Hence the recommendation, only use explicit literals as alphanumeric constants. Because variable names must begin with an alphabetic character (or one of the three special character: ! ? or _), this restriction does not apply to numeric values.

Literals can be delimited by either single (') or double quotes ("), although for any one literal the introductory delimiter also must be used as terminating delimiter. Within a literal, the other delimiter is a normal character (e.g. "O'Brien" represents O'Brien). If the literal delimiter is required within the literal, it must be paired (e.g. 'O''Brien').

REXX variable names are case insensitive; ALPHA, alpha and Alpha represent the same variable.

Although REXX does not have explicit arrays, it does have **compound variables**, that can be used to represent arrays. A compound variable has a **stem** (a variable suffixed with a period, e.g. SALES.) and zero or more **tail** variables, each of which is separated with a period, e.g. SALES.YEAR.MONTH (SALES. is the stem variable, YEAR and MONTH are two tail variables).

The end-of-statement semicolon at the end of the statement is usually optional. End-of-statement is implied at the end of the line, unless statement continuation is implied or explicit. A comma specifies explicit continuation. Implicit continuation occurs when required by the syntax, for example, a THEN clause must follow an IF clause. The end-of-statement delimiter is required if more than one statement is written in the same line.

OS/390 provides two procedure languages: CLISTs and REXX procedures. By default, CLISTs are in the SYSPROC library and REXX procedures are in the SYSEXEC library. If REXX procedures are in a CLIST library, they must be explicitly identified as being REXX procedures (a **comment** as the first statement identifies a REXX procedure). It is in any case good programming practice to identify the procedure with an introductory comment. The /* and */ character-pairs introduce and terminate a REXX comment respectively.

Consequently, our hello world REXX procedure would have the form:

```
/* simple REXX procedure */
SAY 'hello world'
```

This sample procedure can be generalised by requesting the name from the user. It is good programming practice to explicitly prompt when user input is required, otherwise the program will appear to be in an endless loop. As above, the SAY instruction is used to prompt for the user's name, e.g. SAY "Please enter your name".

The PULL instruction gets input from the operating environment. In the TSO environment, this is the REXX queue or from the terminal if the REXX queue is empty.

The statement pair

```
SAY "Please enter your name"
PULL varname
```

would prompt for input and place the returned name in the VARNAME variable. The PULL instruction is actually a shorthand version of the PARSE PULL UPPER instruction, i.e. the input is converted to uppercase when it is stored in the VARNAME variable. To preserve case, the PARSE PULL instruction must be used.

The processing could be further extended by asking the user to input his address. Because addresses often have a variable number of lines (house name, house number and street name, district, city, state and post code, country, etc.), it would be better to write a loop to obtain this information.

As in many programming languages, REXX has a DO instruction (in various forms, DO UNTIL, DO WHILE, DO FOREVER, incremental DO, unconditional DO) that can be used to control a loop.

In this case the incremental DO is the most appropriate; the increment number can be used in the line number prompt.

```
SAY "Please enter your address. Terminate with a null input."
DO i = 1 TO 9
   SAY "Enter address line" i
   PARSE PULL line.i
   IF line.i = '' THEN LEAVE
END
```

The DO statement as coded allows a maximum of 9 address lines. This number is arbitrary. The input address lines are stored in the LINE array (compound variable); the line number is used as index. If a null input line is entered, the LEAVE statement terminates the DO loop. The END statement terminates the DO block. DO-loops can be nested. An unconditional DO can be used where a single statement is expected, for example as a THEN statement.

To enhance code comprehensibility, and to reduce errors in nested DOs, REXX allows the control variable to be used in the associated END statement.

The DO block could then be coded as:

```
DO i = 1 TO 9
   SAY "Enter address line" i
   PARSE PULL line.i
   IF line.i = '' THEN LEAVE
END i
```

It is normally good programming practice to reduce the size of the mainline code as much as possible. REXX allows non-mainline code to be placed in callable routines. Such callable routines can be invoked as functions (with the routine name as function name) or explicitly with the CALL instruction.

Routines may or may not return a result. The RETURN instruction explicitly returns from a routine and must be used if a result (the RETURN operand) is to be returned. The result is the function return value; the RESULT special variable also contains the routine return value.

Routines are identified with the PROCEDURE instruction. In keeping with good programming practice, REXX exhibits data hiding: unless specified otherwise, variables in a routine cannot be accessed outside the routine. The EXPOSE keyword is used to identify global variables. In our case, the LINE. stem variable (and all the associated compound variables) needs to be exposed.

Our procedure could then be coded as follows:

```
SAY "Please enter your address. Terminate with a null input."
CALL GetLine
GetLine: PROCEDURE EXPOSE LINE.
DO i = 1 TO 9
   SAY "Enter address line" i
   PARSE PULL line.i
   IF line.i = '' THEN LEAVE
END i
RETURN
```

As it stands, this program has an error; the GETLINE routine would be invoked twice: directly with the CALL and by being dropped through to. To avoid this second unwanted invocation, an EXIT statement should be included before the routine definition. It is good practice always to place an EXIT statement before the routine definitions.

In the TSO environment, native REXX is often used with a host environment, for example ISPEXEC. In the sample program, the input data could be passed to ISPF for display. The ADDRESS instruction is used to set the current host environment, e.g. ADDRESS ISPEXEC. Commands that are not recognised as being REXX instructions are passed to the host environment. For example, "DISPLAY PANEL(PNO)" would invoke ISPF to display the PNO panel. Because REXX and ISPF have a common variable pool, there is no need to explicitly pass REXX variables to ISPF.

The complete sample program follows:

```
/* simple REXX procedure */
SAY "Please enter your address. Terminate with a null input."
CALL GetLine
ADDRESS ISPEXEC
"DISPLAY PANEL(PNO)"
EXIT
GetLine: PROCEDURE EXPOSE LINE.
DO i = 1 TO 9
   SAY "Enter address line" i
   PARSE PULL line.i
   IF line.i = '' THEN LEAVE
END i
RETURN
```

This small procedure illustrates most of the REXX features.

The rest of the chapter provides a detailed description of the REXX features.

2.2 REXX STRUCTURE

A REXX procedure consists of one or more **statements**. Statements themselves consist of **clauses**. Clauses consist of **tokens**. Tokens may be separated by zero or more blanks or one or more of the special characters. A **comment** is syntactically equivalent to a blank.

In general, a REXX statement is written on a single line that has an implicit end-of-statement delimiter at the end of the line (continuations, implied or explicit, are the exception). Similarly, a line contains a single statement, unless each statement on the line has an explicit end-of-statement delimiter (a semicolon).

Examples:
```
IF a > b THEN SAY 'OK';
```
This statement consists of two clauses: the IF-clause and the THEN-clause.

```
IF a > b
   THEN SAY 'OK';
```
This statement consists of two lines; the statement is implicitly continued after the IF-clause.

```
SAY a b,
c
```
This statement is continued explicitly (with a comma) onto the second line.

```
a = 1; b = 2
```
This line contains two statements.

2.2.1 Token

Tokens are the basic elements of a clause, which in turn form REXX procedure statements. There are several forms of token.

Example:
```
IF a >= b THEN SAY 'OK';
```
This statement consists of eight tokens: IF, a, >=, b, THEN, SAY, 'OK', and ; .

2.2.2 Literal String

A literal string is zero or more characters that are delimited by either a single quote (') or a double quote ("). There is no significance which form of quote is used, both literal strings are equivalent, although the same delimiter that is used to introduce a literal string must terminate the literal string. Within a literal string, the other literal string delimiter has the same significance as a normal character. If the literal string delimiter character is used within a literal, it must be paired; each pair represents a single character. A zero length literal string is a **null literal string**. Literal strings are case-sensitive. A literal string has a maximum length of 250 characters. Literal strings are constant. Hexadecimal and binary literal strings are special forms of literal string.

Examples:

```
'literal string'
"O'Brien"
'O''Brien' /* also O'Brien */
'' /* null literal string */
"This literal",
"is continued"
```

The last literal string consists of two tokens; the comma serves as continuation. The data in a literal string is interpreted as character data, i.e. has its native code. A series of literal tokens is processed as if each token is separated by a single blank, unless the special abuttal continuation operator (||) is used, in which case the literal string tokens are concatenated without any intervening blanks (irrespective of how many blanks are written between the original string tokens).

Example:

```
"part1" ||
"part2"   || 'part3'.
```

This is equivalent to: part1part2part3.

2.2.3 Hexadecimal Literal String

A hexadecimal literal string is a literal string that is suffixed with a x (or x). Only hexadecimal characters can be used within a hexadecimal string. A hexadecimal literal string has a maximum length of 500 characters.

Hexadecimal character digits consist of the following characters:
    0 through 9
    a through f (which represent decimal 10 through 15, respectively)
    A through F.
There is no distinction between lowercase and uppercase characters. Each hexadecimal character is stored as 4 bits.

If a hexadecimal literal string contains an odd number of hexadecimal characters, a 0 is prefixed at the start, i.e. hexadecimal literal strings are right-aligned to a character boundary. For readability, one or more blanks can be placed between hexadecimal-character pairs.

Examples:
```
'1234'x
'12 34'X
'abcde'X /* equivalent to '0A BC DE'X */
''X /* null string */
```

2.2.4 Binary Literal String

A binary literal string is a literal string that is suffixed with a B (or b). Only binary digits (0 or 1) can be used within a binary string.

If a binary literal string does not contain a multiple of 8 binary digits, 0s are prefixed at the start, i.e. binary literal strings are right-aligned to a character boundary. For readability, one or more blanks can be placed between groups of four binary digits.

Examples:
```
'1111 0000'b
'1111'B /* equivalent to '0000 1111'B */
''b /* null string */
```

2.2.5 Symbol

A symbol is one or more English alphanumeric characters (0 through 9, a through z, A through z) and the . ! ? or _ special characters. Symbols are case insensitive (lowercase characters are converted internally to uppercase).
   The meaning of a symbol depends on where it is used (syntax dependence).

Examples:
```
alpha
beta.gamma
Hello!
H2O
79
```

2.2.6 Numeric Symbol

A numeric symbol is a special form of a symbol that represents a numeric constant. A numeric symbol can be used in arithmetic expressions.

A numeric symbol can have four forms:
·   A string of numeric digits. This represents an integer.
·   A string of numeric digits, a decimal point, and a further string of numeric digits. This represents a decimal value.
·   A decimal value suffixed with the E (or e) character and a (signed) integer. This represents an exponential number. The E character denotes the power of ten; the following numeric value is the power. For example, E2 represents 10^2

($=100$) and E-2 represents 10^{-2} ($=0.01$). The exponent can have a maximum of nine digits, i.e. $10^{999999999}$ or $10^{-999999999}$, which is a very large number or small number, respectively.

· A string that starts with a period is equivalent to 0. and can be used in the previous two cases.

Examples:
```
79
12.34
1.23E+3 /* 1230 */
4.56E-2 /* 0.0456 */
0.123
.123
```

Note: E2 (for example) is not a number; to be a number it would have to be written as 1E2 ($=100$).

The **NUMERIC DIGITS** instruction sets the maximum precision (the maximum number of significant digits). The default precision is 9 digits, but can be set as high (or low) as required.

An excessive precision causes more storage to be used to store numeric values and increases the processing time. A precision that is too low can cause processing errors. A numeric symbol is constant.

A numeric literal string (but not a hexadecimal or binary literal, even if it resolves to a numeric EBCDIC value) can be used in arithmetic expressions.

Example:
```
NUMERIC DIGITS 2
SAY (1+100) /* 1.0E+2 */
```

Example:
```
x = 1 + '12'
SAY x /* 13 */
y = 1 + 'F1F2'x /* error */
```

2.2.7 Variables

Variables are non-numeric symbols. REXX variables have their uppercase name as initial value. Although this characteristic can simplify coding, it should not be used as it can lead to unexpected errors (e.g. a program change could use the 'pseudo-literal' symbol as a true variable). A symbol that consists only of alphanumeric characters or ? (and does not start with a numeric digit) is a **simple symbol**.

A **compound symbol** is a special type of symbol. A compound symbol has two parts: the **stem** that is terminated with a period, and an optional **tail**. The tail consists of one or more symbols, each separated with a period. Compound symbols can be used to represent arrays or associative storage. If a value is assigned to the stem, all elements of the compound symbol have by default this value (even those elements that do not yet exist).

The DROP instruction can be used to remove a symbol, i.e. return it to the NOVALUE status. The SIGNAL ON NOVALUE condition clause can be used to detect the use of non-assigned symbols (i.e. symbols with the NOVALUE status).

Example 1:
```
alpha = 1
beta = alpha
```
This is an example for simple assignments.

Example 2:
```
month. = 0 /* initialise */
month.1.rain = 30
month.2.rain = 25
month.march.rain = 20
```
One of the few exceptions using symbol names as constants. REXX semantics do not allow the use of literal strings as tails. However, care must be exercised, for example, if MARCH had the value 2, the assignment month.march.rain = 20 would replace the previous assignment month.2.rain = 25.

Example 3 (associative storage):
```
string = "the rain in spain"
count. = 0 /* initialise count */
j = 0 /* secondary index */
DO i = 1 TO LENGTH(string)
  c = SUBSTR(string,i,1) /* extract character */
  IF count.c = 0 THEN DO /* new entry */
     j = j + 1 /* increment secondary index */
     char.j = c /* store letter */
  END
  count.c = count.c + 1 /* accumulate */
END
DO i = 1 TO j
  c = char.i
  SAY c count.c /* display letter with count */
END
```
This procedure counts the frequency of the individual letters in the specified string. The CHAR. stem variables contain the individual letters, which are used to index the COUNT. stem that contains the count for the particular letter.

In this particular case, a simpler method (given the limited number of possible entries (the 26 letters of the alphabet)) would be to directly index the COUNT. stem without using the intermediate CHAR. associative array. However, this approach is not feasible when the entries that can occur are not known, for example, the word frequency in a book.

2.2.8 Operator

REXX has several special characters that are used as operators.

REXX has six types of operators:
·   prefix operators (+ - \ ¬)
·   arithmetic operators (** * / // % + -)
·   abuttal operator (||)
·   comparison operators (= > < >= <=) — also paired and negated
·   logical operators (& | &&)
·   implicit concatenation operators.

These operators are arranged in order of decreasing priority. Paired comparison operators mean "strictly", e.g. == means strictly equal. Operators that consist of more than one character must be written without embedded blanks, for example, > = is syntactically incorrect. All operators other than the prefix operators are dyadic, i.e. are right-associative and operate on two operands; the prefix operators are monadic, i.e. are left-associative and operate on a single operand.

Note: Non-English languages may have different representations for some non-standard operators. For example, the following German characters are equivalent to the shown operators (the appropriate hexadecimal value is shown in parentheses):

    ! | ('4f'x)
    ¯   ¬ ('5f'x)
    ö   \ ('e0'x)

2.2.9 Prefix Operators

Prefix operators operate on the following symbol. If more than one prefix operator is specified, they are processed from right to left (see Example 2).

REXX prefix operators:
    +   (no affect, present for symmetry with -)
    -     numeric negation
    \   logical negation
    ¬   logical negation.

Logical negation returns the following results:
    \0   1
    \1   0
The logical negation of a non-binary value (e.g. -1, 2) is a syntax error.

Example 1:
```
SAY (1 - -2) /* 3 */
SAY \(2 > 3) /* 1 */
```

In the second example, 2 > 3 is false (i.e. 0), the \ operator negates this false result (i.e. returns 1 (true)).

Example 2:
```
SAY -\\1 /* -1 */
SAY \-\1 /* 1 */
SAY \\-1 /* error (non-binary logical value) */
```
In the second example, 2 > 3 is false (i.e. 0), the \ operator negates this false result (i.e. returns 1 (true)).

2.2.10 Arithmetic Operators

Arithmetic operators are used in **arithmetic expressions** and return a numeric result. The setting for NUMERIC DIGITS determines the precision (default 9 digits).

List of REXX arithmetic operators:
**	exponentiation (power as integer value)
*	multiplication
/	division
//	modulo (integer) division (remainder)
%	quotient
+	addition
-	subtraction.

Examples:
```
2**3 /* 8 */
2**-3 /* 0.125 */
2 * 3 /* 6 */
17 / 3 /* 5.66666667 */
17 // 3 /* 2 */
17 % 3 /* 5 */
2 + 3 /* 5 */
2 - 3 /* -1 */
```

2.2.11 Abuttal Operator

The abuttal operator (||) concatenates two operands without any intervening blanks between the two tokens (any blanks in a token are retained). Also see implicit continuation operators.

Example:
```
'alpha' || 'beta' || ' gamma'
```
This example produces the string: "alphabeta gamma". The two blanks at the start of the third token are retained.

2.2.12 Comparative Operators

Comparative operators are used in **comparative expressions**; the comparison of two operands returns a binary (truth) value:

    0   false
    1   true.

Note: Binary arithmetic values also can be used in place of comparison expressions, e.g. as an IF-clause.

REXX has three basic comparative operators:

    =   equality
    >   first operand greater than the second operand; >= is greater than or equal
    <   first operand less than the second operand; <= is less than or equal.

The three basic operators can be paired to mean "strictly". For example, == strictly equal, >>= strictly greater than or equal.

    A comparison operator can be negated with a logical negation operator. For example, \= (not equal) — /=, <> and >< also can be used for not equal.

Complete list of REXX comparative operators:

    =   equality
    ==   strict equality
    >   first operand greater than the second operand
    >>   first operand strictly greater than the second operand
    >=   first operand greater than or equal to the second operand
    >>=   first operand strictly greater than or equal to the second operand
    <   first operand less than the second operand
    <<   first operand strictly less than the second operand
    <=   first operand less than or equal to the second operand
    <<=   first operand strictly less than or equal to the second operand
    /=   first operand not equal to the second operand
    <>   first operand not equal to the second operand
    ><   first operand not equal to the second operand.

A logical negation prefix operator (\ or ¬) can be used with a comparison operator to negate the condition. For example, \> means not greater than.

Examples:

```
1 > 2; /* 0 - false */
3 > 2; /* 1 - false */
12 = ' 12 '; /* 1 */
12 == ' 12 '; /* 0 (not strictly equal) */
```

2.2.13 Logical Operators

Logical operators operate on binary operands (an operand that has the value 0 or 1). The use of a logical operator with non-binary operands is a syntax error.

REXX has three logical operators:
      &   And
      | Or
      &&   Exclusive Or.

Logical operator truth table:
```
1 && 1 0
0 && 1 1
1 && 0 1
0 && 0 0

1 & 1  1
0 & 1  0
1 & 0  0
0 & 0  0

1 | 1  1
0 | 1  1
1 | 0  1
0 | 0  0
```

Example:
```
IF (two > one) & (three < four) THEN SAY "true"
```
The two operands are logical expressions, each of which evaluates true (1) or false (0). An AND is made on the two truth values, in this case 1 AND 1, which yields 1 (true); it is assumed that the four variables each contains the appropriate value (ONE = 1, TWO = 2, etc.).

2.2.14 Implicit Concatenation Operators

In addition to the explicit (abuttal) continuation operator, two strings not joined by a dyadic operator are implicitly concatenated with each other to form a new string. If the individual strings are separated by one or more blanks, the concatenated string has a single blank, otherwise the strings are concatenated without intervening blanks.

Example:
```
'The' 'rain'  'in'    'Spain' /* "The rain in Spain" */
'The'LEFT('rain')LEFT('in')LEFT('Spain') /* "TheraininSpain" */
'The' || 'rain'  ||  'in'   ||   'Spain' /* "TheraininSpain" */
```

2.2.15 Other Syntax Elements

Other syntax elements are the remaining REXX elements that do not belong to any of the previous categories.

2.2.15.1 Special Characters. Special characters (the operators and , : ; ( )) have syntactical significance. Together with blanks they delimit tokens.

2.2.15.2 Comment. A comment is zero or more characters written between the /* and */ character pairs (the **comment delimiters**). Except for the comment delimiters, any characters can be used in a comment. REXX comments can be nested, each /* initiates a further comment nesting level, which is terminated by the corresponding */. Comments can continue onto subsequent lines without being continued explicitly.

Example:
```
/* This is a simple comment. */
/* This is a comment
that is continued onto a second line. */
/* This is an outer comment /* this is an inner comment */ */
SAY word1/* comment as delimiter */word2
```
In the last statement, the comment separates two tokens.

2.2.15.3 Continuation. In general, a REXX statement consists of a single line. There are three exceptions to this rule:
· If the instruction syntax implies continuation (e.g. an IF-clause must be followed by a THEN-clause).
· A comment is not complete.
· The statement is continued explicitly with a comma.

Examples:
```
IF a > b
  THEN SAY 'OK' /* implicit instruction continuation */
c = 4 /* this comment
continues onto the second line */
SAY a b ,
  c /* explicit continuation */
```

2.3 REXX EXPRESSIONS

Most clauses include **expressions**. Expressions consist of one or more **terms** (literal strings, symbols, function calls, and subexpressions) that are connected by zero or more operators.

Terms:
- Literal string   Character string delimited by single or double quotes.
- Symbol   Symbols that do not begin with a digit or period (implicit 0) are names of variables. Non-initialised variables have the uppercase name as content.
- **Function call**   The name of a function that is immediately followed by parentheses. The parentheses can contain zero or more expressions (arguments), each of which is separated by a comma. After evaluation, the function result (if returned) is used in the expression.
- **Subexpression**   An expression enclosed within parentheses. The evaluated subexpression is used in the expression.

Expressions are evaluated from left to right after taking the operator priority and subexpressions into consideration. Innermost subexpressions are evaluated first, and then the next level, etc. Within an evaluation level, the highest priority operators are evaluated first, then the next priority, etc.

REXX is largely orthogonal, in that the terms used in expressions can themselves be formed from other terms, e.g. the result of a function call can be used in an expression.

Example 1:

```
SAY 34 / -(3 + 4 * 5 - 6) /* -2 */
```

The following processing sequence is performed:

```
1)      (3 + 4 * 5 - 6)
1.1)    4 * 5      = 20
1.2)    3 + 20     = 23
1.3)    23 - 6     = 17
2)      -17        = -17
3)      34 / -17   = -2
```

Example 2:

```
SAY 1 + LEFT(234,5,0) /* 23401 */
```

2.3.1 Arithmetic Expression

Arithmetic expressions are expressions formed using arithmetic operators. An arithmetic expression yields a numeric result string (possibly signed). The NUMERIC DIGITS clause specifies the precision of the result string (the default precision is 9 digits).

Example:

```
x = 1 + 2**3 + 4
```

2.3.2 Comparative Expression

Comparative expressions are expressions formed using comparative operators. Comparative expressions yield a binary truth result string (0 = false, 1 = true) that indicates whether the comparison was satisfied. Comparative expressions are usually used as conditional clauses (e.g. in an IF-clause), although any binary value could be used, similarly comparative expressions can be used in arithmetic expressions (see Example 2).

Example 1:
```
IF (2 < 3) & (3 |= 4)
   THEN SAY "Both true"
```

Example 2:
```
x = 20 + (2 < 3)
SAY x /* 21 */
```
The (2 < 3) comparative expression is true and so yields the result 1, to which 20 is added.

2.3.3 Logical (Boolean) Expression

Logical expressions are expressions formed using logical operators. A logical expression yields a binary result string (0 or 1).

Example:
```
x = (1 | 0) && (1 & 0) /* 1 */
y = (1 < 2) && (3 > 4) /* 1 */
```

2.4 STATEMENTS

Previously, **statement** has been used informally. As mentioned in Section 2.2, REXX procedures consist of statements. In REXX, a statement can be considered to be the smallest entity that has a semantic significance. In contrast, a clause evaluates to (or has) a (string) value, but has no explicit meaning. For example, the clause (1 < 2) evaluates to false (zero), but has significance only when used with an instruction (e.g. IF (1 < 2) THEN ...).

REXX has the following types of statement:
· instruction
· label
· command.

For completeness, a null statement is a special form of statement that consists only of blanks or comments.

Instructions can be classified into:
· keyword instructions
· assignment.

Keyword instructions have the form:
    keyword [clause]...
The keyword identifies the instruction. The keyword determines which clauses can (or must) be present. Keyword instructions are used for control flow, stack processing, parsing, debugging, external environment control (see command), etc.

An **assignment** has the form:
    symbol = expression
The evaluated expression is assigned to the symbol.

A **label** has the form:
    [symbol:]...
The symbol is the target for a CALL or SIGNAL instruction, or the name of an internal routine.

A **command** is a statement that does not fall into one of the previous categories. A command is passed to the current external environment processor (e.g. TSO, MVS).

TSO REXX supplies commands for purposes such as:
· file input/output (EXECIO)
· data stack services (NEWSTACK, etc.)
· procedure processing characteristics (EXECUTIL, HE, etc.).

In addition to these standard TSO REXX commands, users and third-party software providers can implement their own external environment processors. Environment processors are written in a conventional programming language (certain conventions must be met).

An **external function** is a function that is not contained in the procedure. External functions have some similarity to commands in that they can be used to extend the usefulness of the language. But whereas a command is a statement, a function invocation (external function or otherwise) is a term that is used in an expression. REXX offers the following types of external function:
· built-in functions
· TSO external functions.

The built-in functions are the external functions that are specified in the REXX language definition (e.g. ABBREV, ABS, etc.). The TSO external functions are a TSO REXX implementation extension that provides some TSO services for REXX procedures, for example, LISTDSI, OUTTRAP.

In addition to these standard REXX external functions, users and third-party software providers (or other IBM products, e.g. QMF) can implement their own external functions. External functions can be written in REXX or a conventional programming language (provided certain conventions are met).

2.5 INVOCATION OF A REXX EXEC

The invocation of a REXX exec depends on the host environment and on the particular implementation. Chapter 13 describes various methods of invoking a REXX exec.

2.6 COMPARISON WITH CLISTS

CLISTs (command lists) were the predecessors of REXX execs, but have been largely superseded through REXX's improved flexibility and power, and interfacing capabilities, etc. Where CLISTs still exist, it is usually for legacy applications.

This section eases the transition from CLISTs to REXX execs by showing the main similarities and differences between the two languages.

· REXX names (tokens) are variables, rather than literals as in CLISTs. CLIST variables are prefixed with an & (unless they are the target in a SET statement).
· CLIST statement data are processed at execution-time, which can lead to problems if the data contains CLIST syntactical elements (e.g., &'s or)'s).
· REXX can operate in both TSO and batch environments (IRXJCL), whereas CLISTs require TSO (although batch TSO in the form of the IKJEFT01 program is available).
· REXX offers a wide range of publicised interfaces, in particular command environments. There are only a limited number of CLIST interfaces to other products (notably ISPF and TSO). Many products, both IBM and third-party, offer REXX interfaces, both from the product to REXX, and vice versa.
· REXX has powerful parsing services. The PARSE instruction and a large set of related functions (POS, WORD, etc.) are available for string processing.

Because the REXX functionality is a superset of that offered by CLISTs, most well-structured CLISTs can be relatively easily converted to REXX execs (there are products that automate this conversion). However, because the CLIST goto statement has no direct REXX equivalent (the SIGNAL instruction can be used under some circumstances), such CLISTs may need to be rewritten.

3

REXX Processing Elements

The people are the most important element in a nation; the spirits of the land and grain are next; the sovereign is the lightest.

Works
Mencius

3.1 INTRODUCTION

The previous chapter described the fundamental REXX concepts. An executable REXX procedure consists of statements that are made up of clauses formed from these basic elements.

3.2 STATEMENTS

Previously, **statement** has been used informally. As mentioned in Section 2.2, REXX procedures consist of statements. In REXX, a statement can be considered to be the smallest entity that has a semantic significance. In contrast, a clause evaluates to (or has) a (string) value, but has no explicit meaning. For example, the clause (1 < 2) evaluates to false (zero), but has significance when used with an instruction (e.g. IF (1 < 2) THEN ...).

REXX has the following types of statement:
· instruction
· label
· command.

For completeness, a null statement is a special form of statement that consists only of blanks or comments.

Instructions can be classified into:
· keyword instructions
· assignment.

Keyword instructions have the form:
    keyword [clause]...
The keyword identifies the instruction. The keyword determines which clauses can (or must) be present. Keyword instructions are used for control flow, stack processing, parsing, debugging, external environment control (see command), etc.

Example:
    SAY 3 * 4 /* display 12 */

An **assignment** has the form:
    symbol = expression
The evaluated expression is assigned to the symbol.

Example:
    x = 4 * 5 /* assign 20 to X */

A **label** has the form:
    [symbol:]...
The symbol is the target for a CALL or SIGNAL instruction, or the name of an internal routine.

Example:
    funct:

A command is a statement that does not fall into one of the previous categories. A command is passed to the current external environment processor that is set with the ADDRESS instruction (e.g. ISPEXEC, MVS, TSO). The user can implement his own external environment processors.

Example:
    ADDRESS ISPEXEC "DISPLAY PANEL(pn)"

The REXX programming language has statements for:
· assignment
· structured programming constructions
· sequence control
· routine control and invocation
· error processing
· stack (queue) processing

· parsing
· debugging
· miscellaneous instructions.

3.3 ROUTINES

Zero or more REXX statements can be grouped together and assigned a name to form a **routine**. A routine can have one of three forms:
· function
· procedure
· subroutine.

These three forms of routine differ in how they can be invoked, whether they must return a result value, and whether they have access to variables outside the routine.

REXX has three kinds of functions:
· built-in functions
· internal functions
· external functions.

Built-in functions are the functions that the REXX language supplies. Although the user can define functions that have the same name as built-in functions, such functions must be internal functions. **Internal functions** are functions contained in the REXX exec that uses them. **External functions** are functions that external to the current REXX exec. External functions can be written in REXX or in a conventional programming language (e.g. Assembler) programmed in accordance with the specifications described in Chapter 14. A function (or routine name) written as an explicit literal (i.e. within apostrophes or quotes) is invoked as an external function.

When a routine is invoked explicitly, it receives the standard environment (ADDRESS, NUMERIC, SIGNAL and TRACE, and the elapsed time) settings on entry. Any changes made to this standard environment are local to the routine. Because the stack is common to all routines in the current environment, the invoking routine may need to isolate its stack by using the following statements (TSO only):

```
'NEWSTACK' /* create a new stack */
invoke routine
'DELSTACK' /* delete the stack previously created */
```
Such coding should be used if the invoked routine could leave unwanted entries in the stack. A well-behaved routine that uses a stack should protect the original stack, unless it needs access to that stack. Section 3.7 describes stack processing.

Data can be passed to routines in several ways:
· explicitly
· implicitly

· using the stack
· using a specialised product.

Explicit arguments are the parameters specified in the invocation (the parameter list in a CALL instruction or in a function invocation). Implicit arguments are named variables - for procedures, such names must be declared with the EXPOSE clause. Because implicit arguments conflict with data encapsulation, their use should be avoided if possible. The use of an external file to pass parameters is a variation of the use of the stack. In the TSO/SPF environment, the Dialog Manager variable pool is a common method of passing data between external exec (with ISPEXEC VPUT and ISPEXEC VGET). Section 3.3.6 describes the use of arguments.

A routine can return a result with the same general techniques.

The RETURN instruction returns the specified expression (possibly a null string) as explicit result. The result is available at the point of invocation in the RESULT special variable. For a function invocation, this result also is returned as the function value, i.e. is used in place of the function invocation.
   A routine can return values in the stack. A routine can set values implicitly as named variables (a procedure must expose such names) - this method can be used only for routines contained in the same REXX procedure. These two methods must be used if more than one value is to be returned. If the stack is used, the particular stack entry must be identified in some way (e.g. with the implicit position in the stack or the stack entry tagged with an identifier).

Note: The following conventions are used in the next section:
· Brackets ([ ]) indicate an optional entry.
· Ellipses (...) indicate an entry that can be repeated.

3.3.1 Subroutine

A subroutine can be invoked in one of three ways:
· with the CALL instruction, for example, CALL ROUT P1,P2
· with a function invocation, for example, ROUT(P1,P2)
· in the normal processing flow (by being dropped through to).

Syntax:
```
name: [statement]...
RETURN
```

Example:
```
CALL add 1 2;
...
EXIT;
add:
  PARSE ARG parm1 parm2;
  SAY (parm1+parm2);
RETURN;
```

The subroutine ADD is called with two parameters: 1 and 2. The subroutine displays the sum of the two parameters.

3.3.2 Procedure

The PROCEDURE instruction identifies a routine as a procedure.

Compared with a subroutine, a procedure has the following differences:
- A procedure can only be invoked explicitly (that is, with a CALL or function invocation).
- By default, procedure variables are hidden. External variables must be declared explicitly in the EXPOSE clause of the PROCEDURE instruction.

Note: In this book, whereas *procedure* refers to an internal routine, the term *REXX procedure* is used for the "executable" external entity.

Syntax:
```
name: PROCEDURE [EXPOSE [parameter]...]
    [statement]...
    RETURN
```

Example:
```
divisor = 6;
dividend = 2;

CALL div;
...
EXIT;
div: PROCEDURE EXPOSE divisor dividend;
    SAY (divisor/dividend);
RETURN;
```
The procedure DIV is called with two global parameters (variables): DIVISOR and DIVIDEND. The procedure displays the result of dividing DIVISOR by DIVIDEND.

3.3.3 Function

A function is a routine that returns a result value. The RETURN instruction is used to return the function result, for example, RETURN 2. A null value is a valid function result, for example, RETURN ''. The function result is used in place of the explicit function invocation (e.g. funct()) and is set into the RETURN special variable.

For functions invoked with the CALL instruction (e.g. CALL funct), the function result can be obtained from the RESULT special variable. For example, CALL funct; x = RESULT; and x = funct(); are equivalent.

For functions invoked directly (e.g. funct ()), the function result is used in the expression in place of the function invocation.

Syntax:
```
name: [PROCEDURE [EXPOSE [parameter]...]]]
  [statement]...
RETURN expression;
```

Example:
```
x = mult(mult1,mult2);
SAY x
...
EXIT;
mult:
  PARSE ARG parm1,parm2;
  y = parm1*parm2;
RETURN y;
```
The function MULT is called with two parameters: MULT1 and MULT2. The function multiplies these two parameters together and returns the result.

3.3.3.1 Recursive Function. REXX permits functions to be invoked recursively. A recursive function is a function that invokes itself internally once or more times. A recursive function must have some condition to terminate the recursive calling.

Example:
```
factorial:
PARSE ARG n;
IF n < 1 THEN RETURN 1;
RETURN n * factorial(n-1);
```
The FACTORIAL function is called recursively to calculate the factorial of the number passed as parameter. For example, with the invocation: SAY factorial(x); The FACTORIAL function terminates when the argument is less than 1.

3.3.4 Search Order

Routines are searched in the following order:
·   Internal routine (except if the routine name is specified within quotes, in which case it is assumed to be either a built-in function or an external routine);
·   built-in function;
·   external routine.

Example:
```
CALL TIME() /* internal function */
CALL 'TIME'() /* external (built-in) TIME function */
...
EXIT
TIME: /* internal TIME routine */
  RETURN 'TIME'('M')
```

Note that in this example the internal TIME function invokes the standard built-in TIME function with M as argument.

The search for external routines is made in the following order:
· DBCS routines (this book does not discuss the DBCS package);
· function package routines (described in Section 14.9) - contact your system support personnel for details of any system functions available at your installation;
· the load library;
· the procedure library.

Note: The search sequence of load library and procedure library may have been reversed at your installation - contact your system support personnel for details.

3.3.5 Invocation

Procedures and subroutines are invoked using the CALL instruction.

Example:
```
    CALL rout
```
invokes the routine with the name ROUT.

Functions can be invoked in two ways:
· directly using the function name immediately followed with parentheses (even if no arguments are passed to the function);
· indirectly using the CALL instruction with the function name as routine name.

Example:
```
    funct()
```
or
```
    CALL funct
```

At run-time, the function result conceptually replaces the function call. If a function call is not embedded in an instruction, the function result will be passed to the current environment (see Example 3).

Example 1:
```
    x = alpha();
```
The function name must be immediately followed by parentheses, without any intervening blanks, otherwise the parentheses will be interpreted as enclosing an expression (see Example 2). Parameters (arguments) to be passed to the function are included within these parentheses, the individual arguments are separated by a comma. A maximum of 20 parameters can be passed to a function. The parentheses must always be written, even when no arguments are passed to the function.

Example 2:
```
    x = alpha (+3);
```

This statement is not a function invocation; the contents of alpha concatenated with 3 are assigned to x.

Example 3:
```
ADDRESS TSO;
gettime(); /* invoke function and pass result to the cmd processor */
EXIT;
gettime:
   RETURN 'TIME'
```
The GETTIME function result (TIME) is passed to the TSO command processor; i.e., the TSO TIME command will be invoked. This example shows the use of a function invocation as an instruction.

Example 4:
```
CALL putmsg "enter input";
SAY "input msg:" RESULT;
SAY "enter next input";
CALL getmsg;
SAY "input msg:" RESULT;
EXIT;
putmsg:
  PARSE ARG parm;
  SAY parm;
getmsg:
  PARSE PULL parm;
  RETURN parm;
```
This example shows the use of stacked routines. Because the PUTMSG routine does not have a return, it drops through to the following routine (GETMSG), which passes its return value back to the function invocation. A subsequent call invokes GETMSG directly. A sample invocation follows (input is shown in uppercase):
```
 enter input
LINE1
 input msg: LINE1
 enter next input
LINE2
 input msg: LINE2
```

3.3.6 Parameters (Arguments)

As with conventional programming languages, REXX has two basic methods of passing arguments to routines:
- By value. A copy of the argument is passed to the routine. The argument is read-only. The arguments are passed explicitly in the invocation.
- By reference. A named variable is passed as argument. The routine itself obtains the value of the variable. The routine can change the variable. This method can be used only for internal routines. Procedures must expose any

named arguments it uses. The arguments are passed implicitly. Because this is a general REXX programming technique, this method is not discussed here.

Zero, one or more parameters can be passed explicitly to a routine. Each parameter is separated by a comma. The individual parameters may have subparameters that are delimited by any syntactically-correct character other than a comma or semicolon.

Examples:
Invoke a routine without any parameters:

```
CALL rout1;
```

or

```
rout1();
```

Invoke a routine with a single parameter :

```
CALL rout2 "p1";
```

or

```
rout2("p1");
```

Invoke a routine with a single parameter (which consists of two subparameters):

```
CALL rout3 "p1" "p2";
```

or

```
rout3("p1" "p2");
```

Invoke a routine with two parameters:

```
CALL rout4 "p1", "p2";
```

or

```
rout4("p1", "p2");
```

Invoke a routine with two parameters (the first of which consists of two subparameters):

```
CALL rout5 "p1 p2", "p3";
```

or

```
rout5("p1 p2", "p3");
```

The parameters are retrieved in the invoked routine with the ARG function or the PARSE ARG (or ARG) instruction.

The ARG function has two forms:
·   The ARG() function returns the number of parameters passed to the routine.
·   The ARG(n) function returns the nth parameter passed to the routine.

The usual parsing operations can be used on the retrieved parameters, for example, to obtain the subparameters.

Example 1:
```
CALL funct "p1" "p2";
...
funct:
  SAY ARG(); /* 1 - no. of parameters */
  SAY ARG(1); /* 'p1 p2' */
  ...
RETURN;
```

Example 2:
```
CALL funct "p1", "p2";
...
funct:
  SAY ARG(); /* 2 - no. of parameters */
  SAY ARG(1); /* 'p1' */
  SAY ARG(2); /* 'p2' */
  ...
RETURN;
```

Example 3:
```
CALL funct "p1 p2", "p3";
...
funct:
  SAY ARG(); /* 2 - no. of parameters */
  SAY ARG(1); /* 'p1 p2' - parameter 1 */
  SAY ARG(2); /* 'p3' - parameter 2 */
  ...
RETURN;
```

Example 4 (using the PARSE ARG instruction):
```
CALL funct "p1", "p2";
...

funct:
  PARSE ARG parm1, parm2;
  SAY parm1; /* 'p1' */
  SAY parm2; /* 'p2' */
  ...
RETURN;
```

3.3.7 Return

A routine returns to the statement that immediately follows the invocation in one
of two ways:
· at the physical end of the exec
· with the RETURN instruction.

If the routine was invoked directly from the operating environment, return from
the exec returns to the operating environment. The EXIT instruction terminates the
exec.

   If the routine was not invoked as a function (i.e. not with the CALL instruction),
it must use the RETURN instruction with an expression to return a result. A null
expression is allowed (i.e. RETURN '';).

   The value of the expression specified in the RETURN instruction is also set into
the RESULT special variable. The RESULT variable does not contain a value if no
expression was specified (i.e. RETURN;).

Examples:

```
        x = funct();
        SAY x; /* 4 */

        ...

        funct:
        RETURN 4;
or
        CALL funct;
        SAY RESULT; /* 4 */

        ...

        funct:
        RETURN 4;
```

3.3.8 Communication Between Execs

Although execs can invoke other execs that are not physically contained within
each other, REXX offers only limited means of sharing data.

REXX execs have two methods of passing data between external execs:
·   explicit data transfer (invocation arguments or return value)
·   data transfer via the queue.

The use of an external file to buffer (transfer) data is basically the same as using
the queue, and so it will not be discussed. Strictly speaking, these two methods do
not share data, because in both cases a copy of the data is passed.

   To directly share data between external execs, non-REXX products must be
used; for example, the ISPF Dialog Manager shared variable pool or IEANXXX token
services. However, neither of these approaches is ideal, ISPF Dialog Manager
requires TSO, and a REXX-aware program must be written to use the IEANXXX token
services, although such a program can be written as a general REXX function or
command.

3.3.8.1 Explicit Data Transfer. The invoking exec passes data to the invoked exec as invocation arguments (CALL or function arguments). The invoked exec returns data to the invoking exec (RETURN operand). Figure 3.1 illustrates explicit data transfer. This method is suitable for limited amounts of data. Although, if 'objects' (name and data) are passed, the receiving exec can recreate the original data (see example).

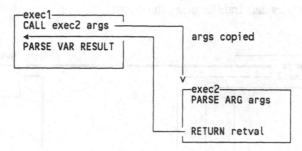

Figure 3.1 - Explicit data transfer

Example:
```
alpha = 'beta'
gamma = 'delta'
/* create 'object string' containing the variable names and associated
data (together with their respective lengths) */
objstr = '005ALPHA004beta005GAMMA005delta'
CALL funct objstr /* pass the object-string to funct */
EXIT
funct: PROCEDURE
  PARSE ARG str /* get object-string */
  /* parse the object-string */
  DO WHILE LENGTH(str) > 0
    PARSE VAR str VNL 4 str
    n = VNL+1
    PARSE VAR str VN =(n) str
    PARSE VAR str VDL 4 str
    n = VDL+1
    PARSE VAR str VD =(n) str
    stmt = VN '="'VD'"'
    INTERPRET stmt
  END
  SAY alpha /* beta */
  SAY gamma /* delta */
  RETURN
```

This example shows how objects can be passed to a function, which can then recreate the original data. This method can also be used when the variable names are not known. Although there are no standard REXX exec facilities to obtain the variable names, the IRXEXCOM service (SHVNEXTV function) can be used in a REXX program to retrieve the REXX variables (see Chapter 14).

3.3.8.2 Data Transfer Using the Queue. The queue (or an external file) is the most suitable means of passing large amounts of data between external execs. Figure 3.2 illustrates data transfer using the queue.

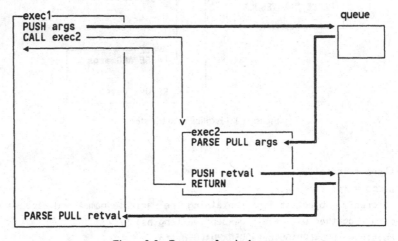

Figure 3.2 - Data transfer via the queue

3.3.8.3 Data Sharing Using Dialog Manager. For execs that run in the ISPF environment, the Dialog Manager variable pools (shared or profile) can be used to directly share data between external execs.

Note: Dialog Manager has restrictions on the use of REXX variable names: names cannot be longer than 8 characters and there is limited support for compound symbols (e.g. VGET/VPUT cannot be used).

Example:

```
/* REXX - ex1 */
ADDRESS ISPEXEC /* set ISPEXEC environment */
var1 = 'alpha'
"VPUT (var1) SHARED" /* set var1 into ISPF shared pool */
CALL ex2 /* invoke external exec */
"VGET (var1) SHARED" /* get updated var1 from ISPF shared pool */
SAY var1 /* beta */
```

```
/* REXX - ex2 */
ADDRESS ISPEXEC /* set ISPEXEC environment */
var1 = 'alpha'
"VGET (var1) SHARED" /* get var1 from ISPF shared pool */
SAY var1 /* alpha */
var1 = 'beta'
"VPUT (var1) SHARED" /* set updated var1 into ISPF shared pool */
RETURN /* return to invoking exec */
```

3.4 TYPES OF INSTRUCTION

REXX has two forms of instruction:
· simple instructions
· instruction blocks.

Most instructions are simple instructions. An instruction block is syntactically equivalent to a single (simple) instruction. An instruction block (DO or SELECT instruction) is terminated with an END clause. Instruction blocks can contain blocks (**nested blocks**).

3.4.1 Conditional Control

REXX provides three instructions for conditional control:
· IF instruction
· SELECT instruction
· conditional DO instruction.

The IF instruction specifies a single conditional clause (which may consist of several conditional expressions). The associated THEN clause is performed if the condition is satisfied. The associated (optional) ELSE clause is performed if the condition is not satisfied.

The SELECT instruction introduces a series of conditional (WHEN) clauses and an optional OTHERWISE clause: a SELECT-block. Only the first satisfied clause is processed — a syntax error results if no clause is satisfied. An END clause terminates a SELECT-block.

There are two forms of conditional DO instruction: DO UNTIL and DO WHILE. Each of these clauses introduces a DO-block. A DO UNTIL loop is performed until the specified condition is satisfied; the condition testing is made at the end of the loop, i.e. the loop is performed at least once. A DO WHILE loop is performed provided that the specified condition is satisfied; the condition testing is made at the start of the loop. An END clause terminates a DO-block.

3.4.2 Loop Control

The REXX DO instruction is used for processing loops.

REXX provides four basic types of DO-loop:
- simple DO
- endless DO
- iterative DO
- conditional DO.

The forms of a DO-block other than the simple DO (endless DO, iterative DO, and controlled repetitive DO) constitute a **DO-loop**. An iterative and conditional DO-loop can be combined as a single DO-loop.

DO-loops can terminate themselves with the LEAVE instruction or any instruction that terminates an exec or routine (EXIT or RETURN), although the latter means will terminate not only the loop by also the exec or routine (as appropriate). The ITERATE instruction terminates the current loop iteration (cycle).

3.4.2.1 Simple DO. A **simple DO** is a block of statements that are syntactically equivalent to a single statement.

Example:
```
IF (a < b) THEN
DO
   alpha = 1
   SAY alpha "beta"
END
```
The two instructions: alpha = 1 and SAY alpha "beta" are syntactically equivalent to a single statement.

3.4.2.2 Endless DO. The FOREVER operand specifies an **endless DO**. The loop will continue until some condition terminates the loop. This condition is usually internal but may be external (e.g. INTERRUPT key).

Example:
```
DO FOREVER;
   PULL line;
   IF line = '' THEN LEAVE;
   SAY 'LINE:'line;
END;
```
This code performs the statements between the DO and END until a null entry is input.

3.4.2.3 Iterative DO. An **iterative DO** is a DO-block that is performed repetitively. For a **simple iterative DO-loop**, the number of iterations is constant, unless the loop terminates itself prematurely. A **controlled iterative DO-loop** has a **control variable** that is assigned an initial value (specified with the = keyword). The control variable is incremented by a fixed amount (specified with the BY keyword) for each iteration until the limit value (specified with the TO keyword) is reached or until the loop terminates itself prematurely; alternatively, the FOR keyword can be used to specify the number of iterations. To improve the understandability of the exec, the control variable can be specified on the associated END instruction (this can also help to avoid unbalanced DO-END constructions).

Example 1:
```
DO 5;
    PULL line;
    IF line = '' THEN LEAVE;
    SAY 'LINE:'line;
END;
```
This code accepts a maximum of five input entries. The processing also terminates if a null entry is input.

Example 2:
```
DO i = 1 TO 4 BY 2;
    SAY i;
END i;
```
This code displays: 1 and 3.

Example 3:
```
DO i = 1 FOR 3 BY 2;
    SAY i;
END i;
```
This code displays: 1, 3 and 5.

3.4.2.4 Conditional DO. A **conditional DO** is a DO-block with a conditional expression that controls the loop. The loop condition can be at the start of the loop (WHILE condition) or at the end of the loop (UNTIL condition). The WHILE condition specifies the condition that has to be satisfied for the loop to be continued. The UNTIL condition specifies the condition that has to be satisfied for the loop to be terminated; a loop with an UNTIL condition is always performed at least once.

Example 1:
```
i = 1;
DO WHILE i < 5;
    SAY i;
    i = i+2;
END;
```

Example 2:
```
    i = 1;
    DO UNTIL i >= 5;
      SAY i;
      i = i+2;
    END ;
```

3.4.2.5 Composite Iteration Condition. The iteration condition can be augmented with a conditional expression to form a composite condition that controls the loop iteration as well as an index to the loop iteration. If the loop limit is set to a very large value (e.g. 999999999, although regard must be made for the precision implied with the NUMERIC DIGITS setting), this is in effect a DO FOREVER loop with a conditional loop expression.

Example 1:
```
    j = 0;
    DO i = 1 TO 10 WHILE j < 21;
      j = i * 7;
      SAY i j;
    END i;
```
This code performs three cycles.
Note: In this particular example, j must be initialised before the loop, otherwise it is undefined for the first loop. Compare this with Example 2 (UNTIL condition) which does not require that j be initialised, because the condition is tested at the end of the loop.

Example 2:
```
    DO i = 1 TO 10 UNTIL j > 21;
      j = i * 7;
      SAY i j;
    END i;
```

3.4.2.6 Modification of DO-Loop Processing. In many cases the processing of a DO-loop is not controlled just by the condition specified in the DO statement but also by internal logic in the loop (e.g. as the result of command). This modification of the loop processing can have many forms:

·   Terminate the current cycle (ITERATE instruction); i.e. make an implicit branch to the associated END instruction.
·   Terminate the current DO-loop (LEAVE instruction); i.e. make an implicit branch to the statement following the associated END instruction.
·   Terminate the exec (EXIT instruction).
·   Terminate the routine (RETURN instruction).
·   Change the condition that controls the DO-loop, e.g. change the value of the control variable or limit variable.

· Exit from the current DO-block by passing control to some routine outside the DO-block (by using the CALL or SIGNAL instruction); this is unstructured programming that should not normally be used.

With the exception with the first two cases, these methods also can be used for simple DO-blocks.

3.5 CONTROL PROCESSING FLOW

The SIGNAL instruction can be used to control the processing flow in one of three ways:
· enable a trap to be taken should the specified condition arise (ON parameter);
· disable a trap (OFF parameter);
· pass control to a specified label.

The statement number of the statement which caused the SIGNAL to be invoked (not the statement number where the SIGNAL instruction was enabled) is set into the SIGL special variable.

The CALL instruction can be used to a large extent in the same way, except that the conditions which can be trapped are limited compared with the SIGNAL instruction.

Tip
Reserve the CALL instruction for invoking routines, unless the RETURN instruction is used to return control to the point of invocation.

3.6 ASSIGNMENT

Assignment occurs when a value is assigned to a variable.

REXX has two methods of performing assignment:
· explicit assignment with the = operator, or
· implicit assignment with the PARSE instruction.

The assignment operator differs from the other instructions in that it is not a keyword at the start of the statement. The assignment operator (=) is placed between two operands; the right-hand operand is assigned to the left-hand operand.

The =-operator is not used just as assignment operator, but also as comparison operator (comparison for equality). The assignment of the initial value for the control variable in an iterative DO-loop is a special form of assignment. The following parsing logic is used to process statements that have =-operators:
· The sequence: symbol =   as the first two items in a statement (ignoring any labels) or after the DO instruction is interpreted as being the assignment of the expression following this = assignment operator to the symbol.

· In all other cases, the =-operator is interpreted as being the comparison operator.
· A single statement can use the =-operator in both ways (see examples).

Example 1:
```
y = 3;
x = y = 2;
```
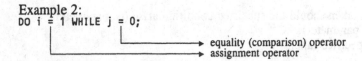
equality (comparison) operator
assignment operator

The comparison (y = 2) has higher priority than the assignment. The result of this comparison (1 = true, 0 = false; 0 in this case) is assigned to x.

Example 2:
```
DO i = 1 WHILE j = 0;
```
equality (comparison) operator
assignment operator

3.7 STACK (QUEUE) PROCESSING

The REXX stack is a temporary storage medium that can contain zero (empty stack) or more entries. The stack is also referred to as the **queue**. Entries can be added at the head (start) or tail (end) of the stack. Entries can be removed only from the head of the stack. Reading a stack entry is destructive. TSO REXX allows multiple stacks to exist concurrently, although only one stack can be active at any one time.

The stack can be used for the following purposes:
· buffer for terminal input;
· store data (intra-exec communication);
· pass data between execs (inter-exec communication);
· file buffer for EXECIO command.

The following three instructions explicitly use the stack:
· PARSE PULL (or PULL). Obtain the first entry from the stack. If the stack is empty, obtain input from the terminal.
· PUSH. Set an entry at the start of the stack.
· QUEUE. Set an entry at the end of the stack.

TSO REXX has several host REXX commands for stack processing.

3.7.1 Stack as Terminal Input Buffer

The stack is used as buffer for terminal input. When data input is requested from the terminal (PARSE PULL instruction), the stack is used in preference. That is, if the stack contains data, the data entry is first retrieved from the stack before data is obtained from the terminal. This means that an exec can pre-empt terminal input by placing data in the stack before it is required. It also means that any data still in the stack at the end of the exec will be passed to the **command processor**.

Tip
Clear the stack before the exec terminates or use an exec-specific stack (NEWSTACK and DELSTACK commands), unless the remaining entries in the stack are to be used as commands for the command processor. The QUEUED function can be used to obtain the number of entries in the stack.

3.7.2 Stack Used for General Data Storage

Although the stack can be used to store data items within an exec, it is usually better to use variables.

3.7.3 Stack Used for Passing Data Between Execs

Other than passing data explicitly with routine invocation or with the RETURN instruction, the stack is the only REXX-specific means of passing data between execs (inter-exec communication).

3.7.3.1 TSO Stack Processing. The TSO environment has a number of extensions to better support the use of the stack in a multi-tasking environment. These facilities are also useful for normal processing. Figure 3.3 illustrates the organisation of TSO stacks.

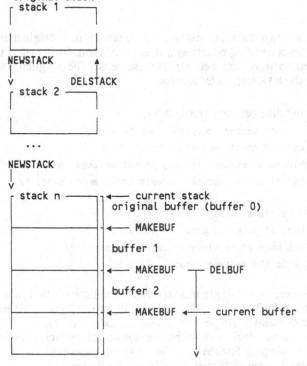

Figure 3.3 - TSO stack organisation

· A new stack is created when the TSO session is initiated. This stack is deleted when the TSO session terminates.
· Sub-stacks can be created. Each of these sub-stacks can be used in the same way as the original stack. The NEWSTACK (New Stack) command creates a new stack, which becomes the **current stack**. The DELSTACK (Delete Stack) command deletes the current stack and all entries contained within it, the previous stack becomes the current stack. The QSTACK (Query Stack) command returns the number of stacks.
· The current stack is the stack used when the REXX exec terminates. REXX execs initiated within the same TSO session can access any higher-level stacks which have been created using the usual stack commands.
· A stack can be subdivided into one or more buffers. The MAKEBUF (Make Buffer) command creates a new buffer in the current stack, this buffer then becomes the **current buffer**. The DROPBUF (Drop Buffer) command deletes the specified buffers and all entries contained within them. The QBUF (Query Buffer) command returns the number of buffers in the current stack which have been created with the MAKEBUF command and have not been deleted. The QELEM (Query Elements) command returns the number of entries in the current buffer.
· Buffers are only a conceptual subset of a stack, and have no fundamental significance. The entries in the various buffers of a stack can be directly processed as entries of the stack.
· A stack or buffers in a stack, together with all their elements, can be explicitly deleted.

ISPF performs its own stack processing, and creates a new original stack for each invocation - screen splitting counts as a new invocation. This means that the stack cannot be used to pass data between ISPF screens. The original TSO stacks are restored when the ISPF session terminates.

Example (passing data between execs, tasks):

```
/* REXX - pass message between execs */
"NEWSTACK"; /* create new stack */
PUSH "this is a message" TIME(); /* set message into stack */
"NEWSTACK" /* protect stack - create (new) empty stack */

/* REXX- retrieve message */
"DELSTACK"; /* point to previous stack */
PARSE PULL msg; /* retrieve message from stack */
SAY "this is the message" msg;
```

The first REXX exec sets a single message (with the time of day) into a new stack, and then creates a further stack, which at this point is empty. This means that the previous stack contains a single entry. The second REXX exec deletes the empty stack, i.e. the current stack is now the previous stack, which contains the passed message. This message is fetched with the PARSE PULL instruction.
Note: This method is not restricted to passing a single message.

3.7.4 File Buffer

The current stack can be used as buffer for the EXECIO command.

3.8 PARSING

Because parsing (string analysis) is one of REXX's features, a complete chapter is devoted to this topic. Many built-in functions for string processing complement the PARSE instruction. The PARSE instruction has several instructions that are a subset: ARG, PULL and UPPER.

REXX offers the following forms of string parsing:
- at a particular location (absolute or relative)
- at a particular delimiter
- at a word boundary.

3.9 DEBUGGING

Although TSO REXX does not provide a full-screen debugging tool, the REXX language offers the following debugging facilities:
- trace statements
- trace intermediate results produced when expressions are evaluated
- trace final results of evaluated expressions
- trace those statements with commands that caused an error return
- trace labels
- perform syntax check (without execution)
- disable the execution of host commands
- pause after the execution of the traced statement (equivalent to single-step).

With the exception of the last tracing mode, all these tracing facilities can be used both in dialogue and batch. The debugging mode can be set in the exec or interactively after interrupting the execution of the exec.

3.10 MISCELLANEOUS INSTRUCTIONS

The miscellaneous instructions are those instructions that do not belong in any of the previous groupings.

·	ADDRESS	Set the current environment. Commands are passed to the active environment.
·	ARG	Fetch argument.
·	DROP	Free variable or stem.
·	INTERPRET	Interpret statement. Process a statement that has been built at execution-time. For example, if the target variable name is determined dynamically.

· NOP	No-operation. The NOP instruction is used when a clause is required for syntax reasons (e.g. for a null THEN clause in an IF instruction). A NOP instruction can be necessary when interactive tracing is set dynamically.
· NUMERIC	Define numeric formats (e.g. precision, display form).
· OPTIONS	Pass special parameters to the language processor.
· SAY	Display.
· UPPER	Transform lowercase characters to uppercase.

3.11 COMMANDS

Strictly speaking, a command is not a REXX instruction. A command is any statement that the REXX interpreter does not recognise as being an instruction. Commands are passed to the currently active command processor, which is set by the ADDRESS instruction. The TSO REXX implementation supplies several host commands (e.g. ISPEXEC, MVS, TSO). User-written command processors can augment the standard command processors; see Chapter 14.

If necessary, quotes must be used to distinguish commands that have the same name as REXX instructions. For example; 'EXIT' is passed to the command processor.

EXECIO is the most important standard command. EXECIO is used to perform file-oriented input/output (see Example 2).

Example 1:
```
ADDRESS LINK
"IEBGENER" /* invoke the IEBGENER utility program */
ADDRESS TSO "LISTDS (EX.ISPPLIB) MEMBERS" /* invoke the TSO LISTDS
command */
```

Example 2:
```
"ALLOC F(MYFILE) DSN(TEST.DATA) SHR"
"EXECIO 10 DISKR MYFILE"
```
Read the first ten records from the TEST.DATA file into the stack.

3.12 SPECIAL VARIABLES

REXX has three special variables:
· RC
· RESULT
· SIGL

3.12.1 RC - Return Code
The return code can be set in one of two ways:

· If the command cannot be invoked (e.g. command not found), the command invocation routine sets a failure return code (negative).
· If the command was invoked, the return code is that set by the command. By convention, commands set the return code in accordance with the following scheme:
0   successful processing
4   successful processing, but some warning condition
8   error condition
12 (and higher), severe error.

Example:

```
ADDRESS ISPEXEC
"DISPLAY PANEL(pn)"
IF RC = 0 THEN DO
   /* processing */
END
```

3.12.2 RESULT - Function Result

The function result is the value of the expression that the most-recently invoked routine set in the RETURN instruction.

Example 1:

```
CALL rout
SAY RESULT /* abc */
EXIT
rout:
  RETURN 'abc'
```

Example 2:

```
x = rout()
SAY x /* abc */
SAY RESULT /* abc */
EXIT
rout:
  RETURN 'abc'
```

3.12.3 SIGL - Source Line Number

The source line number is the number of the source line which caused the current exception condition to be raised. SIGL can be used as index to obtain the corresponding source line.

Example:

```
/* REXX */
SIGNAL ON NOVALUE NAME ERR
x = y
```

```
EXIT
ERR:
   SAY 'NOVALUE exception at statement' SIGL
   SAY 'Source statement:" SOURCELINE(SIGL)
   EXIT
```

Because the Y variable is not initialised, it will raise the NOVALUE exception. This code would display the messages:

```
NOVALUE exception at statement 3
Source statement: x = y
```

4

REXX Instructions

The villainy you teach me I will execute, and it shall go hard but I will better the instruction.

The Merchant of Venice

William Shakespeare

4.1 INTRODUCTION

The REXX language provides the following instructions:

·	ADDRESS	Set current command environment
·	ARG	Get argument
·	CALL	Invoke routine (exception handler)
·	DO	Start of DO-block
·	DROP	Free variable
·	EXIT	Exit
·	IF - THEN - [ELSE]	Conditional processing
·	INTERPRET	Process run-time statement
·	ITERATE	Iterate DO-loop
·	LEAVE	Leave DO-loop
·	NOP	No-instruction
·	NUMERIC	Set numeric options
·	OPTIONS	Set language processor options
·	PARSE	Parse data
·	PROCEDURE	Define start of procedure
·	PULL	Retrieve element from stack
·	PUSH	Place element at end of the stack
·	QUEUE	Place element at start of the stack

· RETURN   Return from routine
· SAY   Display
· SELECT   Define start of SELECT-block
· SIGNAL   Exception handler processing
· TRACE   Set debugging option
· UPPER   Transform to uppercase
· =   Assign
· commands.

A library of powerful functions and commands appropriate for the host
environment (e.g. input/output processing routines) augment these basic program
elements. The terminating semicolon (;) shown in the syntax diagrams is optional
unless more than one instruction is written in a single line; the record end (except
for statements that are implicitly or explicitly continued) implies a semicolon (see
Example 1).

For instructions that have keywords, the keywords are interpreted as being a
self-defining literal, i.e. it is not necessary to specify such keywords in quotes.
The INTERPRET instruction must be used if the keyword parameter is to be set at
run-time (see Example 2).

Example 1:
```
TRACE ?R; NOP /* 2 instructions in a single line */
IF a > b /* implicit continuation */
   THEN SAY 'condition satisfied'
msg = "part 1" , /* explicit continuation */
      "part 2"
```

Example 2:
```
ADDRESS ISPEXEC
"DISPLAY PANEL(pn)"
```
The following code can be used to set the environment dynamically:
```
handler = 'ISPEXEC'
stmt = 'ADDRESS' handler
INTERPRET stmt
"DISPLAY PANEL(pn)"
```

4.2 INSTRUCTION DESCRIPTIONS

4.2.1 ADDRESS – Set Environment

The ADDRESS instruction sets the system component environment to that which the
non-REXX statements are to be passed. Chapter 14 explains how to write
application-specific environment handlers.

The ADDRESS instruction without a statement sets the global environment, which applies, until changed, to all subsequent non-REXX statements. The ADDRESS clause prefixed to a statement sets the local environment only for that statement.

Syntax:

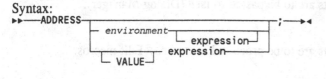

environment:

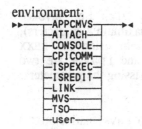

The default environment is MVS and TSO for OS/390 (MVS) batch and TSO, respectively.

expression

The statement which is to be passed to the specified local **environment**.

VALUE expression

Expression is a character expression which defines the global environment. The VALUE keyword can be omitted when **expression** is enclosed within parentheses.

If no operands are specified, the global environment is set back to what it was before the last change was made – see Example 3.

ATTACH

Non-REXX statements are to be processed via ATTACH, i.e. invoked asynchronously as a sub-task. The first item is the program name (maximum 8 characters), subsequent items are passed to the invoked program using the REXX parameter convention (see Section 14.7). ATTACHMVS and ATTACHPGM are two variations of ALLOC that use a different convention for passing the parameters.

CONSOLE

The CONSOLE environment supports OS/390 system and subsystem commands during an extended MCS console session. CONSOLE command authority is a requirement for use of the CONSOLE environment.

CPICOMM

The CPICOMM environment supports SAA Common Programming Interface (CPI) communication (APPC). The LU62 environment supports APPC/MVS calls based on the SNA LU 6.2 architecture. The APPCMVS environment allows APPC transaction execs to invoke APPC/MVS callable services.

ISPEXEC

Non-REXX statements are to be passed to ISPF (Dialog Manager).

ISREDIT

Non-REXX statements are to be processed as ISPF/PDF Edit macros.

LINK

Non-REXX statements are to be processed via LINK, i.e. invoked synchronously. The first item is the program name (maximum 8 characters), subsequent items are passed to the invoked program using the REXX parameter convention (see Section 14.7). LINKMVS and LINKPGM are two variations of LINK that use a different convention for passing the parameters.

MVS

Non-REXX statements are to be processed as OS/390 (MVS, native REXX) commands. The worked example shown in Section 15.3 illustrates the use of this instruction. This parameter returns the address environment to its initial value.

TSO

Non-REXX statements are to be processed as TSO commands. The first item is the command name (maximum 8 characters), with subsequent items being passed to the invoked command (see Section 14.7).

user

The name of a user command environment. User in this context means a command environment other than one of the standard environments; such environments can be user-written (see Chapter 14) or application-specific (applications can be written by product developers, etc.).

Note: The ADDRESS instruction does not check the environment for validity.

Example 1:
```
ADDRESS ISREDIT;
ADDRESS ISPEXEC "VPUT (ALPHA) SHARED";
"(lno,colno) = CURSOR";
```
The first instruction sets the global environment to ISREDIT. The second instruction passes the "VPUT (ALPHA) SHARED" statement to the local ISPEXEC environment. The "(lno,colno) = CURSOR" statement is passed to the ISREDIT environment (the current global environment).

Example 2:
```
env = "ISPEXEC";
ADDRESS (env);
```
This example sets the global environment to ISPEXEC.

Note: At least one blank must follow the ADDRESS keyword, otherwise the ADDRESS function would have been invoked.

Example 3:
```
SAY ADDRESS(); /* display current environment */
ADDRESS MVS; /* set OS/390 environment */
SAY ADDRESS(); /* display current environment */
ADDRESS; /* set previous environment */
SAY ADDRESS(); /* display current environment */
```
This example displays, for example, TSO, MVS and TSO, respectively.

4.2.2 ARG – Fetch Argument

The ARG instruction parses the argument passed via the CALL instruction or function invocation. The ARG instruction is a subset of the PARSE ARG instruction.
Note: This instruction largely duplicates the ARG function.

Syntax:

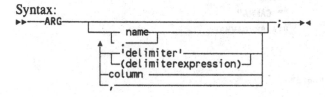

name
> The symbol to be assigned the parsed data.

.
> Placeholder. The data are parsed but no assignment is made.

'delimiter'
> The delimiter which is to be used as search argument for the source data.
> **Delimiter** is not restricted to being a single character.

(delimiterexpression)
> A character expression which is to be used as delimiter for the source data.

column
> The position at which the source data is to be split, 1 is the first position in the source data.
> If column is prefixed with either a '+' or '-' sign, this column is relative to the last location parsed.

,
> A comma specifies that the next argument in the source data is to be processed.

Example 1:
```
      alpha = "beta ** gamma";
      CALL funct alpha;
      ...
      funct:
        ARG a b;
        ARG a '**' b;
        ARG a '*' b;
        ARG a 3 b;
      RETURN;
```

returns the following results:

a	b
"BETA"	"** GAMMA"
"BETA "	" GAMMA"
"BETA "	"* GAMMA"
"BE"	"TA ** GAMMA"

Example 2:
```
      CALL funct "alpha", "beta";
      ...
      funct:
        ARG a, b;
        SAY a b; /* ALPHA BETA */
        ARG a b;
        SAY a b; /* ALPHA */
      RETURN;
```

4.2.3 CALL - Invoke Routine

The CALL instruction explicitly invokes a routine. The invoked routine returns to the statement following the CALL instruction. The CALL instruction can explicitly pass zero or more parameters to the called routine. The called routine can (but need not) return a result to the point of invocation. The calling routine can access this returned value in the RESULT special variable.

The called routine may be either internal or external to the calling exec; external execs must be located in a procedure library known to REXX (either in one of the standard libraries (typically SYSEXEC or SYSPROC) or in an ALTLIB-allocated library).

Example:
```
CALL rout1;
SAY "return from rout1";
...
rout1:
SAY "rout1 entered";
RETURN;
```
This code displays "rout1 entered" and "return from rout1".

Syntax:

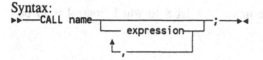

name
>   The name of the routine to be invoked.

expression
>   The argument (parameter) to be passed to the called routine. The individual arguments are separated by commas. Each argument may contain subparameters, which can be parsed in the usual way.

Example:
```
CALL funct alpha;
SAY RESULT;
...
funct:
parm = ARG(1);              /* fetch argument */
SAY parm;
...
RETURN beta;
```
The funct routine is invoked with argument alpha.

4.2.3.1 CALL - Exception Handling

The CALL ON or OFF instruction can be used to enable or disable and exception some condition handlers. In contrast with the SIGNAL instruction, the condition handler can be either an internal or external routine. The CALL exception handler can process only the ERROR, FAILURE and HALT conditions.

If an exception condition has been enabled, control is passed to the specified routine should the particular exception condition occur; multiple exception conditions can be active at any one point of time. The setting of any particular exception condition overrides any previous setting for that condition.

Syntax:

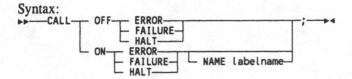

labelname
>   The name of a label to which control is to be passed.

VALUE expression
>   The evaluated **expression** is the name of a label to which control is to be
>   passed.

OFF
>   The following trap condition is disabled.

ON

>   The following trap condition is enabled. If the trapped condition is raised,
>   control is passed to the label having the condition name. For example, if the
>   ERROR condition is enabled, control is passed to the label ERROR if this
>   condition is raised. A syntax error is signalled if the required label does not
>   exist.

ERROR
>   The error condition (positive non-zero return from host command) is
>   disabled or enabled according as to whether OFF or ON has been specified.

FAILURE
>   The failure condition (negative return from host command) is disabled or
>   enabled according as to whether OFF or ON has been specified.

HALT
>   The halt condition is disabled or enabled according as to whether OFF or ON
>   has been specified. The halt condition can be raised in several ways, for
>   example, with the HI command.

Example:
```
CALL ON ERROR NAME ERR_RTN;
"nocmd";

   ...
EXIT;
ERR_RTN: SAY "ERROR exit taken at statement" SIGL;
EXIT;
```

4.2.4 DO – Define Start of DO-Block

The DO instruction defines the start of a DO-block; the DO-block is terminated with
an END instruction.

Syntax:

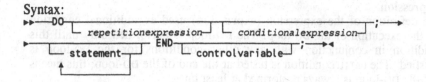

repetitionexpression:

conditionalexpression:

name=expression
> The assignment of the initial value (**expression**) to the control variable (**name**) used for the DO-loop.

TO toexpr
> The definition of the final value (**toexpr**) of the control variable used for the DO-loop.

BY byexpr
> The definition of the increment value (**byexpr**) to be added to the control variable for each cycle through the DO-loop. The increment may be either positive or negative. Default: 1

FOR forexpr
> The definition of the number of cycles (**forexpr**) to be performed in the DO-loop. The **forexpr**, if present, takes priority over any other loop counts which are specified.

FOREVER
> The FOREVER keyword specifies that an endless DO-loop is to be performed. Normally the DO-loop will be terminated using the LEAVE, RETURN or EXIT instruction on some condition.

repexpr
> The assignment of the repetitive expression (**repexpr**) to be used for the DO-loop. This expression specifies the number of cycles to be performed.

WHILE expression
> The definition of the expression (**expression**) used as additional condition for the execution of the DO-loop. The DO-loop is performed only when this condition in conjunction with any other conditions for the DO-loop is satisfied. The WHILE condition is tested before the DO-loop is performed.

UNTIL expression
>The definition of the expression (**expression**) used as additional condition for the execution of the DO-loop. The DO-loop is performed only until this condition in conjunction with any other conditions for the DO-loop is satisfied. The UNTIL condition is tested at the end of the DO-loop; this means that the DO-loop is always performed at least once.

Example 1:
```
DO i = 1 TO 10;
...
END;
```
This code performs 10 iterations.

Example 2:
```
J = 3
DO i = 1 TO 10 FOR J;
...
END;
```
This code performs 3 iterations.

Example 3:
```
DO FOREVER;
...
END;
```
This code performs an endless iteration.

4.2.5 DROP – Free Variable

The DROP instruction frees the specified variables, i.e. resets the variables to the uninitialised state and releases the associated storage areas. The NOVALUE condition is signalled if a dropped variable is used without having been assigned a value.

Tip
Because the amount of storage used for compound variables can be extensive, a DROP should be made for such variables when they are no longer required. For example, if the EXECIO command has been used to read the complete contents of a dataset into a stem variable.

Syntax:

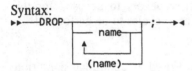

name
>The name of the variable to be freed. If **name** is a written within parentheses, the contents of **name** are processed as a list of names (see Example 2).

Example 1:
```
alpha = "beta";
SAY alpha; /* beta */
DROP alpha;
SAY alpha; /* ALPHA */
DROP 'S.'; /* drop all S. stem variables */
```

Example 2:
```
str = "alpha beta";
DROP (str); /* drop ALPHA and BETA variables */
```

Example 3:
```
ADDRESS TSO "ALLOC F(fn) DSN(user.file) SHR"
"EXECIO * DISKR fn (STEM r. FINIS"
/* ... processing ... */
DROP 'R.'
```

4.2.6 EXIT – Terminate Exec

The EXIT instruction terminates the execution (logical end) of the current REXX exec – control is returned to the invoking exec, program, etc. A REXX exec may have more than one EXIT. An EXIT is automatically generated at the physical end of the REXX exec, i.e. after the last statement.

Tip
It is good programming practice to explicitly specify the exec EXIT. This is especially true before subroutine definitions, which could be inadvertently executed by being dropped through to (see Example 2).

Note: Many host environments (e.g. QMF) also have an EXIT command. Commands that have the same name as REXX instructions must be written in quotes (i.e. "EXIT") to distinguish them from the REXX instruction.

Syntax:
```
►►──EXIT──────────────────;──►◄
          └ expression ┘
```

expression
    The numeric value to be returned to the point of invocation.

Example 1:
```
EXIT 8;
```

Example 2:
```
i = 1;
CALL funct;
```

```
funct:
  i = i+1;
  SAY i;
  RETURN;
```

The omitted EXIT before the funct function, causes funct to be invoked twice: once with the CALL and once by being dropped through to.

4.2.7 IF – Conditional Execution

The IF instruction specifies the processing to be performed based on the result of the tested condition. The IF instruction has two branches; the THEN-branch is taken when the condition is satisfied, the ELSE-branch, if present, is taken when the condition is not satisfied.

Syntax:
```
►►──IF expression; THEN statement;─┬─────────────────┬──►◄
                                   └─ ELSE statement;─┘
```

expression
> The condition to be tested. **expression** must evaluate to either 1 (true) or 0 (false).

THEN statement
> The statement to be performed if **expression** evaluates to 1 (true). The NOP instruction can be used as statement and so satisfy the syntax, if no processing is to be performed (see Example 2).

ELSE statement
> The statement to be performed if **expression** evaluates to 0 (false). The ELSE clause is optional.

Note: **Statement** may be a simple DO-block, if more than one statement is to be performed.

Example 1:
```
IF alpha < 2
  THEN
    SAY "alpha lt 2";
  ELSE DO;
    SAY "alpha ge 2";
    SAY "line 2";
  END;
```
This example uses a simple DO-block as ELSE clause.

Example 2:
```
IF alpha < 2 & beta > 3
  THEN NOP;
  ELSE SAY "condition not satisfied";
```
This code illustrates the use of the NOP instruction. The use of the NOP can simplify the writing of negated complex conditional expressions. This code could also be written as:
```
IF alpha >= 2 | beta <= 3
  THEN SAY "condition not satisfied";
```

4.2.8 INTERPRET – Interpret Statement

The specified expression is interpreted at run-time. The INTERPRET instruction should be restricted to those statements that can be created only at run-time (INTERPRET instructions are more complicated than the equivalent instructions, and there is increased processing overhead). It is typically required when variable names can be determined only at run-time (e.g. the variable names are obtained from a file). In such a case stem variables can often be used (see Example 2).

Note: The VALUE function that returns the run-time value of the specified expression often can be used instead of the INTERPRET instruction.

Syntax:
```
►►——INTERPRET expression;——►◄
```

expression
> The statement to be performed. **expression** must be a valid REXX statement, the final semicolon (";") is not specified.

Example 1:
```
vn = 'alpha';
INTERPRET vn "= 'beta'";
```
is equivalent to:
```
alpha = 'beta';
```

Example 2:
```
vn = 'alpha';
a.vn = 'beta';
```
is equivalent to:
```
a.alpha = 'beta';
```
This example shows how stem variables can avoid the use of the INTERPRET instruction.

Example 3:
```
IF op = 1
  THEN fn = 'add';
  ELSE fn = 'sub';
INTERPRET 'CALL' fn;
```
This example performs a computed procedure call; depending on the value of op, either ADD or SUB is called.

4.2.9 ITERATE - Terminate the Current Cycle in the DO-Loop

The ITERATE instruction passes control to the associated END instruction, i.e. the current DO-loop cycle is terminated.

Syntax:
```
▶▶──ITERATE──┬──────┬──;──▶◀
             └ name ┘
```

name
> The name of the control variable for the associated DO-loop. If omitted, the iteration is performed on the current DO-loop.

Example 1:
```
DO i = 1 TO 2;
  DO j = 1 TO 4;
    IF j = 3 THEN ITERATE j; /* inner loop */
    SAY i j;
  END;
END;
```

This code displays:
```
1 1
1 2
1 4
2 1
2 2
2 4
```

Example 2:
```
DO i = 1 TO 2;
  DO j = 1 TO 4;
    IF j = 3 THEN ITERATE i; /* outer loop */
    SAY i j;
  END;
END;
```

This code displays:

```
1 1
1 2
2 1
2 2
```

4.2.10 LEAVE - Terminate DO-loop

The LEAVE instruction causes the current DO-loop to be terminated, i.e. control is passed to the statement following the END instruction of the current DO-loop.

Syntax:

```
►►——LEAVE————————;——►◄
          └─ name ─┘
```

name

      The name of the control variable for the associated DO-loop. If omitted, the leave is performed on the current DO-loop.

Example 1:

```
DO i = 1 TO 2;
  DO j = 1 TO 4;
    IF j = 3 THEN LEAVE j; /* inner loop */
    SAY i j;
  END;
END;
```

This code displays:

```
1 1
1 2
2 1
2 2
```

Example 2:

```
DO i = 1 TO 2;
  DO j = 1 TO 4;
    IF j = 3 THEN LEAVE i; /* outer loop */
    SAY i j;
  END;
END;
```

This code displays:

```
1 1
1 2
```

4.2.11 NOP - No-Operation

The NOP instruction serves as statement placeholder. It is principally used in the following situations:

· In a THEN clause when no processing is required, but the clause must be present to satisfy the syntax requirements (see Example 1).

· When tracing is set dynamically (for example, when an exception condition is signaled). In such a situation, tracing is effective from the next statement onwards (see Example 2).

Syntax:
```
►►——NOP;——►◄
```

Example 1:
```
SELECT;
  WHEN alpha < 2;
    THEN SAY "alpha lt 2";
  WHEN alpha = 2;
    THEN NOP;
  OTHERWISE
    SAY "alpha gt 2";
END;
```
In this example processing is required only when alpha is not equal to 2.

Example 2:
```
SIGNAL ON NOVALUE NAME err
SAY a
EXIT
err:
  TRACE ?R; NOP;
```

4.2.12 NUMERIC - Define Numeric Formats

The NUMERIC instruction is used to define the format of numeric values. The NUMERIC instruction duplicates the functions: DIGITS, FORM and FUZZ.

Syntax:
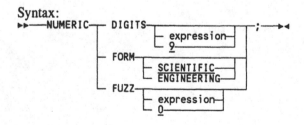

DIGITS expression

The **expression** is a numeric value which specifies the precision of numeric values.

Default: 9.

FORM

The external (display) form of numeric values whose size exceeds the DIGITS value. Such large, or very small, values are represented in exponential notation. There are two forms of exponential notation:

SCIENTIFIC – only one non-zero digit appears before the decimal point of the mantissa, e.g. 1.2E+4

ENGINEERING – the exponent is always a power of three, e.g. 12E+3

FUZZ expression

The **expression** is a numeric value which specifies the number of digits to be ignored during numeric comparisons.

Default: 0.

Example 1:

```
n = 123456;
NUMERIC DIGITS 4;
NUMERIC FORM ENGINEERING;
SAY n*2; /* displays 246.9E+3 */
NUMERIC FORM SCIENTIFIC;
SAY n*2; /* displays 2.469E+5 */
NUMERIC DIGITS 6;
SAY n*2; /* displays 246912 */
```

Example 2:

```
NUMERIC DIGITS 4;
SAY (2.004 = 2); /* displays 0 (= false) */
NUMERIC FUZZ 1;
SAY (2.004 = 2); /* displays 1 (= true) */
SAY (1.998 = 2); /* displays 0 (= false) */
```

FUZZ is equivalent to:

```
ABS(value1-value2) = 0
```

4.2.13 OPTIONS – Pass Special Parameters to the Language Processor

The OPTIONS instruction is used to pass special parameters to the language processor. The form of these parameters is implementation dependent, for example, the OPTIONS instruction is used in the TSO/E implementation to set the DBCS (Double Byte Character Set) environment. This book does not discuss the DBCS operations.

Syntax:
```
►►──OPTIONS expression;──►◄
```

4.2.14 PARSE – Assign Data

The PARSE instruction assigns the source data to the specified variables or
placeholders. The assignment can be made according the following criteria:
· words
· delimiter
· position.

Syntax:

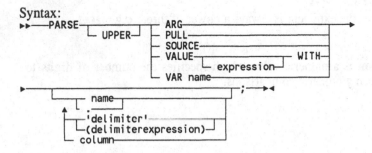

UPPER
The assigned data are converted to uppercase.
Default: The case of the source data is retained.

ARG
The current argument is used as the source data. The argument is set in one
of the following ways:
· argument passed to the REXX exec
· argument passed to a routine (subroutine, procedure or function).

PULL
The entry at the head of the stack (or the input data stream, if the stack is
empty) is fetched and used as the source data.

SOURCE
The current program source is used as the source data. Table 4.1 shows the
program source format. Each entry is separated by a blank. "?" is set for
entries where no information is available.

VAR name
The **name** is the symbol containing the source data.

VALUE expr
The evaluation of **expr** is used as the source data.

name
The symbol to be assigned the parsed data.

.

A placeholder. The data are parsed but no assignment is made.

Table 4.1   — Program source

TSO
invocation of the program
name of the exec
DDname from which exec was loaded
dataset from which exec was loaded
name of invoked exec
initial host environment
name of address space
user token

'delimiter'

The delimiter which is to be used as search argument for the source data.
Delimiter is not restricted to being a single character.

(delimiterexpression)

A character expression which is to be used as delimiter for the source data.

column

The position at which the source data is to be split, 1 is the first position in
the source data.
The column may also be a displacement, i.e. prefixed with either a '+' or
'-' sign. This column is then relative to the last location parsed.

,

A comma specifies that the next argument in the source data is to be
processed. This operand may only be used in conjunction with the ARG
keyword.

The following non-SAA parameters are available in the TSO implementation:

EXTERNAL

The data from the input data stream (terminal or input dataset) is used as the
source data.

NUMERIC

The current numeric attributes (DIGITS, FORM, FUZZ) are used as the source
data.

VERSION
> The identifier containing REXX version information is used as the source
> data. Table 4.2 shows the version format (5 words).

Table 4.2 – Version format

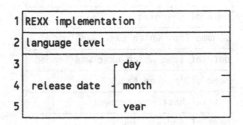

Example:
```
CALL alpha "beta gamma";
EXIT;
alpha:
PARSE ARG a b;
SAY a b; /* displays alpha beta */
PARSE UPPER ARG a b;
SAY a b; /* displays ALPHA BETA */
RETURN;

alpha = "beta gamma";
PARSE VALUE alpha WITH a b;
SAY a b; /* display beta gamma */
```

4.2.15 PROCEDURE – Define Internal Procedure

The PROCEDURE instruction defines the start of an internal procedure. A procedure
differs from a subroutine in that it can only be invoked explicitly and that global
variables used in the procedure must be defined with the EXPOSE keyword.

Syntax:

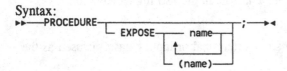

name
> The **name** is a global variable. If **name** is a written within parentheses, the
> contents of **name** are processed as a list of exposed names (see Example 2).

Example 1:
```
beta = "gamma";
CALL funct;
EXIT;
funct: PROCEDURE;
   SAY beta; /* displays BETA */
RETURN;
```
BETA is displayed, because the variable beta is not initialised for the funct procedure.


```
beta = "gamma";
CALL funct;
EXIT;
funct: PROCEDURE EXPOSE beta;
   SAY beta; /* displays gamma */
RETURN;
```
The variable beta has been exposed for funct procedure, hence its contents are available in the procedure.

Example 2:
```
names = "beta gamma";
beta = "delta";
CALL funct;
EXIT;
funct: PROCEDURE EXPOSE (names);
   SAY beta; /* displays delta */
RETURN;
```
Because the EXPOSE parameter is written within parentheses, it is processed as a list of names. This procedure instruction is equivalent to: funct: PROCEDURE EXPOSE beta gamma;

4.2.16 PULL – Fetch Data Element from the Head of the Stack

The PULL instruction is equivalent to the PARSE UPPER PULL instruction. The entry at the head of the stack (or the input data stream, if the stack is empty) is fetched and used as the source data.

Syntax:

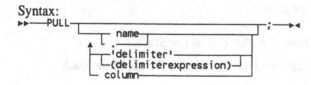

name
   The symbol to be assigned the parsed data.

.

A placeholder. The data are parsed but no assignment is made.

'delimiter'

The delimiter which is to be used as search argument for the source data. Delimiter is not restricted to being a single character.

(delimiterexpression)

A character expression which is to be used as delimiter for the source data.

column

The position at which the source data is to be split, 1 is the first position in the source data.
If **column** is prefixed with either a '+' or '-' sign, this column is relative to the last location parsed.

Note: PULL without any operand is equivalent to PULL . , i.e. the next entry is fetched. For example, this can be used to wait for operator intervention.

Example:

```
PULL . alpha .;
```
This instruction assigns the second word from the head of the stack to the variable alpha. Two placeholders (".") are used: one for the first word, and one for all words after the second word.

4.2.17 PUSH - Set Data Element at the Head of the Stack

The PUSH instruction places the specified data element at the head of the stack.

Syntax:

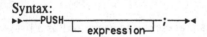

expression

The data element to be put into the stack. If no expression is specified, a null entry is entered into the stack.

Example:

```
PUSH "alpha";
PUSH "beta";
```
This code sets two entries into the stack.

4.2.18 QUEUE - Set Data Element at the Tail of the Stack

The QUEUE instruction places the specified data element at the tail of the stack.

Syntax:

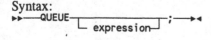

expression

The data element to be put into the stack. If no expression is specified, a null entry is entered into the stack.

Example:

```
QUEUE "alpha";
QUEUE "beta";
```

This code sets two entries into the stack.

4.2.19 RETURN - Return from Routine

The RETURN instruction either:

· returns to the statement following the invoking statement; or
· exits from the exec, if the issuing routine was not invoked with a CALL or as function invocation.

Syntax:

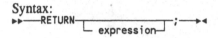

expression

The value to be passed back to the point of invocation. If the RETURN is equivalent to an EXIT, the expression must evaluate to a numeric value.

Example:

```
CALL funct;

...

funct:

...

   RETURN 4;
```

The value 4 is passed back to the statement following CALL funct.

4.2.20 SAY - Display

The SAY instruction displays the evaluated expression on the terminal.

Syntax:

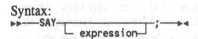

expression

The data to be displayed. The **expression** is evaluated before being displayed.

Example:

```
alpha = 10;

SAY "value of alpha is:" alpha;
```

This code displays the 'value of alpha is: 10' message.

4.2.21 SELECT - Select One Condition from a Series of Conditions

The SELECT instruction performs one (and only one) logical statement from a Select-block. The SELECT and END keywords specify the limits of the Select-block. A Select-block has one or more conditional statements that the WHEN keyword introduces. If the when-condition is satisfied, the statement following the associated THEN is executed and the Select-block terminated. A Do-block can be used as then-statement. If none of the select conditions is satisfied, control is passed to the OTHERWISE group of statements. The OTHERWISE group of statements are all statements up to the END keyword. Although the OTHERWISE group is optional, a run-time error occurs if no OTHERWISE group is present when none of the select conditions is satisfied. The OTHERWISE group can be empty.

Syntax:

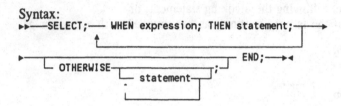

WHEN

Introduce a conditional clause.

expression

The condition to be tested. **expression** must evaluate to either 1 (true) or 0 (false).

THEN statement

The statement to be performed if the WHEN **expression** evaluates to 1 (true). If more than one statement is to be performed, a simple DO-block must be used. The NOP instruction can be used if no processing is to be performed.

OTHERWISE

Introduce the statements to be performed if none of the conditional clauses are true. The following **statements** (up to the Select END) are performed if the OTHERWISE clause is executed – this is an implicit Do.

The OTHERWISE clause must be present if none of the previous WHEN clauses have been satisfied, even when no processing is to be done. However, the OTHERWISE does not need to have any entries – in such a case the NOP instruction can be used to emphasise that no processing is to be performed.

Example 1:
```
a = 2;
SELECT
  WHEN a < 2;
    THEN SAY "a lt 2";
  WHEN a > 1;
    THEN SAY "a gt 1";
  OTHERWISE
    SAY "a not gt 1";
END;
```
This code displays the message "a gt 1".

Example 2:
```
a = 2;
SELECT
  WHEN a < 2;
    THEN SAY "a lt 2";
  WHEN a > 1;
    THEN DO;
      SAY "a gt 1";
    END;
  OTHERWISE;
    SAY "a not gt 1";
END;
```
The simple DO-block used to display the message "a gt 1" is illustrative, a single SAY statement could have been used.

4.2.22 SIGNAL - Enable (or Disable) an Exception Condition, or Cause Control to be Passed to a Routine (or Label)

The SIGNAL instruction can be used in one of three ways:
·   pass control to a routine or labelled statement;
·   enable an exception condition;
·   disable an exception condition.

If an exception condition has been enabled, control is passed to the specified routine should the particular exception condition occur; multiple exception conditions can be active at any one point of time. The setting of any particular exception condition overrides any previous setting for that condition.

Note: Whereas the handler associated with the SIGNAL instruction must be contained with the procedure, the CALL instruction can have external condition handlers.

Syntax:

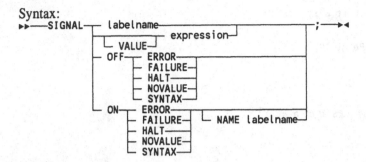

labelname
>   The name of a label to which control is to be passed.

VALUE expression
>   The evaluated **expression** is the name of a label to which control is to be passed.

OFF
>   The following trap condition is disabled.

ON

>   The following trap condition is enabled. If the trapped condition is raised, control is passed to the label having the condition name. For example, if the NOVALUE condition is enabled, control is passed to the label NOVALUE if this condition is raised. A syntax error is signaled if the required label does not exist.

ERROR
>   The error condition (positive non-zero return from host command) is disabled or enabled according as to whether OFF or ON has been specified.

FAILURE
>   The failure condition (negative return from host command) is disabled or enabled according as to whether OFF or ON has been specified.

HALT
>   The halt condition is disabled or enabled according as to whether OFF or ON has been specified. The halt condition can be raised in several ways, for example, with the HI command.

NOVALUE
>   The no-value condition (non-initialised variable used in a statement) is disabled or enabled according as to whether OFF or ON has been specified.

SYNTAX

The syntax condition is disabled or enabled according as to whether OFF or ON has been specified. The syntax-error condition can be raised in several ways, for example, a non-numeric value is used in an arithmetic expression.

Example:

```
SIGNAL alpha;
SAY "beta";
alpha: SAY "gamma";
SIGNAL ON NOVALUE;
SAY delta;
EXIT;
NOVALUE: SAY "NOVALUE exit taken at statement" SIGL;
EXIT;
```

This code displays (in sequence):

```
gamma

no value raised
```

The SAY delta statement raises the NOVALUE exception condition; the delta variable has not been initialised. The 'NOVALUE exit taken at statement 5' message will be displayed.

4.2.22.1 SIGNAL Used as GoTo.

The SIGNAL instruction can be used as a GoTo, but it should not be used to cause a branch into a DO or SELECT construction – this will cause an error, see the following code segment.

```
DO i = 1 TO 5;
  IF i = 3 THEN SIGNAL a1;
a2: END;
  ...
a1: SIGNAL a2;
```

The first SIGNAL (to a1) functions correctly, the second SIGNAL (to a2) results in an error situation – the END is misplaced.

The SIGNAL target can also be a character expression – this is similar to a computed GoTo.

Example:

```
target = "alpha";
SIGNAL (target||1);
```

causes control to be passed to the label alpha1.

Warning

The SIGNAL instruction having the function of an implicit branch should be used with caution. Where possible, the SIGNAL instruction should be reserved for the setting (or disabling) of trap conditions.

Example:
```
    SIGNAL ON NOVALUE;
    ...
    NOVALUE:
```

4.2.23 TRACE   – Set Debugging Options

The TRACE instruction is used to set the debugging option.

Syntax:

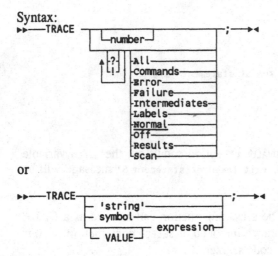

number
>   > 0 – this is the number of pauses to be bypassed;
>   < 0 – this is the number of trace outputs to be suppressed.

Only the first character of the following alphabetic keywords is significant.

ALL
>   All expressions are displayed before being executed.

COMMANDS
>   Host commands are displayed before being executed.

ERROR
>   Host commands which return a non-zero code are displayed after being executed.

FAILURE
>   Host commands which return a negative code are displayed after being executed. This is the same as the **Normal** setting.

INTERMEDIATE

All expressions are displayed before being executed, intermediate results are also displayed.

LABELS

Labels are displayed as they are reached.
Tip: This setting is useful for following the program paths.

NORMAL

Host commands which return a negative code are displayed after being executed. This is the default.

OFF

Stop trace.

RESULTS

All expressions are displayed before being executed, end results are also displayed.
Tip: This setting is recommended for general debugging purposes.

SCAN

Check the syntax without processing the statements. *Note*: This is no longer an SAA parameter.

?

Turn on interactive debugging.

!

Suppress the execution of host commands. The return code is set to zero for each host command which would have been performed.
Tip: This setting is useful for testing an exec when the host commands are either not available or erroneous.

Note: "?" and "!" are binary switches (toggles), i.e. each setting reverses the current setting of the option.

'string'

A literal that contains the trace option, e.g. TRACE '?R';

symbol

A symbol (not the value of the symbol) that is used as the trace option, e.g. TRACE ?R;

expression

The evaluated expression as the trace option, e.g. SYM = '?R'; TRACE VALUE SYM;.

Example 1:
```
TRACE ?R;
```
This statement causes the exec to execute in single-step mode.

Example 2:
```
opt = '?R';

...

TRACE (opt);
```
This code is equivalent to that shown in Example 1, but sets the tracing option dynamically.

4.2.24 UPPER – Transform Lowercase Characters into Uppercase

The UPPER instruction transforms the contents of the specified variables from lowercase to uppercase.
Note: This instruction duplicates the PARSE UPPER and TRANSLATE functions.

Syntax:

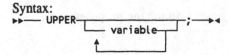

variable
> The name of a variable which is to be fetched and transformed to uppercase.

Example:
```
alpha = "beta";
SAY alpha; /* displays beta */
UPPER alpha;
SAY alpha; /* displays BETA */
```

Tip
A statement of the form
```
UPPER alpha;
```
can be replaced with either
```
PARSE UPPER VAR alpha alpha;
```
or
```
alpha = TRANSLATE(alpha);
```

4.2.25 = – Assign

The = operator assigns the specified expression to the target variable.

Syntax:
```
▶▶──target=expression;──▶◀
```

target
> The variable to which the evaluated expression is to be assigned.

expression

The expression which is to be assigned to the specified **target**.

Example:

```
x = 3 * 4
```
Assign 12 to x.

4.2.26 Command

A command is any statement that is not a keyword instruction or assignment. Commands are passed to the current environment handler, which is set with the ADDRESS instruction.

If the command has the same name as a REXX instruction or keyword (e.g. EXIT, END), the command must be written in quotes (see Example 3).

There a several standard command handlers supplied with REXX (MVS, TSO, ISPEXEC, etc.). Other command handlers can be provided by third-party products or as user-written interfaces.

Example 1:

```
ADDRESS TSO
"ALLOC F(TABFILE) DSN(USER.TABLE) SHR"
ADDRESS ISPEXEC
"TBOPEN TEMP NOWRITE LIBRARY(TABFILE)"
```

Example 2:

```
ADDRESS ISPEXEC
"LMDINIT LISTID(lid) LEVEL(tsou001)"
IF rc = 0 THEN DO
  "LMDDISP LISTID("lid") VIEW(ATTRIB)"
  "LMDFREE LISTID("lid")"
END
```
Example 2 illustrates the use of a global environment, ISPEXEC in this case. All commands (here, LMDINIT, LMDDISP, LMDFREE) are passed to this current environment.

Example 3:

```
ADDRESS TSO
/* TSO commands */
"EXIT" /* TSO EXIT */
EXIT /* REXX EXIT */
```

4.3 EXAMPLES

The following two examples illustrate the use of REXX instructions. These two examples are not typical REXX execs in that they do not make use of REXX built-in functions (Section 10.3 contains examples of execs that use built-in functions).

4.3.1 Example 1

This example calculates annual compound interest. Each year's interest and the new accumulated capital are displayed. The three variables (initial capital, annual interest rate, and number of years) are specified as invocation parameters.

```
/* REXX - interest calculation */
/* C(N) = C * Q ** N */
PARSE ARG c, p, n;
/* c = initial capital */
/* p = interest rate */
/* n = number of years */
NUMERIC DIGITS 6; /* precision */
q = p/100;
ac = c; /* initialise accumulated capital */
DO i = 1 TO n;
  ai = ac * q; /* annual interest */
  ac = ac + ai;
  SAY i ai ac; /* display */
END;
```

For the invocation parameters: 1000 (initial capital), 5 (interest rate), and 10 (years), the first and last lines are

```
1 50.00 1050.00
10 77.5670 1628.91
```
respectively.

4.3.2 Example 2

This somewhat more extensive example calculates the trigonometric sine of the specified invocation argument.

The sine is calculated using the following series:

$$\sin(x) = x/1! - x^3/3! + x^5/5! - \ldots$$

where x is expressed in radians (π (3.14159) radians = 180 degrees).

```
/* REXX - sine calculation */
PARSE ARG x; /* get invocation argument */
pi = 3.14159; /* define pi constant */
y = x * pi / 180; /* convert degrees to radians */
m = 20; /* number of terms */
z = 0; /* initialise result accumulator */
```

```
DO i = 1 TO m;
  termi = term(y, (2*i-1)); /* ith term */
  IF (i//2 = 0)
    THEN z = z - termi; /* even */
    ELSE z = z + termi; /* odd */
END;
SAY 'sine' x '=' z; /* display result */
EXIT; /* terminate */
term: PROCEDURE;
  PARSE ARG x, n;
  y = power(x,n) / factorial(n);
  RETURN y;
power: PROCEDURE; /* calculate power */
  PARSE ARG x, n; /* POWER(x**n) */
  y = 1; /* initialise result accumulator */
  DO i = 1 TO n;
    y = y * x;
  END;
  RETURN y;
factorial: PROCEDURE; /* calculate factorial */
  PARSE ARG n; /* factorial(n) = n * (n-1) * ... * 3 * 2 * 1 */
  y = 1; /* initialise result accumulator */
  DO i = n TO 1 BY -1;
    y = y * i;
  END;
  RETURN y;
```

The number of terms that are used in the series is specified as an exec constant (here m is 20). For the invocation parameter: 45, the result sine 45 = 0.707106312 is displayed.

5

Exception Handling
No rule is so general, which admits not some exception.

The Anatomy of Melancholy

Robert Burton

5.1 INTRODUCTION

REXX provides optional exception handlers that can trap various error situations.

The individual traps can be activated (set ON) or deactivated (set OFF). If the appropriate user trap has not been enabled, standard processing is performed.

Standard trap processing:
· For HALT or SYNTAX, an appropriate message is displayed and execution is terminated.
· For all other traps, the condition is ignored and processing continues normally.

Exception handlers are activated and deactivated with the CALL or SIGNAL instruction. When an exception trap is activated, the name of the associated handler routine can be specified explicitly; if no routine is specified, the trap is made to the handler routine that has the same name as the condition.
    Handlers are not stacked. If a condition is re-enabled, the original handler is disabled. A subsequent disable of the condition reactivates the default handler.

CALL trap processing varies from SIGNAL trap processing in several ways:
· CALL trap handlers can be either internal or external (SIGNAL trap handlers are only internal to the procedure).

- CALL traps can be set only for the ERROR, FAILURE and HALT conditions.
- If an exception occurs, the corresponding condition trap is set in the delayed state before the CALL is made. The delay is reset on return from the handler or if the condition is explicitly activated or deactivated. For SIGNAL, the condition trap is deactivated until explicitly enabled.
- If a CALL trap handler specifies RETURN data, unlike a normal CALL routine, this data value is ignored.

When a trap handler is invoked, the SIGL special variable contains the line number of the source statement that caused the condition. The SOURCELINE function can be called to obtain the corresponding procedure statement. The RC special variable is set before the condition handler is invoked when an ERROR or FAILURE condition occurs.

5.2 CONDITION TRAPS

REXX supports the following condition traps:
- ERROR
- FAILURE
- HALT
- NOVALUE
- SYNTAX

5.2.1 ERROR Condition

The ERROR condition is raised when a command returns a non-zero return code. If a FAILURE condition is active, it takes precedence over the ERROR condition.

Example:
```
SIGNAL ON ERROR NAME ERR5
ADDRESS TSO "FREE F(X)"
EXIT
ERR5:
   SAY 'ERROR at statement' SIGL
   SAY CONDITION() /* SIGNAL */
   SAY CONDITION('D')
   EXIT
```

This example displays the following:
```
ERROR at statement 2
SIGNAL
FREE F(X)
```

5.2.2 FAILURE Condition

The FAILURE condition is raised when a command returns a negative return code. If a FAILURE condition is active, it takes precedence over the ERROR condition.

Example:
```
SIGNAL ON FAILURE NAME ERR5
"nocmd"
EXIT
ERR5:
   SAY 'FAILURE at statement' SIGL
   SAY CONDITION() /* SIGNAL */
   SAY CONDITION('D')
   EXIT
```

This example displays the following:
```
FAILURE at statement 2
SIGNAL
"NOCMD"
```

5.2.3 HALT Condition

The HALT condition is raised by an external interrupt (PA1 key to pause processing and HI intermediate command to halt interpretation or with the EXECUTIL HI command).

Example:
```
SIGNAL ON HALT NAME ERR3
DO i = 1 TO 1000
   SAY i
END
EXIT
ERR3:
   SAY 'HALT at statement' SIGL
   EXIT
```

This example displays the following:
```
| (PA1 - interrupt)
IRX0920I ENTER HI TO END, A NULL LINE TO CONTINUE, ...
```
hi (user input — halt interpretation)
```
76 (the current value)
HALT at statement 3
```

5.2.4 NOVALUE Condition

The NOVALUE condition is raised when a symbol is used that has not been assigned a value (or if the symbol has been dropped after being assigned a value).

Example:
```
/* REXX */
SIGNAL ON NOVALUE NAME ERR1
x = 1
SAY y
EXIT
ERR1:
  SAY 'NOVALUE error in statement' SIGL
  /* NOVALUE error in statement 4 */
  EXIT
```

5.2.5 SYNTAX Condition

The SYNTAX condition is raised when a language processing error is detected. For example, a non-numeric value is used in an arithmetic expression.

Example:
```
SIGNAL ON SYNTAX NAME ERR4
a = 'alpha'
SAY a + 1
EXIT
ERR4:
  SAY 'SYNTAX ERROR at statement' SIGL
  SAY 'SOURCE:' SOURCELINE(SIGL)
  EXIT
```

This example displays the following:
```
SYNTAX ERROR at statement 3
SOURCE: SAY a + 1
```

5.2.6 Stacked Conditions

If the same condition occurs in a handler, standard condition processing is performed unless a new condition handler has been activated in the handler. If a new handler is specified for a condition, the previous handler is deactivated; a deactivation of this new handler does not reactivate the previous handler, but causes the standard system condition processing to apply.

Example 1:
```
/* REXX */
SIGNAL ON FAILURE NAME ERR5
"NULLCMD1"
EXIT
ERR5:
  "NULLCMD2"
  SAY 'FAILURE at statement' SIGL
```

```
SAY CONDITION() /* SIGNAL */
SAY CONDITION('D')
SAY CONDITION('S')
EXIT
```

This code displays:

```
IKJ56500I COMMAND NULLCMD1 NOT FOUND
    3 *-* "NULLCMD1"
      +++ RC(-3) +++
IKJ56500I COMMAND NULLCMD2 NOT FOUND
    6 *-* "NULLCMD2"
      +++ RC(-3) +++
FAILURE at statement 3
SIGNAL
NULLCMD
OFF
```

Example 2:

```
/* REXX */
CALL ON FAILURE NAME ERR5
"NULLCMD1"
EXIT
ERR5:
  "NULLCMD2"
  SAY 'FAILURE at statement' SIGL
  SAY CONDITION() /* CALL */
  SAY CONDITION('D')
  SAY CONDITION('S')
  EXIT
```

This code displays:

```
IKJ56500I COMMAND NULLCMD1 NOT FOUND
    3 *-* "NULLCMD1"
      +++ RC(-3) +++
FAILURE at statement 3
CALL
NULLCMD1
DELAY
IKJ56500I COMMAND NULLCMD2 NOT FOUND
    6 *-*  "NULLCMD2"
      +++ RC(-3) +++
```

Example 3:

This example illustrates the reactivation of a trap condition in the error handler. The unknown "ABC" command signals an ERROR trap, which is handled by the ERR1 routine. The ERR1 condition handler reactivates ERR2 as the ERROR condition handler. Within the ERR1 handler, the unknown "DEF" command signals an ERROR trap, which now is handled by the ERR2 routine.

```
/* REXX */
CALL ON ERROR NAME err1
"abc"
EXIT
err1:
   SAY 'ERR1 error trap'
   CALL ON ERROR NAME err2
   "def"
   SAY "return from ERR2"
   RETURN
err2:
   SAY 'ERR2 ERROR TRAP'
   RETURN
```

This code displays:

```
IKJ565001 COMMAND ABC NOT FOUND
    3 *-* "ABC"
       +++ RC(-3) +++
ERR1 ERROR TRAP
IKJ565001 COMMAND DEF NOT FOUND
    8 *-*  "DEF"
       +++ RC(-3) +++
ERR1 error trap
return from ERR2
```

Example 4:

```
/* REXX */
CALL ON ERROR NAME err1
CALL ON ERROR NAME err2
"abc"
CALL OFF ERROR
"xyz"
EXIT
err1: SAY 'ERR1 ERROR TRAP'
   RETURN
err2: SAY 'ERR2 ERROR TRAP'
   RETURN
```

The ERR2 routine handles the "ABC" command error. Standard condition processing is performed for the "XYZ" command error.

5.3 EXPLICIT INVOCATION

Condition handlers can be invoked directly using CALL or SIGNAL with the handler
label.

Example:

```
DO i = 1 TO 100
   IF i > 50 THEN SIGNAL HANDLER1
END
EXIT
HANDLER1:
   SAY 'Handler invoked; stmt:' SIGL
   SAY 'I:' i
   EXIT
```

This code displays:

```
Handler invoked; stmt: 2
I: 51
```

6

String Processing
Harp not on that string

King Richard

William Shakespeare

6.1 INTRODUCTION

String processing is one of REXX's most powerful features.

REXX provides two forms of string processing:
- the PARSE instruction
- built-in functions.

Although the PARSE instruction duplicates some of the functionality of certain built-in functions, the processing areas of the PARSE instruction and the built-in string processing functions are largely distinct. If either can be used, the PARSE instruction usually offers reduced processing overhead.

The built-in string processing functions have two forms:
- functions that process words (a REXX word is series of characters delimited by one or more blanks)
- functions that process strings (a string in this context being a series of characters).

The PARSE instruction operates on a source string. The parsing operation splits data in the source according to the specified template (pattern). The parsed data can be

Example 1:
This example illustrates the parsing significance of the last-variable.

```
str = " alpha  beta   gamma     "
PARSE VAR str p1 p2
SAY p1 /* alpha */
SAY p2 /* --beta---gamma---- */


str = " alpha  beta   gamma     "
PARSE VAR str p1 p2 p3
SAY p1 /* alpha */
SAY p2 /* beta */
SAY p3 /* ---gamma---- */


str = " alpha  beta   gamma     "
PARSE VAR str p1 p2 p3 .
SAY p1 /* alpha */
SAY p2 /* beta */
SAY p3 /* gamma */
```

Note the use of a placeholder as the "last-variable" in the template.

```
str = " alpha  beta   gamma     "
PARSE VAR str p1
SAY p1 /* -alpha--beta---gamma---- */
```

Note the use of a single variable in the template, which is then the "last-variable".

Note: In the above examples, - represents a blank.

Example 2:
This example illustrates the equivalent of the two forms of word parsing.

```
str = "alpha beta gamma"
PARSE VAR str p1 p2
SAY p1 /* alpha */
SAY p2 /*  beta gamma */
PARSE VALUE str WITH p1 p2
SAY p1 /* alpha */
SAY p2 /*  beta gamma */
```

Example 3:
This example illustrates the use of recursive parsing with stem variables.

```
DO i = 1 TO 999 UNTIL str = ''
  PARSE VAR str p.i str
  SAY i p.i
END
```

Example 4:

This example illustrates the use of a dynamically created template, for example when the number of words in the string is not known and stem variables cannot be used.

```
n = WORDS(str) /* get number of words */
stmt = "PARSE VAR str"
DO i = 1 TO n
  stmt = stmt 'P'i
END
INTERPRET stmt
SAY p1
SAY p2 /* and so on */
```

6.3 DELIMITER PARSING

Delimiter parsing splits the source string into two parts: before and after the delimiter. If the delimiter is not present, the second part is null. The delimiter is one or more characters that can be specified as either a literal string or as an alphanumeric variable (written within parentheses); a numeric variable is interpreted as positional parsing (see Section 6.4).

Delimiter parsing can be combined with other forms of parsing (e.g. word-parsing) to achieve dynamic parsing, i.e. parsed results are used to affect the subsequent parsing (see Section 6.5).

Template syntax:
```
▶▶─────────┬───────────┬──'literal'──┬──templateitem──▶◀
           ├ variable──┤  ├"literal"──┤
           └placeholder┘  └(variable)─┘
```

Example 1:
```
str = "x := alpha"
PARSE VAR str p1 ':=' p2
SAY p1 /* x- */
SAY p2 /* -alpha */
```

Example 2:
```
str = "x := alpha"
dlm = ':='
PARSE VAR str p1 (dlm) p2
SAY p1 /* x- */
SAY p2 /* -alpha */
```

Note: In the above examples, - represents a blank.

6.4 POSITIONAL PARSING

Positional parsing uses a numeric argument to split the parsed string. The position
argument can be either absolute (in the parsed string) or relative to the current
position in the parsed string. The numeric argument can be either a numeric
constant or a variable written in parentheses. Relative positions are written with a
prefixed sign (+ or -). The optional =-prefix can be used to explicitly specify an
absolute position. If the next parsing position (either absolute or relative) lies
before the previous parsing position, the remaining string is assigned (see Example
3).

Template syntax:

Example 1:
```
str = "epsilon lambda"
PARSE VAR str p1 3 p2 +3 p3 -2 p4
SAY p1 /* ep */
SAY p2 /* sil */
SAY p3 /* on lambda */
SAY p4 /* ilon lambda */
```

Example 2:
```
str = "epsilon lambda"
m = 3
n = 2
PARSE VAR str p1 =(m) p2 +(m) p3 -(n) p4
SAY p1 /* ep */
SAY p2 /* sil */
SAY p3 /* on lambda */
SAY p4 /* ilon lambda */
```

Example 3:
```
str = "epsilon lambda"
PARSE VAR str p1 4 p2 -2 p3
SAY p1 /* eps */
SAY p2 /* ilon lambda */
SAY p3 /* psilon lambda */
```

6.5 DYNAMIC PARSING

Dynamic parsing involves using one or more values from the parsed string in the parsing template.

Example 1:

```
str = "05alpha"
PARSE VAR str len 3 var +(len) .
SAY len var /* display length and data */
```

In this example, the parsed string consists of a pair of items: a two-character length item that contains the length of the following data field, and the data field itself. The extracted length (the parsed string split at the 3rd character) is assigned to the LEN variable. This relative position specifies the end of the variable length DATA variable. Worked Example 2 (Section 6.7.2) shows a practical example of this processing.

Example 2:

```
str = '"O''Brien"' 'Dublin'
PARSE VAR str dlm 2 name (dlm) city .
say name /* O'Brien */
say city /* Dublin */
str = "'Smith'" 'London'
PARSE VAR str dlm 2 name (dlm) city .
say name /* Smith */
say city /* London */
```

This example uses the first character from the parsed string as delimiter for the NAME item.

Note: The first delimiter (' or ", respectively) is the REXX delimiter to define a literal.

6.6 ARGUMENT PARSING

The PARSE ARG or ARG instruction can process multiple templates, each of which is separated with a comma. ARG differs from PARSE ARG only in that it automatically converts the result to uppercase. Each template can have a different format.

Example:
This example also illustrates two different uses of the comma in a template: to separate arguments and as a delimiter.

```
CALL funct 2,"alpha,beta"
EXIT
funct:
  PARSE ARG n, parmlist
  SAY n /* 2 */
```

```
SAY parmlist /* alpha,beta */
PARSE VAR parmlist p1 ',' p2
SAY p1 /* alpha */
SAY p2 /* beta */
RETURN
```

6.7 WORKED EXAMPLES

6.7.1 Worked Example 1

Depending on the processing required, built-in word processing functions sometimes can be used instead of the PARSE instruction. The following example illustrates equivalent processing with the SUBWORD function and the PARSE instruction.

Note: The use of built-in functions in preference to PARSE is normally only of theoretical interest; the PARSE instruction normally provides better performance.

Procedure code:
```
str = "alpha beta gamma delta epsilon"
newstr = SUBWORD(str,2,3)
SAY newstr /* beta gamma delta */
PARSE VAR str . word2 word3 word4 .
newstr = word2 word3 word4
SAY newstr /* beta gamma delta */
```

6.7.2 Worked Example 2

This example illustrates dynamic parsing. Each logical item in the string contains two pairs of entries; each entry contains a length field, which contains the length of the following data item. The first entry pair represents the variable name (the length field is two characters). The second entry pair represents the variable data (the length field is three characters). The invoked routine (SETVAR) uses the parameter string to create REXX variables with the specified data. The example also shows the use of recursive parsing; the number of items in the parameter string is unlimited.

To avoid overcomplicating the code, a simplifying assumption is made that the variable data entry does not contain a single quote; such data would cause a syntax error in the interpreted statement.

Note: This method can be used to pass REXX variables between external procedures.

Procedure code:

```
str = "05alpha004beta05gamma011DELTA OMEGA"
CALL setvar str
EXIT
setvar: PROCEDURE
  PARSE ARG parmstr
  DO UNTIL parmstr = ''
    PARSE VAR parmstr vl 3 vn +(vl) parmstr
    PARSE VAR parmstr vl 4 vd +(vl) parmstr
    stmt = vn "='"vd"'"
    INTERPRET stmt
  END
  SAY alpha /* beta */
  SAY gamma /* DELTA OMEGA */
RETURN
```

6.7.3 Worked Example 3

This example illustrates the use of parsing to analyse and process list output. The IDCAMS utility PRINT function lists selected records in one of three formats: character, hexadecimal or dump. If only a listing of the keys is required, the print report contains much superfluous information (namely the listing of the record's contents). Similarly, depending on the key format, none of these standard formats may be suitable; it may be appropriate to display the key in some application-specific format. This sample code displays the key in one of two formats: in character format if the key contains only alphanumeric data, otherwise in hexadecimal format (a non-alphanumeric key is displayed as a hexadecimal value).

Procedure code:

```
alphanum = '0123456789', /* alphanum. chars */
           'abcdefghijklmnopqrstuvwxyz',
           'ABCDEFGHIJKLMNOPQRSTUVWXYZ'
CALL OUTTRAP 'r.','*','NOCONCAT' /* trap PRINT output */
"PRINT INDATASET(test.ksds) HEX" /* IDCAMS print */
/* process PRINT output */
IF RC = 0 THEN DO i = 1 TO r.0
  /* analyse record */
  PARSE VAR r.i . 'KEY OF RECORD - ' key .
  IF key <> '' THEN DO /* key record */
    xkey = X2C(key)
    IF VERIFY(xkey,alphanum) = 0
      THEN SAY xkey /* alphanumeric key */
      ELSE SAY "X'"key"'" /* nonalphanumeric key */
  END
END
```

Sample output:

```
X'A2A281A281A281A28100000000000000'
A1
X'C1F1F04040404040404040409585A6409985'
A2
A3
A4
X'C1F94040404040404040409585A6409985'
CAA
```

7

Numbers and Arithmetic

"Reeling and Writing, of course, to begin with," the Mock Turtle replied, "and the different branches of arithmetic - Ambition, Distraction, Uglification, and Dirision."

Alice's Adventures in Wonderland

Lewis Carroll

7.1 INTRODUCTION

The concepts of a number and of arithmetic operators were introduced in Section 2.2.

A REXX number can be written either as a fixed-point value (e.g. `2`, `2.3`, `0.4`) or in exponential notation (e.g. `2E3` or `3E-4`) or as a combination (e.g. `2.3E-5`). In exponential notation, `E` (or `e`) represents the power of ten (e.g. `2E3` is equivalent to `2*1000 = 2000`).

The processing of arithmetic expressions in REXX generally follows the usual rules (e.g. multiplicative operators have precedence over additive operators), although there are certain rules with regard to:
· precision
· representation
· sequence of operations.

7.2 NUMBER

A REXX number has the format:

```
▶▶──────────┬─DecimalNumber─┬──────────▶◀
     └─Sign─┘               └─Exponent─┘
```

Sign

The optional sign is either + (default) or -

DecimalNumber

A decimal number contains one or more decimal digits and may have a decimal point that is represented by a period. The NUMERIC DIGITS instruction specifies the maximum precision (default 9 digits). If the number of digits exceeds this precision, the number is represented in exponential form.

Decimal number syntax:

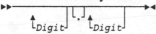

Examples:

    1
    1.2
    0.1
    .2
    -12.3
    +4

Exponent

A leading E (or e) indicates an exponent. If an exponent is specified, the prefixed decimal number is interpreted as the mantissa. The exponent is an integral power of ten (positive or negative) with which the mantissa is multiplied.

Exponent syntax:

Examples:

    1E1 /* 10 */
    1.2E2 /* 120 (= 1.2*100) */
    0.1E-1 /* 0.01 (= 0.1*0.1) */
    0.1E+1 /* 1 */

7.3 ARITHMETIC OPERATORS

REXX has the following arithmetic operators:
** exponentiation (power)
* multiplication
/ division
% integer division (modulo)

// remainder
+ addition
- subtraction.

7.3.1 Power (Exponentiation)

The power operator (**) raises the specified number by the specified integer power. The power can be either positive or negative. A negative power returns the reciprocal.
Exponentiation is performed from left to right. This also applies if the exponentiation operator is applied twice (see Example 2).

Example 1:
```
SAY 2**3 /* 8 */
SAY 2**-3 /* 0.125 */
```

Example 2:
```
SAY 2 ** 3 ** 4 /* (2**3=8)**4 = 4096 */
SAY 2 ** (3 ** 4) /* 2.4E+24 */
```

7.3.2 Multiplication

The multiplication operator (*) multiplies two numbers together. The precision of the result has a maximum precision of the sum of the individual precisions of the multiplier and multiplicand.

Example:
```
SAY 3.2*4.3 /* 13.76 */
```

7.3.3 Division

The division operator (/) performs a signed division by dividing the dividend by the divisor. If necessary, the dividend is successively multiplied by 10 until its numeric value (without regard to decimal value) is larger than the numeric value of the divisor.

Example:
```
NUMERIC DIGITS 4
SAY 1 / 6 /* 0.1667 */
SAY 10 / 6 /* 1.667 */
SAY 100000 / 6 /* 1.667E+4 */
```

7.3.4 Modulo (Integer) Division

The modulo (integer) division operator (%) returns the integer quotient that results from dividing the dividend by the divisor. The result is truncated, i.e. any remainder is ignored. The rules as specified for division apply.

Example:
```
NUMERIC DIGITS 4
SAY 1 / 6 /* 0 */
SAY 10 / 6 /* 1 */
SAY -1000 / 6 /* -166 */
SAY -1000 / -6 /* 166 */
SAY 100000 / 6 /* error, invalid whole number (precision exceeded) */
```

7.3.5 Remainder of Division

The remainder division operator (//) returns the remainder that results from an integer division.

Example:
```
NUMERIC DIGITS 4
SAY 1 // 6 /* =1; 6 * 0 + 1 = 1 */
SAY 10 // 6 /* =4; 6 * 1 + 4 = 10 */
SAY -1000 // 6 /* =-4; 6 * -166 - 4 = -1000 */
SAY -1000 // -6 /* =-4; -6 * 166 - 4 = -1000 */
```

7.3.6 Numeric Comparison

A numeric comparison is made when two numeric values are compared with a comparison operator (the "strictly" comparison operators (==, >>, >>=, <<, <<=) do not perform a numeric comparison). The numeric comparison is made by subtracting the second operand from the first operand. The precision of this temporary result is reduced by the fuzz setting (NUMERIC FUZZ instruction) before it is compared with 0 to return the comparison result.

Example:
```
NUMERIC DIGITS 4
SAY 12.34 = 12.345 /* 0 = unequal */
NUMERIC FUZZ 2
SAY 12.34 = 12.345 /* 1 = equal with regard to fuzz setting */
```

7.4 PRECISION AND REPRESENTATION

The precision is determined by the value specified in the NUMERIC DIGITS instruction. The default precision is 9 digits.

The NUMERIC DIGITS instruction specifies how many digits are to be retained as the result of a numeric operation, and is also directly concerned with how the result is represented in external format, e.g. how the number is displayed with the SAY function. The DIGITS function returns the current NUMERIC DIGITS setting.

Do not set the precision higher than it need be:
·   Increasing the precision increases the computation time.

· Increasing the precision also increases the amount of storage required for numeric fields, even when the higher precision is not used.

Similarly, do not set the precision less than required. The set numeric precision is used for all numeric operations, including loops; if the precision is set too low, the loop condition may not be satisfied. It may be better to set an extended precision only in those sections of code that require it.

Rule
If the number of digits before the decimal place is greater than the value specified for DIGITS, the number is represented in exponential format. If the number of digits after the decimal place is greater than twice the value specified for DIGITS, the number is represented in exponential format.

This rule is best illustrated with an example. If DIGITS has been set to 2 (e.g. x = DIGITS(2);), the following results of multiplying 12.5 by 5 (to various numbers of decimal places) are displayed:

```
NUMERIC DIGITS 2
SAY 12.5 * 500          6.3E+3
SAY 12.5 * 50           6.3E+2
SAY 12.5 * 5            63
SAY 12.5 * 0.5          6.3
SAY 12.5 * 0.05         0.63
SAY 12.5 * 0.005        0.063
SAY 12.5 * 0.0005       0.0063
SAY 12.5 * 0.00005      6.3E-4
SAY 12.5 * 0.000005     6.3E-5
```

Note in this particular example, the number of digits would need to be set to at least 3 to avoid loss of significant digits (12.5 * 5 = 62.5).

Example:
```
NUMERIC DIGITS 1
DO i = 1 TO 12
   SAY i
END
```
This example of setting the precision too low results in an endless loop because the i control variable can never attain the value 12.

Exponential format is a mathematical way of representing both very large and very small numbers. The "E" (or "e") in REXX represents the power ten with the following number as the exponent.

Example:
E2   represents $10^2 = 100$
E-2 represents $10^{-2} = 1/100 = 0.01$

The mantissa, the number preceding the "E", is multiplied by this power of ten to give the end result.

Example:
6.3E2   represents $6.3 * 10^2 = 6.3 * 100 = 630$
6.3E-2   represents $6.3 * 10^{-2} = 6.3 * 0.01 = 0.063$

7.4.1 Computational Base

The base used in computation depends on the form of the numbers involved in the arithmetic operation (as shown in the following list).

decimal,decimal	decimal
decimal,exponential	exponential
exponential,exponential	exponential

Example:
```
SAY (2+3) /* 5 */
SAY (2+4.0) /* 6.0 */
SAY (4.0+5.0) /* 9.0 */
```

7.4.2 Retention of Significance

REXX arithmetic operations retain the maximum number of significant digits of the operands that take part in the computation.

Example:
```
SAY 12.3+1 /* 13.3 */
SAY 12.3+1.00 /* 13.30 */
SAY 1.2/0.6 /* 2 */
SAY 1.2/2 /* 0.6 */
SAY 1.20/2 /* 0.6 */
SAY 1.2*0.5 /* 0.60 */
```

7.4.3 Arithmetic Exceptions

Because REXX adjusts its internal precision accordingly and stores very large and small numbers in exponential form (base 10) with up to nine exponential digits (i.e. maximum exponent: e999999999, and minimum exponent: e-999999999), arithmetic exceptions (such as overflow and underflow) rarely occur. These arithmetic exceptions are signalled as bad arithmetic conversion conditions.

Example 1:
```
NUMERIC DIGITS 3
x1 = 123
SAY x1+1 /* 124 */
x2 = .1234
SAY x2+1 /* 1.12 */
y = 2e9999999999
SAY y+1 /* (overflow) */
```

Example 2:
```
a = 'X'
SAY (a+1) /* non-numeric operand */
```

7.5 SEQUENCE OF OPERATIONS

General mathematics has the rule that multiplicative (which includes division) operations are performed before additive (which includes subtraction) operations; REXX also adheres to this rule.

Example:
```
x = 12 + 4*2;
```
This expression assigns 20 to x.

As in general mathematics, parentheses can be used to explicitly specify the order of performing operations; the parenthesised expression is calculated first. For example,
```
x = (12 + 4)*2;
```
This expression assigns 32 to x.

If the parenthesised expression itself contains parentheses, the innermost parentheses are resolved first. For example,
```
x = (3+(12 + 4)*2);
```
This expression is calculated in the following manner:
12 + 4 = 16; 16 * 2 = 32; 3 + 32 = 35

7.6 NUMERIC FORMATTING

Although numeric formatting is not directly concerned with arithmetic operations, numeric formatting is important for display of results. By default, numbers are formatted in accordance with the implied NUMERIC DIGITS setting (see Section 4.2.12).

The following functions and instruction influence the formatting:

· NUMERIC FORM instruction. The NUMERIC FORM instruction specifies whether the scientific (default) or engineering representation is to be used for the exponent. Engineering exponents are always a multiple of three.

· TRUNC function. The TRUNC function specifies the number of decimal places to be shown. Trailing zeros are inserted when the current precision (NUMERIC DIGITS setting) is exceeded.

· FORMAT function. The FORMAT function specifies the number of digits and decimal places to be shown. Trailing zeros are inserted when the current precision is exceeded. Furthermore, the FORMAT function can specific a trigger for the exponential display representation and the number of digits to be used.

Example:

```
NUMERIC DIGITS 4
SAY (1234+0) /* 1234 */
SAY (12345+0) /* 1235E+4 */
SAY (1.234+0) /* 1.234 */
SAY (1.2345+0) /* 1.235 */
x = 1.234+0
SAY TRUNC(x,2) /* 1.23 */
SAY TRUNC(x,4) /* 1.2340 */
y = 234.56+0
SAY FORMAT(y,3,4) /* 234.6000 */
SAY FORMAT(y,4,3) /*  234.600 */
SAY FORMAT(y,3,4,,2) /* 2.3460E+2 */
SAY FORMAT(y,3,4,2,2) /* 2.3460E+02 */
z = 12345+0
NUMERIC FORM ENGINEERING
SAY z /* 12.35E+3 */
NUMERIC FORM SCIENTIFIC
SAY z /* 1.235E+4 */
```

8

Input/Output

Tiny differences in input could quickly become overwhelming differences in output ...

Chaos
James Gleick

8.1 INTRODUCTION

Input/output (I/O) statements, other than simple terminal operations (PULL and SAY instructions), are not part of the SAA REXX implementation. Although simple procedures using REXX may be able to be written without using I/O statements, most practical REXX programs will require I/O operations.

Whereas many REXX implementations (for example, the REXX Standard) have character and line-oriented REXX functions (for example, CHARIN and LINEOUT), the mainframe-based REXX implementations (VM and OS/390) have just the record-oriented EXECIO command, although this single command is very powerful.

The OS/390 I/O facilities can be classified into two groups:
· simple terminal operations (PULL and SAY instructions);
· operations at the file level (EXECIO command), although the EXECIO command can also be used to process single records and for file positioning.

This chapter describes the general I/O facilities. The following chapters contain detailed descriptions of the I/O operations:
· this chapter - I/O terminal instructions;
· Chapter 11 - EXECIO command.

8.2 DATA BUFFERING

The data buffering is related to the level (line or file) at which the input/output operation is performed. Input terminal data can be buffered in the stack. For line operations, REXX variables are used to contain the data. For operations at the file level, either the stack or stem variables can be used as the data buffer.

8.3 OPENING AND CLOSING THE DATA FILES

REXX files are automatically opened when they are first used; the OPEN operand can be specified to explicitly open a file. They are also automatically closed when the REXX exec terminates. For processing at the file level, i.e. with the EXECIO command, files can be explicitly closed with the FINIS operand. This can be used to reprocess a file from the start (in OS/390, the disposition specifies how a file is to be reprocessed).

In general, a file should be closed when it is no longer needed. This has two advantages:
· main-storage is freed;
· if the file has been reserved for exclusive use by the processing exec, it is then available for use by other programs.

Example 1:
```
"EXECIO 0 DISKW DDN (OPEN"; /* open */
```
This command opens the file that has DDN as ddname; the 0 specifies that no records are to be written.

Example 2:
```
"EXECIO 2 DISKW DDN (FINIS"; /* write and close */
```
This command writes records from the stack to the DDN file, which it subsequently closes (FINIS operand).

8.4 TERMINAL OPERATIONS

The PULL and SAY instructions are used to perform basic transfer from and to the terminal, respectively.

Terminal input is taken by default from the stack - this means that a request for terminal input is first satisfied by taking data from the stack; if the current stack is empty, the program awaits input from the terminal. The carriage-return character ends a terminal input line (the stored data item does not contain this carriage-return character, i.e. the carriage-return character entered by itself results in a null data item).

This use of the stack has two consequences:
- Responses can be pre-stored with the PUSH or QUEUE instruction - this can be useful to provide information for host environment commands and functions.
- When the REXX terminates, any entries remaining in the stack will be interpreted as being commands (the DELSTACK command can be used to remove the stack).

Tip
Always precede a request for terminal input data with a message to the terminal. This avoids the application program seeming to wait for no apparent reason.

Example 1:
```
QUEUE 'TIME';
```
Pass the TIME command to the currently active command processor. The command processor is invoked when a non-REXX instruction is processed or on completion of the exec.

Example 2:
```
SAY "Enter command";
PARSE PULL cmd; /* get command */
SAY 'cmd:'cmd; /* display command */
QUEUE cmd; /* pass command to the Command Processor */
```
Request the user to enter a command, which is displayed and passed to the currently active command processor.

8.5 FILE-MODE OPERATIONS

The EXECIO command is used for file-mode (record-oriented) input/output operations.

The EXECIO command as implemented in REXX is based on the VM/CMS EXECIO command, although not all the parameters are supported.

The TSO implementation supports only the following record formats:
- fixed length records
- variable length records.

The records may be either blocked or unblocked; data being written is formatted as appropriate, e.g. fixed length records are automatically padded on the right with blanks.

Warning
The EXECIO command is optimised. Consequently, the output file is opened only when data are to be written. However, a null variable contains no data - this also means that such a file is not closed on termination of the exec, normally the end-of-file marker would have been written.

8.5.1 File Positioning

File positioning can be made in two ways:
· the SKIP operand skips the specified number of records;
· the starting record number can be specified.

Example:

```
"EXECIO 2 DISKR DDNAME (SKIP" /* skip */
"EXECIO * DISKR DDNAME" /* line 3, 4, ... */
```

These two commands are equivalent to the following command:

```
"EXECIO * DISKR DDNAME 3" /* line 3, 4, ... */
```

In both cases the first two records are skipped. Whereas the first commands explicitly skip these two records, the last command starts processing with the third record.

8.5.2 Write Operation

The DISKW operation writes zero or more records from the stack or a named stem to a file. If no explicit record count is specified, the first null record terminates the write operation. The file remains open unless the FINIS option is specified.

Example:

```
QUEUE 'line1'
QUEUE 'line2'
QUEUE '' /* null variable */
"ALLOC F(DDN) DSN(DATA.FILE) NEW REUS"
"EXECIO * DISKW DDN"
```

This example writes all the stack records (here two records) to the specified file.

The equivalent processing using stem variables follows:

```
s. = '' /* null variable */
s.1 = 'line1'
s.2 = 'line2'
"ALLOC F(DDN) DSN(DATA.FILE) NEW REUS"
"EXECIO * DISKW DDN (STEM s."
```

8.5.3 Delete Data Operation

A DISKW operation that writes zero records and closes (FINIS option) the file will delete all the data records from the file.

Example:

```
"ALLOC F(DDN) DSN(DATA.FILE) OLD"
"EXECIO 0 DISKW DDN (FINIS"
```

8.5.4 Read Operation

The DISKR (or DISKRU for update) operation reads zero or more records from a file into the stack or a named stem. The read records can be placed at either the head (LIFO operand) or the tail (FIFO operand) of the stack. If the file is read into stem variables, the stem.0 variable is set to contain the number of records read. Unless the FINIS option is specified, the file remains open.

Example:
```
"ALLOC F(DDN) DSN(DATA.FILE) SHR REUS"
"EXECIO * DISKR DDN (FIFO"
SAY QUEUED() /* number of records */
```
This example reads the file into the queue and displays the number of records.

The equivalent processing using stem variables follows:
```
"ALLOC F(DDN) DSN(DATA.FILE) SHR REUS"
"EXECIO * DISKW DDN (STEM s."
SAY s.0 /* number of records */
```

8.5.5 Update Operation

If a record is read for update (DISKRU operation), it can be updated by performing a write operation (DISKW) as the next operation on the file.

Example:
```
"ALLOC F(DDNAME) DSN(DATA.FILE) OLD"
"EXECIO 1 DISKRU DDNAME 2 (STEM s."
s.1 = STRIP(s.1,'T') 'updated'
"EXECIO 1 DISKW DDNAME (STEM s. FINIS"
```
This example appends the text "updated" at the end of the record.

9

Debugging

Yet let me flap this bug with gilded wings,
This painted child of dirt, that stinks and stings; ...

Epitaph on Gay
Alexander Pope

9.1 INTRODUCTION

Debugging described in this chapter deals with the mechanics involved, i.e. the tools which REXX makes available. The techniques used for debugging are largely an art, which can only be learnt to a limited degree - a good "debugger" (the person who debugs) does it largely by intuition. For those people who do not fall into this category, the best help is information. This chapter describes the REXX facilities available to supply this information.

Unlike many conventional programming languages, standard REXX does not have a full-screen debugger. This means that debugging REXX execs involves the display of trace information, contents of variables, etc.

REXX supports three forms of debugging:
· Signal the processing to be performed if a specified exception condition occurs (SIGNAL instruction).
· Trace statement execution. The TRACE instruction (or TRACE function) allows many levels of information display (label tracing, statement execution tracing, display intermediate results, etc.). The TRACE instruction offers a flexible form of tracing; tracing can be activated only for critical code sections or the tracing option can be set as a variable, which enables the tracing level to be set **parametrically** (possibly externally, and so allow productive exec code to be debugged if operational errors occur).

· Simple display with the SAY instruction. This technique can be used for the selective display of a literal or the contents of a variable, and is especially appropriate for large execs, which otherwise would result in excessive trace output.

REXX offers two means of obtaining information:
· statically
· dynamically (interactively).

Static means build the debugging statements into the REXX exec. **Dynamic** or **interactive** means interrupt the REXX exec while it is executing and invoke the appropriate debugging statements from the terminal. All REXX statements are available in interactive debugging mode, for example, the assignment instruction can be used to alter the contents of a variable.

9.2 EXCEPTION CONDITIONS

Exception conditions are:
· ERROR   A non-zero return code from a host command.
· FAILURE   A negative return code from a host command.
· HALT   The interpretation of the REXX exec is halted, for example, with the HI command.
· NO VALUE A symbol has been used which has not been initialised (i.e. has not received data).
· SYNTAX   An invalid REXX statement has been invoked (this can have invalid syntax, or an operand contains invalid data (e.g. non-numeric data in an arithmetic expression, etc.)).

These exception conditions are trapped by the SIGNAL instruction. If exception conditions are not trapped, messages are displayed only in the following circumstances:
· a host command returns the failure condition;
· syntax error (and processing is terminated).

Tip
To avoid unexpected processing occurring, the NO VALUE exception condition should always be set, even though this may increase the program coding to some extent.

One of the features of the REXX language which makes coding easier is that each symbol is initialised by default to have its own name as content (in upper case). The hidden danger is that when such symbols are used as parameters, rather than using explicit literals, their value may be altered somewhere in the program - possibly when modifications are made at some later point in time.

9.3 TRACING OPTIONS

One of the following tracing options can be set:
- ALL
- COMMANDS
- ERROR
- FAILURE
- INTERMEDIATE
- LABELS
- RESULTS
- SYNTAX

These options specify what tracing is to be performed, i.e. under what circumstances a trace message is to be displayed. Only one tracing option can be active at any one time. However, the setting of the trace option may be altered during the course of running the REXX exec. The above tracing options can be abbreviated to their initial letter, for example, A instead of ALL.

There are also two prefix operators:
- ?
- !

These prefix operators may be prefixed before any of the options specified above.

? invokes interactive debugging, which means that execution pauses when the set option occurs, e.g. TRACE ?ALL stops before each statement is executed, and is equivalent to operating in single-step mode. ! suppresses the execution of host commands. The return code is set to 0 for each host command which would have been executed. This can be useful for testing a REXX exec when the required host commands are not available.

The two prefix operators (? and !) are binary switches (toggles). Each setting reverses the previous setting.

There is also a special form of the TRACE instruction that can be used in interactive tracing mode: a numeric operand suppresses intervention.

9.3.1 ALL - Display All Expressions Before Execution

The ALL option is used to display all expressions before they are executed.

Example:
```
/* REXX */
TRACE ALL
i = 1
A1:
 CALL compute
A2:
 EXIT
```

```
compute:
c1:
 j = i + 1
 RETURN
```

Trace output:

```
 3 *-* i = 1
 4 *-* A1:
 5 *-* CALL compute
 8 *-*  compute:
 9 *-*  c1:
10 *-*  j = .i + 1
11 *-*  RETURN
 6 *-* A2:
 7 *-* EXIT
```

9.3.2 COMMANDS - Display All Commands Before Execution

The COMMANDS option is used to display all commands before they are executed.

Example:

```
/* REXX */
TRACE COMMANDS
ADDRESS TSO
"SUBCOM USER"
"SUBCOM TSO"
```

Trace output:

```
4 *-* "SUBCOM USER"
  >>>    "SUBCOM USER"
  +++ RC(1) +++
5 *-* "SUBCOM TSO"
  >>>    "SUBCOM TSO"
```

9.3.3 ERROR - Display All Commands Which Return an Error Condition

The ERROR option is used to display all commands which return a non-zero code after being executed.

Example:

```
/* REXX */
TRACE E
ADDRESS TSO
"FREE F(FILE)"
NOP
```

Trace output:

```
IKJ56247I FILE FILE NOT FREED, IS NOT ALLOCATED
    4 *-* "FREE F(FILE)"
       +++ RC(12) +++
```

9.3.4 FAILURE - Display All Commands Which Return a Negative Error Condition

The FAILURE option is used to display all commands which return a negative code after being executed. This is the default setting.

Example:

```
/* REXX */
TRACE F
ADDRESS TSO
"NOFREE F(FILE)"
NOP
```

Trace output:

```
IKJ56500I COMMAND NOFREE NOT FOUND
    4 *-* "NOFREE F(FILE)"
       +++ RC(-3) +++
```

9.3.5 INTERMEDIATE - Display All Expressions (With Intermediate Results) Before Being Executed

The INTERMEDIATE option is used to display all expressions before being executed; intermediate results are also displayed. This is the option usually used for general debugging.

Example:

```
/* REXX */
TRACE I
i = 1
A1:
 CALL compute
A2:
 EXIT
compute:
c1:
 j = i + 1
 RETURN
```

Trace output:
```
 3 *-* i = 1
   >L>    "1"
 4 *-* A1:
 5 *-* CALL compute
 8 *-* compute:
 9 *-* c1:
10 *-* j = i + 1
   >V>    "1"
   >L>    "1"
   >O>    "2"
11 *-* RETURN
 6 *-* A2:
 7 *-* EXIT
```

9.3.6 LABELS - Display All Labels As They Are Reached

The LABELS option is used to display the names of labels as they are reached. This option is useful for tracing the program flow. The displayed labels are automatically nested, i.e. each hierarchy is indented.

Example:
```
/* REXX */
TRACE L
i = 1
A1:
  CALL compute
A2:
  EXIT
compute:
c1:
  j = i +1
  RETURN
```

Trace output:
```
 4 *-* A1:
 8 *-* compute:
 9 *-* c1:
 6 *-* A2:
```

9.3.7 RESULTS - Display All Expressions (With End Results) Before Being Executed

The RESULTS option is used to display all expressions before being executed; the end results are also displayed.

Example:

```
/* REXX */
TRACE R
i = 1
A1:
 CALL compute
A2:
 EXIT
compute:
c1:
 j = i + 1
 RETURN
```

Trace output:

```
 3 *-* i = 1
   >>>    "1"
 4 *-* A1:
 5 *-* CALL compute
 8 *-* compute:
 9 *-* c1:
10 *-* j = i + 1
   >>>    "2"
11 *-* RETURN
 6 *-* A2:
 7 *-* EXIT
```

9.3.8 SYNTAX - Check Syntax Without Processing the Statements

The SYNTAX option is used to check the syntax of the complete program. The program is not executed. SYNTAX cannot be invoked in the following circumstances:
· from within a construction (Do-group or Select-block);
· from the interactive debugging mode.

Tip
With exception of compiled REXX execs, execs are interpreted. This means that the statements are first processed when they are executed, with the result that erroneous statements may be hidden in parts of the program which are not normally executed, e.g. error handling routines. TRACE SYNTAX detects such errors, and so should be used before important applications are put into production.

9.3.9 n - Suppress Trace Intervention

The TRACE instruction with a numeric operand suppresses intervention. The numeric operand specifies the number of trace operations that are to be processed without requiring intervention; if the operand is negative, this number of trace operations are processed with neither intervention nor trace output. This option can only be used in the interactive tracing mode.

In the following examples, input is shown italicised.

Example:
```
/* REXX */
TRACE ?L
DO i = 1 TO 5
  a1:
END
```

Trace output 1:
```
        4 *-* a1:
     IRX0100I +++ Interactive trace.  TRACE OFF to end debug, ENTER to
     continue. +++

     (ENTER)
            *-* a1:
     (ENTER)
            *-* a1:
     (ENTER)
            *-* a1:
     (ENTER)
            *-* a1:
```

This example shows the output from a normal interactive trace session; each trace output is confirmed with ENTER.

Trace output 2:
```
        4 *-* a1:
     IRX0100I +++ Interactive trace.  TRACE OFF to end debug, ENTER to
     continue. +++

     trace 2
        4 *-* a1:
          *-* a1:
          *-* a1:
     (ENTER)
          *-* a1:
```

This example shows the output from an interactive trace session with suppression of trace intervention.

Trace output 3:

```
      4 *-*  a1:
    IRX0100I +++ Interactive trace.  TRACE OFF to end debug, ENTER to
continue. +++

trace -2
      4 *-*  a1:
  (ENTER)
          *-*  a1:
```

This example shows the output from an interactive trace session with suppression of trace intervention and output.

9.4 TRACE OUTPUT

Trace output is prefixed with a three-character code which identifies the contents of the following trace line. There are two forms of prefix:
·   those used for trace data;
·   those used for (intermediate) results.

9.4.1 Trace Data Prefixes

The prefixes used for trace data:

-	the program source line
+++	trace message
>>>	result
>.>	value assigned to a placeholder.

9.4.2 Trace Intermediate Data Prefixes

The following prefixes are used only when TRACE INTERMEDIATES has been specified:

>C>	The data are the name of a compound variable.
>F>	The data are the result of function invocation.
>L>	The data are a literal.
>O>	The data are the result of an operation.
>P>	The data are the result of a prefix operation.

>V>   The data are the contents of a variable.

The displayed data are shown in character form within double quotes; "?" denotes
non-character data.

9.4.3 Trace Output Example

Sample REXX exec:
```
1        /* REXX trace */
2        TRACE I;
3        i = 1;
4        PARSE VALUE DATE('E') WITH day.i '/' .;
5        x = day.1 * -2;
6        SAY x;
7        FUNCT();
```

The corresponding (annotated) output follows; the number in the left-hand column
refers to the statement number in the REXX exec. Annotations are written in italics
and immediately follow the trace output to which they refer.

>   3 *-* i = 1
source statement 3
>   >L>   "1"
contents of numeric literal
>   4 *-* PARSE VALUE DATE('E') WITH day.i '/' .
source statement 4
>   >L>   "E"
contents of character literal, parameter for DATE *function*
>   >F>   "24/10/94"
result of evaluating the DATE *function*
>   >C>   "DAY.1"
resolved name of compound variable, "1" has been substituted for "i" in
"day.i"
>   >>>   "24"
first parsed operand from the evaluated DATE('E'); *"/" has been used as*
delimiter
>   >.>   "10/94"
remainder after parsing to the "/" delimiter, this has been assigned to a
placeholder
>   5 *-* x = day.1 * -2
source statement 5
>   >V>   "24"
contents the variable "day.1"
>   >L>   "2"
contents of numeric literal
>   >P>   "-2"

result of performing the prefix operator (-) on 2

    >O> "-48"

result of the operation of multiplying 12 by -2

    6 *-* SAY x

source statement 6

    >V> "-48"

contents the variable "x"

  -48

output from the SAY *instruction*

    7 *-* FUNCT()

source statement 7

    7 +++ FUNCT()

trace message

IRX0043I Error running RXTRACE, line 7: Routine not found

The IRX0043I *REXX error message specifies that the* FUNCT() *routine
(function) was not found. The line number refers to the original source
instruction.*

9.5 INTERACTIVE DEBUG

Interactive debug mode is invoked in one of two ways:
- The exec can invoke a TRACE ?option instruction, where option is one of the
  trace options, e.g. TRACE ?ALL;
- The user can interrupt the REXX exec while it is executing, for example, by
  pressing the PA1 key (in TSO).

On entry to interactive debug mode, a message similar to the following is
displayed:

    +++ Interactive trace. 'Trace off' to end debug

In interactive debug mode, one of the following actions can be performed:
- Enter a null line (i.e. press the Enter key without having entered any input
  data). This causes the REXX exec to proceed to the next trace point, when it
  will again pause. For example, the TRACE ?COMMAND will stop at the next
  command.
  TRACE ?ALL stops at each statement, i.e. causes single-stepping through the
  REXX exec.
- Enter a single equals sign ("=") to re-execute the last statement traced.
  Processing will pause after this statement has been re-executed, irrespective of
  the setting of trace option.
- The TRACE OFF instruction terminates interactive tracing. This is a special case
  of processing described in the following action.
- The EXIT instruction terminates the REXX exec.

· Any other input data will be interpreted as being a REXX statement and will be immediately processed as if it were contained within a Do-End group. The input can be multiple REXX statements, each separated by a ";" (semicolon).

9.5.1 Interactive Debugging Example

The sample REXX exec invokes interactive debug if an error condition arises. Note that the statement numbers at the start of each line are for identification purposes only, and are not present in the actual code.

```
1      /* REXX debug */
2      SIGNAL ON SYNTAX;
3      x = funct();
4      EXIT;
5      SYNTAX:
6      SAY "debug invoked";
7      SAY "condition" CONDITION('C');
8      TRACE ?a
9      SAY "source line" SIGL " " SOURCELINE(SIGL);
10     SAY "debug end";
11     EXIT;
```

2   The SIGNAL instruction specifies that the SYNTAX exception condition is to be set.

3   Force a syntax error; the funct() function is undefined.

4   Terminate normal processing.

5   The entry point for the interactive debug routine.

6   Display a message to the user indicating that an exception condition has arisen.

7   Display the name of the condition which has arisen. The CONDITION built-in function with operand 'C' supplies this information.

8   Activate interactive trace. This enables the user to input his own debugging commands, if required. The text specifying that interactive trace has been invoked is displayed after the next text line is output.

9   Display the line number (contained in the SIGL special variable) and source data (obtained with the SOURCELINE built-in function) in error.

10   Display a message to indicate that debugging has terminated.

11   Terminate processing.

Typical output arising from a syntax error using the above interactive debug processing follows.

```
debug invoked
condition SYNTAX
```

```
        9 *-* SAY "source line" SIGL " " SOURCELINE(SIGL)
source line 3   x = funct();
IRX0100I +++ Interactive trace.  TRACE OFF to end debug, ENTER to
continue

trace off
debug end
```

9.6 PARAMETRIC DEBUG

Parametric debug is a means of making the setting of the trace options dependent on a parameter. If this parameter can be set at execution-time (for example, with an invocation parameter), operational execs can be programmed to contain the necessary debugging code that is activated only when necessary. Such a "trapdoor" should be incorporated into all non-trivial operational execs (see Example 2).

Example 1:
```
/* REXX - TRACE setting is an optional invocation argument */
ARG traceopt .;
IF opt <> '' THEN TRACE(traceopt);
   ...
```

This exec fragment allows an argument to be specified on invocation. This argument, if specified, is used as trace option; for example, ?R would initiate interactive tracing with results display.

Example 2:
Because the method shown in Example 1 does not allow for selective debugging, it is less suitable for large applications. It would be better if such code can be activated when the procedure name has been set in a global variable (TRACENAM in the sample code). If TRACENAM is set dynamically (invocation parameter, execution-time dialogue, etc.), the trace code is activated at will. For maximum flexibility, TRACENAM can specify a list of the procedure names for which tracing is to be activated. The sample code uses Dialog Manager to set the variable.

Procedure code:
```
/* TRACE-Block */
ADDRESS ISPEXEC "VGET (tracenam)"
PARSE SOURCE . . procname .
IF WORDPOS(procname,tracenam) > 0 THEN TRACE ?r;NOP
/* TRACE-Block */
```

9.7 ERRORS WITH HOST COMMANDS AND FUNCTIONS

Many host commands and functions return a list of results in the queue or as stem variables. Because most such commands or functions are often resource dependent, they are subject to failure. Well-defined commands and functions return a status in the RC special variable or as function return value, respectively. This status should be checked before the results are processed. In particular, the stem0 variable (normally set to contain the number of returned stem variables) then contains no value (which is not the same as 0) if no stem variables can be set because of a command or function error.

Example:
```
CALL OUTTRAP 's.',,'NOCONCAT'; /* trap display output */
"LISTDSI L(TSOUSER)";
IF RC = 0 THEN DO i = 1 TO s.0; /* process if no error occurred */
  SAY s.i; /* list entries */
END;
```

10

REXX Built-In Functions
Form ever follows function.

from Lippincott's Magazine [March, 1896]
Louis Henri Sullivan

10.1 INTRODUCTION

The REXX language has an extensive library of functions known as **built-in functions**. There are two classes of built-in functions:
- those which are part of SAA (Systems Application Architecture);
- additional functions defined in the book *The REXX Language* or in other implementations (e.g. TSO/E).

A third class of function, host command functions, that pertain to the host environment are described in Chapter 12. Because the SAA functions are common to all REXX implementations, only such functions should be used if portability is a consideration; the non-SAA functions in this chapter are indicated as such.

Some of the REXX host commands described in Chapter 12 also provide function-like services, in particular, the EXECIO command performs record-oriented input/output processing.

Many functions have keyword operands, of which only one letter, usually the initial letter, is significant. These keyword operands may be written in either uppercase or lowercase. For example, the uppercase operand for the DATATYPE function can be written as either 'Uppercase' or 'U', or even U. The last form (U) should not be used, because there is always the possibility that the symbol has been used as a variable somewhere else. This recommendation is not restricted to functions, as all keyword operands should be written as literals.

REXX adopts the following conventions:
- · The first position of a string is position 1.
- · A word is a string of characters delimited by one or more blanks.

Functions can be invoked either directly with the function name, in which case the function result must be used, or with the CALL statement, in which case the RESULT special variable contains the function result (see Section 3.3).

In this book I have normally used literals to simplify the examples, although variables could have been used. For example, the following three function calls are all equivalent:

```
string = "translate";
phrase = "trans";
x = ABBREV(string,phrase);
y = ABBREV(string,"trans");
z = ABBREV("translate",phrase);
```

Similarly, for simplicity, most of the examples in this chapter use the SAY instruction to display the function result. The example in the next section shows how the function result can itself be used as argument in a function call.

10.1.1 Function-Like (Direct) Invocation

A function-like invocation must use the function result in some statement (e.g. assignment or in an expression).
   A direct function invocation must include the parentheses, even when no arguments are to be passed to the function. The open-parenthesis ("(") must immediately follow the function name without any intervening blanks. If this requirement is not met, the function name is interpreted as being a symbol.

Example:

```
x = D2X(X2D('a0')+16);
```
This example shows how a function value (here X2D('a0')) can be used in an expression (**orthogonality**).

10.1.2 Call Invocation

A call invocation is made with the CALL instruction. The RESULT special variable contains the function result.

Example:

```
CALL X2D 'a0';
CALL D2X (RESULT+16);
x = RESULT;
```
This example, which is equivalent to the previous example, shows the CALL invocation instead of the direct function invocation. In this case the parentheses are not strictly necessary, but are used to emphasise the operand grouping (at least one

blank must precede the left parenthesis here, otherwise it would be interpreted as a function invocation).

10.1.3 Internal Functions

There are occasions when internal functions within an exec must override a standard (external) function that has the same name. If the function exists within the exec, the external function name must be written in quotes to distinguish it from the internal function.

Example:

```
SAY 'TIME'(); /* external */
SAY TIME(); /* internal */
EXIT;
TIME: /* internal TIME function */
    CALL OUTTRAP 's.','*','NOCONCAT';
    "TIME"; /* invoke TSO TIME command */
    RETURN s.1;
```

This sample exec invokes two TIME functions. The first invocation is to the built-in TIME function. The second invocation is to the internal TIME function, which in turn invokes the TSO TIME command whose output it traps and returns as function result.

Sample display output:

```
19:49:03
IKJ56650I TIME-07:49:03 PM. CPU-00:00:04 SERVICE-364809 SESSION-00:05:51
FEBRUARY 2,1995
```

10.1.4 Function Side-Effects

Function arguments remain unchanged during the execution of the REXX function. This means that the same data field may be used as both an operand and as the result; the result is set only on completion of the function.

Note: This does not apply to exposed variables used in a user-written function.

Example:

```
newstr = DELSTR(str,2,1);
```

This statement creates an intermediate variable that contains a copy of str from which the second word has been removed, and then assigns the contents of this intermediate variable to newstr (the contents of str remain unchanged). If the actual contents of str are to be changed, the result must be reassigned, for example,

```
str = DELSTR(str,2,1);
```

10.1.5 Invocation Errors

The most frequent error is caused by passing incorrect arguments to a function. Typical errors are:
·   The number of arguments is incorrect.
·   The size or type of individual arguments is incorrect (e.g. some function arguments must be a single character).
·   The function result is too large (e.g. the precision set by the NUMERIC DIGITS instruction is insufficient to contain the conversion result of the C2D function).

REXX displays the offending statement and sets the IRX00401 error message, for example,

```
3 +++ newstr= SPACE(str,2,"**")
    IRX00401 Error running A02, line 3: Incorrect call to routine
```
This particular error is caused by passing a two-character fill-string.

Note: Unlike some other programming languages (e.g. CLISTs), it is not an error to try to access beyond the limits of the data.

Example:
```
str = "The rain in Spain";
newstr = DELWORD(str,5); /* ok */
```

10.1.6 Internal Data Format

Several REXX built-in functions (e.g. C2X) process character data. The term character data is a misnomer; character data in REXX refers to the internal representation, i.e. the data that can be stored in the smallest directly addressable unit (= byte).

The character functions are code-dependent, i.e. different results are returned in the mainframe (EBCDIC) and personal computer (ASCII) environments. For example, the uppercase character 'A' has the ASCII code '41'X and the EBCDIC code 'C1'X.

Example:
```
SAY C2X("123"); /* F1F2F3 */
SAY D2C(193); /* A (193 = X'C1' = character A) */
SAY D2C(193+256*194); /* BA */
```

10.2 FUNCTION DEFINITIONS

·   ABBREV   Test whether string is an abbreviation
·   ABS   Return absolute value
·   ADDRESS   Return name of current environment
·   ARG   Return argument
·   BITAND   Logical And

·	BITOR	Logical Or
·	BITXOR	Logical Exclusive-Or
·	B2X	Convert binary data to hexadecimal
·	CENTRE (CENTER)	Centralise data
·	COMPARE	Compare
·	CONDITION	Return condition
·	COPIES	Replicate data
·	C2D	Convert character data to decimal
·	C2X	Convert character data to hexadecimal
·	DATATYPE	Determine data type
·	DATE	Return current date
·	DELSTR	Delete substring
·	DELWORD	Delete one or more words
·	DIGITS	Return the NUMERIC DIGITS setting
·	D2C	Convert decimal data to character
·	D2X	Convert decimal data to hexadecimal
·	ERRORTEXT	Return message text
·	FIND	Search for word (non-SAA)
·	FORM	Determine NUMERIC FORM setting
·	FORMAT	Format numeric value
·	FUZZ	Determine NUMERIC FUZZ setting
·	INDEX	Search for substring (non-SAA)
·	INSERT	Insert substring
·	JUSTIFY	Justify string of words (non-SAA)
·	LASTPOS	Determine last position of phrase
·	LEFT	Left-align string
·	LENGTH	Determine length of string
·	LINESIZE	Return the (maximum) width of a terminal line (non-SAA)
·	MAX	Determine the maximum of a series of numeric values
·	MIN	Determine the minimum of a series of numeric values
·	OVERLAY	Overlay part of a string with a phrase
·	POS	Search for substring
·	QUEUED	Determine the number of entries in the queue
·	RANDOM	Generate a (pseudo-)random number
·	REVERSE	Reverse the sequence of data
·	RIGHT	Right-align string
·	SIGN	Determine numeric sign
·	SOURCELINE	Return "program line"
·	SPACE	Insert fill-character between words
·	STRIP	Remove padding-characters at the start or end of a string
·	SUBSTR	Extract substring
·	SUBWORD	Extract series of words from word-string
·	SYMBOL	Determine the status of a symbol
·	TIME	Return the current time-of-day

·	TRACE	Return (and set) the current trace mode
·	TRANSLATE	Translate
·	TRUNC	Truncate numeric value
·	USERID	Return Userid (non-SAA)
·	VALUE	Return (and set) the contents of a symbol
·	VERIFY	Test whether only characters in a phrase are present in string
·	WORD	Fetch word
·	WORDINDEX	Determine the character position of a word in a string of words
·	WORDLENGTH	Determine word length
·	WORDPOS	Determine word-number of a word in word-string
·	WORDS	Determine number of words in word-string
·	RANGE	Define a range of hexadecimal values
·	X2B	Convert hexadecimal to binary
·	X2C	Convert hexadecimal to character
·	X2D	Convert hexadecimal to decimal.

10.2.1 ABBREV – Test Whether String is an Abbreviation

The ABBREV function tests whether a substring is an abbreviation of the specified string, i.e. whether the specified number of characters at the start of **string** are identical to the **substring**.

The function returns:
· 1 – **substring** corresponds to **string**;
· 0 – **substring** does not correspond to **string**.

Syntax:
```
►►——ABBREV(string,substring—————————)——►◄
                          └,length┘
```

string
 The string to be tested.

substring
 The argument.

length
 The minimum number of characters that must correspond.
 Default: The length of **substring**.

Example:
```
SAY ABBREV("translate","trans"); /* 1 */
SAY ABBREV("translate","trans",4); /* 1 */
SAY ABBREV("translate","transform"); /* 0 */
```

10.2.2 ABS - Return Absolute Value

The ABS function returns the absolute (unsigned) value of the specified argument.

Syntax:
```
►►——ABS(number)——►◄
```

number
>   The argument to be converted.

Example:
```
SAY ABS(-123); /* 123 */
SAY ABS(4567); /* 4567 */
```

10.2.3 ADDRESS - Return Name of Current Environment

The ADDRESS function returns the name of the current environment. The environment is set with the ADDRESS instruction; the default environment name is returned if no environment has been set (i.e. TSO or MVS for TSO or batch, respectively).

Syntax:
```
►►——ADDRESS()——►◄
```

Example:
```
SAY ADDRESS(); /* for example, TSO */
```

10.2.4 ARG - Return Argument

The ARG function processes the arguments that were passed to the invoking routine.

The ARG function can be used in one of the following four ways:
· return the number of arguments;
· return a specific argument;
· determine whether a specific argument is present;
· determine whether a specific argument is not present.

Syntax:
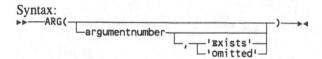
```
►►——ARG(─┬─────────────────────────────┬─)——►◄
          └─argumentnumber─┬──────────┬─┘
                          └─,─┬─'Exists'─┐
                              └─'omitted'─┘
```

argumentnumber
>   The number of the argument whose value is to be returned.
>   Default: All the arguments.

'Exists'
>   Return 1 (true) if the specified argument exists.
>   Return 0 (false) if the specified argument does not exist.

'Omitted'
>   Return 1 (true) if the specified argument does not exist.
>   Return 0 (false) if the specified argument exists.

Example:

```
CALL alpha beta, gamma;
...
alpha:
SAY ARG();     /* 2 (the number of arguments) */
SAY ARG(1)     /* beta */
SAY ARG(3,'E') /* 0 (3rd argument is not present) */
SAY ARG(3,'O') /* 1 (3rd argument is omitted) */
```

10.2.5 BITAND – Logical And

The BITAND function performs a Logical And on the contents of the first argument using the contents of the second argument. The operation is performed bit by bit from left to right. The & operation (see Section 2.2.13) performs a Logical And on the complete fields, which must have either 0 or 1 as content.

Syntax:

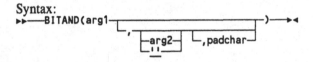

arg1
>   The first argument.

arg2
>   The second argument.
>   Default: The null string ('' or "").

padchar
>   The padding character **padchar**, which, if specified, is added to **arg2**, if it
>   is shorter than **arg1**.

Example:

```
SAY BITAND("125","22","4"); /* 024 */
```

```
'F1F2F5'x
'F2F2F4'x ('F4'x = pad character)
------- AND
'F0F2F4'x ( "024")
```

10.2.6 BITOR – Logical Or

The BITOR function performs a Logical Or on the contents of the first argument using the contents of the second argument. The operation is performed bit by bit from left to right. The | operation (see Section 2.2.13) performs a Logical Or on the complete fields, which must have either 0 or 1 as content.

Syntax:

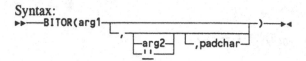

arg1

>   The first argument.

arg2

>   The second argument.
>   Default: The null string ('' or "").

padchar

>   The padding character **padchar**, which, if specified, is added to **arg2**, if it is shorter than **arg1**.

Example:

```
SAY BITOR("125","22","4"); /* 325 */

'F1F2F5'x
'F2F2F4'x ('F4'x = pad character)
------- OR
'F3F2F5'x ( "325")
```

10.2.7 BITXOR – Logical Exclusive-Or (XOR)

The BITXOR function performs a Logical XOR on the contents of the first argument using the contents of the second argument. The operation is performed bit by bit from left to right. The && operation (see Section 2.2.13) performs a Logical Exclusive-Or on the complete fields, which must have either 0 or 1 as content.

Syntax:

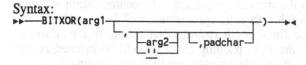

arg1

>   The first argument.

arg2

>   The second argument.
>   Default: The null string ('' or "").

padchar
> The padding character **padchar**, which, if specified, is added to **arg2**, if it is shorter than **arg1**.

Example:
```
SAY BITXOR("125","0202"x,"04"x); /* 301 */


'F1F2F5'x
'020204'x ('F4'x = pad character)
------- XOR
'F3F0F1'x ( "301")
```

10.2.8 B2X - Convert Binary Data to Hexadecimal

The B2X (binary-to-hexadecimal) function converts a binary-coded data argument (0's and 1's) to its hexadecimal equivalent. The hexadecimal code (one hexadecimal digit) for each group of four binary digits in the data argument is returned as function result. The binary string may contain embedded blanks at half-byte (four-digit) boundaries. Binary strings whose length is not a multiple of four will be left-padded with 0's.

Syntax:
```
►►——B2X(arg)——►◄
```

arg
> The argument to be processed.

Example:
```
SAY B2X("11110001"); /* F1 */
SAY B2X("0101 0000 1010"); /* 50A */
SAY B2X("101"); /* 5 (left-pad) */
```

10.2.9 CENTRE (CENTER) - Centralise Data

The CENTRE function centralises the specified argument. The centralisation is made by filling the data to the specified length with equal numbers of padding characters on each side of the data. If the final length requires that an unequal number of padding characters be inserted, the extra padding character will be inserted at the right. Any padding characters in the original string count towards its length.

Note: The British and American spellings (CENTRE and CENTER, respectively) refer to the same function.

Syntax:
```
►►——┌CENTER┐(arg,length┬──────────────┬)——►◄
     └CENTRE┘           └,┬padchar┬──┘
                          └' '┘
```

arg
> The data to be centralised.

length
> The length of the centralised data.

padchar
> The padding character. Default: ' '.

Example:
```
SAY CENTRE("abcde",9); /* '  abcde  ' */
SAY CENTER("abcde  ",9); /* 'abcde    ' */
```

10.2.10 COMPARE - Compare

The COMPARE function compares two arguments. The arguments are compared character by character from left to right, with a shorter field being right-padded. The position of the first non-equal character is returned; 0 indicates that the two data fields (padded, if necessary) are equal.

A character comparison is also made for numeric fields. For example, COMPARE returns the not equal condition for the two numeric fields 1.2E+1 and 12, even though these two fields are numerically equal.

Syntax:
```
▶▶──COMPARE(arg1,arg2─────────────)──▶◀
                     └─,─┬─padchar─┘
                        └─' '─┘
```

arg1
> The first argument.

arg2
> The second argument.

padchar
> The padding character. Default: ' '.

Example:
```
SAY COMPARE("translate","translation"); /* 9 */
SAY COMPARE("transl","translation",'a'); /* 8 */
SAY COMPARE("translate ","translate"); /* 0 */
SAY COMPARE("translate ","translate",'a'); /* 10 */
```

10.2.11 CONDITION - Return Condition

The CONDITION function returns the setting of the specified condition. This function is usually used in an error exit to determine the cause of error.

Syntax:

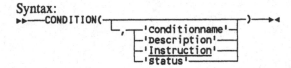

'Conditionname'
Return the current condition setting, which is one of the following entries:
- ERROR
- FAILURE
- HALT
- NOVALUE
- SYNTAX

'Description'
Return any descriptive text associated with the condition; the name of the symbol that caused the condition is an example of descriptive text.

'Instruction'
Return the type of the invoking instruction: CALL or SIGNAL. This is the default.

'Status'
Return the status of the trapped condition:
- DELAY   any new occurrence is delayed;
- OFF   the condition is disabled;
- ON   the condition is enabled.

Note: The status may change during the course of execution.

Section 9.5.1 shows an example of the use of the CONDITION function.

10.2.12 COPIES - Replicate Data

The COPIES function replicates the contents of the specified argument.

Syntax:
```
▶▶──COPIES(arg,number)──▶◀
```

arg
The argument to be processed.

number
The number of copies to be created.

Example:
```
x = COPIES("abcd",2); /* abcdabcd */
y = COPIES(" ",80); /* eighty blanks */
z = COPIES("abcd",0); /* the null character */
```

10.2.13 C2D - Convert Character Data to Decimal

The C2D (character-to-decimal) function converts the specified argument to its decimal equivalent. The sign of the converted data is taken from the leftmost bit of the data field (padded or truncated).

Syntax:

```
►►──C2D(arg──────────)──►◄
            └,length─┘
```

argument

> The argument to be processed.

length

> The length of the argument. If necessary, **arg** will be padded on the left with hexadecimal zeros to achieve the specified **length**. If **length** is less than the implicit argument length, **arg** will be truncated from the left.

Example:

```
SAY C2D("0"); /* -240 */
SAY C2D("0",1); /* -240 */
SAY C2D("0",2); /* 240 */
SAY C2D("03",1); /* -243 */
```

The argument ("0") has an implicit length of one character and the '1111 0000'b EBCBIC code, i.e. the leftmost bit is set. When the explicit length is longer than the implicit length, the argument is left-padded with binary zeros, i.e. the argument is processed as '0000 0000 1111 0000'b. When the explicit length is shorter than the implicit length, the argument is truncated from the left, i.e. the "03" ('1111 0000 1111 0011'b) argument is processed as '1111 0011'b.

10.2.14 C2X - Convert Character Data to Hexadecimal

The C2X (character-to-hexadecimal) function converts the specified argument to its hexadecimal equivalent. The hexadecimal code (two hexadecimal digits) for each character of the argument field is returned.

Syntax:

```
►►──C2X(arg)──►◄
```

arg

> The argument to be processed.

Example :

```
SAY C2X("0"); /* F0 */
```

10.2.15 DATATYPE – Determine Data Type

The DATATYPE function can be used in two ways:
·   return the form of the data (numeric or character, character is non-numeric);
·   confirm (or otherwise) that the data is of a particular class.

Syntax:

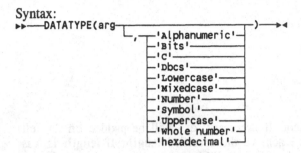

arg
>   The data field to be tested. The optional keyword specifies the class of data
>   to be tested. If **arg** contains valid data for the specified class, 1 (true) is
>   returned, otherwise 0 (false). If no class keyword is specified, the value NUM
>   or CHAR is returned, depending on whether **arg** contains numeric data or not,
>   respectively.

class
>   The class to be tested. The uppercase letter can be used in place of the
>   complete class name (e.g. x instead of hexadecimal).

'Alphanumeric'
>   The characters a through z, A through Z, and 0 through 9.

'Bits'
>   The digits 0 and 1.

'C'
>   SBCS/DBCS data.

'Dbcs'
>   DBCS data.

'Lowercase'
>   The characters a through z.

'Mixedcase'
>   The characters a through z, and A through Z.

'Number'
>   A valid REXX number.

'Symbol'
> A valid REXX symbol.

'Uppercase'
> The characters A through Z.

'Whole number'
> A non-decimal number, e.g. 123 or 1.23E2, but not 1.23 or 1.234E2.

'heXadecimal'
> The characters a through f, A through F, and 0 through 9.

Example:
```
SAY DATATYPE("ag",'X'); /* 0 (false) */
SAY DATATYPE(1.2E4); /* NUM */
SAY DATATYPE(1.2F4); /* CHAR */
SAY DATATYPE("01",'B'); /* 1 (true) */
```

10.2.16 DATE - Return Current Date

The DATE function returns the current date in the specified format.

Syntax:

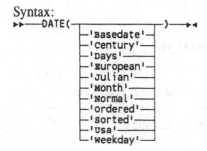

Dateformat
> The form with which the current date is to be returned. The uppercase letter can be used in place of the complete date format (e.g. E instead of European).

'Basedate'
> Return the number of days (including the current day) since January 1, 0001. The remainder of dividing the basedate by 7 is the day of the week (0 = Monday).

'Century'
> Return the number of days (including the current day) since January 1 of the start of the current century.

'Days'
> Return the number of days (including the current day) since January 1 of the current year.

'European'
> Return the date in the European form (dd/mm/yy).

'Julian'
> Return the date in the form yyddd.

'Month'
> Return the English name of the current month, e.g. January.

'Normal'
> Return the date in default format: dd mon yyyy ("mon" is the 3-character English abbreviation for month, e.g. Jan for January.

'Ordered'
> Return the date in the sortable format: yy/mm/dd.

'Sorted'
> Return the date in the sortable format: yyyymmdd. Sorted is also known as 'Standard'.

'Usa'
> Return the date in the American form (mm/dd/yy).

'Weekday'
> Return the English name of the current day of the week, e.g. Sunday.

Example 1 (assuming that the current date is February 2, 1995):

```
SAY DATE(); /* 2 Feb 1995 */
SAY DATE('J'); /* 95033 */
SAY DATE('W'); /* Thursday */
```

Example 2:

```
n = DATE('B')//7; /* day of week */
Tag = POS("Mon Die Mit Don Fri Sam Son", (n+1) );
```
This example gets the German weekday.

10.2.17 DELSTR – Delete Substring

The DELSTR function deletes a substring from the specified argument.

Syntax:
```
►►──DELSTR(string,position─┬─────────┬─)──►◄
                          └,length─┘
```

string

> The data field from which the substring is to be deleted.

position

> The starting position in the data field of the substring to be deleted. The first character in the field is at position 1. If **position** lies outside the **string** limits, the complete **string** is returned.

length

> The length of the substring to be deleted.
> Default: The remaining string.

Example:

```
SAY DELSTR("abcde",3,2); /* abe */
SAY DELSTR("abcde",3); /* ab */
SAY DELSTR("abcde",6); /* abcde */
```

10.2.18 DELWORD - Delete Words

The DELWORD function deletes one or more words from a string of words.

Syntax:

```
►►──DELWORD(string,wordnumber─┬──────────────┬─)──►◄
                             └─,wordcount─┘
```

string

> The data field from which the words are to be deleted.

wordnumber

> The starting position (word number) of the first word to be deleted. If **wordnumber** specifies a word that is not contained in **string**, the complete **string** is returned.

wordcount

> The number of words to be deleted.
> Default: All the remaining words in the string.

Example:

```
SAY DELWORD("a bb ccc",2,1); /* 'a ccc' */
SAY DELWORD("a bb ccc",2); /* 'a' */
SAY DELWORD("a bb ccc",4,1); /* 'a bb ccc' */
```

10.2.19 DIGITS - Return the NUMERIC DIGITS Setting

The DIGITS function returns the current precision for numeric values. The NUMERIC DIGITS instruction sets the precision.

Syntax:

```
►►──DIGITS()──►◄
```

Example:
```
NUMERIC DIGITS 4;
SAY DIGITS(); /* 4 */
```

10.2.20 D2C - Convert Decimal to Character

The D2C (decimal-to-character) function converts a decimal value to its character code. The sign of the converted number is propagated to the specified length.

Syntax:
```
►►──D2C(arg────────────)──►◄
          └─,length─┘
```

arg

The argument to be processed.

length

The length (in characters) of the result. The sign of **arg** will be propagated if necessary. An error results if no **length** is specified for a negative **arg**. Default: If no **length** is specified, the length of the result is such that no leading '00'x characters are present in the result field.

Example 1:
```
SAY D2C(241) /* 1 */
SAY D2C(241,2) /* ' 1' */
SAY D2C(241,0) /* '' */
x = D2C(-241,2)
SAY x C2X(x) /* FF0F */
x = D2C(10)
SAY C2X(x) /* 0A */
SAY D2C( (241+242*256),2) /* 21 */
SAY D2C( (241+242*256),3) /* ' 21' */
SAY D2C( (241+242*256),1) /* 1 (left-truncate) */
x = D2C(241,0)
SAY 'LEN:'LENGTH(x) C2X(x) /* '' */
```

Example 2:
```
SAY D2C(-241) /* error */
```
Because no explicit length is specified for a negative argument, this invocation causes the "Incorrect call to routine" error.

10.2.21 D2X - Convert Decimal to Hexadecimal

The D2X (decimal-to-hexadecimal) function converts a decimal value to the hexadecimal digits representing its internal code. The sign of the binary number is propagated to the specified length.

Syntax:
```
▶▶────D2X(arg──────────)───▶◀
            └─,length─┘
```

arg

> The argument to be processed.

length

> The length (in characters) of the result. The sign of **arg** will be propagated
> if necessary. An error results if no **length** is specified for a negative **arg**.
> Default: If no **length** is specified, the length of the result is such that no
> '00'x characters are present at the start of the result field.

Example 1:
```
SAY D2X(241) /* F1 */
SAY D2X(241,1) /* 1 (left-truncate) */
SAY D2X(241,3) /* 0F1 */
SAY D2X(-241,2) /* 0F */
SAY D2X(-241,3) /* F0F */
SAY D2X( (241+242*256),4) /* F2F1 */
SAY D2X( (241+242*256),5) /* 0F2F1 (left-pad) */
SAY D2X( (241+242*256),3) /* 2F1 (left-truncate) */
SAY D2X(10) /* A */
SAY D2X(241,0) /* '' (null) */
```

Example 2:
```
SAY D2X(-241) /* error */
```
Because no explicit length is specified for a negative argument, this invocation
causes the "Incorrect call to routine" error.

10.2.22 ERRORTEXT - Return Message Text

The ERRORTEXT function returns the message text associated with the specified
message number. No text is returned for a non-existent message number.

Syntax:
```
▶▶────ERRORTEXT(errornumber)───▶◀
```

Example:
```
SAY ERRORTEXT(40);
```
This example displays the message: Incorrect call to routine.

10.2.23 FIND - Search for Word

The FIND function searches for the first occurrence of the specified phrase in the
specified word-string. FIND returns the first position of the phrase in the searched
string; 0 = phrase not found.

Note: The SAA function WORDPOS should be used instead.

Syntax:
▶▶────FIND(string,phrase)────▶◀

string
> The string that is to be searched.

phrase
> The phrase being searched for.

10.2.24 FORM - Determine NUMERIC FORM Setting

The FORM function returns the current display form for numeric values. The NUMERIC FORM instruction sets the current display form.

Syntax:
▶▶────FORM()────▶◀

Example:
```
NUMERIC FORM SCIENTIFIC;

SAY FORM(); /* SCIENTIFIC */
```
This example returns SCIENTIFIC.

10.2.25 FORMAT - Format Numeric Value

The FORMAT function formats a numeric value for display. Default formatting is performed if the FORMAT function is not used. The TRANSLATE function can also be used for certain formatting operations.

Syntax:

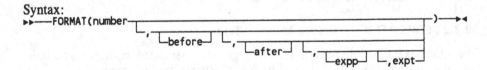

before
> The number of digits to be formatted before the decimal point; leading zeros (except for a single zero before the decimal point) are suppressed.

after
> The number of digits to be formatted after the decimal point.

expp
> The number of digits to be used for the exponential. If omitted, the minimum number of digits necessary to represent the exponent is used.

expt
> The number of digits to trigger the exponential representation.

Example:

```
SAY FORMAT("12.3",3,2); /* ' 12.30' */
SAY FORMAT("1234",,,2,2); /* 1.234E+03 */
SAY FORMAT("1234",,,,2); /* 1.234E+3 */
```

10.2.26 FUZZ – Determine NUMERIC FUZZ Setting

The FUZZ function returns the current number of digits to be ignored for numeric comparisons. The NUMERIC FUZZ instruction sets the fuzz setting.

Syntax:
```
▶▶──FUZZ()──▶◀
```

Example:

```
NUMERIC FUZZ 2;
SAY FUZZ(); /* 2 */
```

10.2.27 INDEX – Search for Substring

The INDEX function searches for the first occurrence of the specified substring in the specified string. INDEX returns the first position of the substring in the searched string; 0 = substring not found.

Note: The SAA function POS is recommended.

Syntax:
```
▶▶──INDEX(phrase,string─┬─────────────────────┬─)──▶◀
                        └─,─┬─startposition─┬──┘
                            └─1─────────────┘
```

string
    The string that is to be searched.

phrase
    The phrase being searched for.

startposition
    The starting position in the string. Default: 1.

Example:

```
SAY INDEX("The rain in Spain","in",8); /* 10 */
SAY INDEX("The rain in Spain","in"); /* 7 */
SAY INDEX("The rain in Spain","in",18); /* 0 (outside string limits) */
SAY INDEX("The rain in Spain","snow"); /* 0 */
```

10.2.28 INSERT – Insert Substring

The INSERT function inserts a substring at the specified position of a data field.

Syntax:

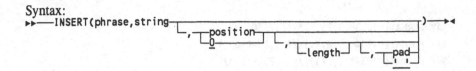

phrase
> The data field which is to be inserted into the specified **string**.

string
> The data field into which the **phrase** is to be inserted.

position
> The position in **string** after which **phrase** is to be inserted.
> Default: 0 (i.e. **phrase** is inserted before the start of **string**).

length
> The length of the **phrase** to be inserted.

pad

> The padding character to be used if the specified **length** is greater than the
> implicit length of **phrase**.
> Default: ' ' (blank).

Example:
```
SAY INSERT("abcde","fghi",3); /* fghabcdei */
SAY INSERT("abcde","fghi"); /* abcdefghi */
SAY INSERT("abcde","fghi",5); /* fghi abcde */
```

10.2.29 JUSTIFY - Justify String of Words

The JUSTIFY function adjusts the individual words in a string of words so that all
the words are equally spaced and the first and last words are justified to the
specified bounds. The number of blanks that separate the words in the original
string has no significance.

Syntax:

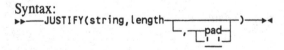

string
> The string that contains the words to be adjusted.

length
> The final length of the adjusted **string**.

pad

> The padding character to be used if the specified **length** is greater than the implicit length of **string**.
> Default: ' ' (blank).

Example:

```
SAY ("a b   cc",8); /* 'a b   cc' */
```

10.2.30 LASTPOS - Determine Last Position of Phrase

The LASTPOS function determines the last position of a phrase in a string. This is done by searching backwards starting from the specified position.
0 is returned if the phrase is not found.

Syntax:

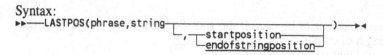

phrase

> The argument used as search argument.

string

> The argument to be searched.

startposition

> The position from which the search is to start. The search is made from right to left.
> Default: The last position in **string**.

endofstringposition

> The position from which the search is to stop.
> Default: The first position in **string**.

Example 1:

```
SAY LASTPOS("ai","the rain in Spain"); /* 15 */
SAY LASTPOS("ai","the rain in Spain",10); /* 6 */
```

Example 2:

```
n = LASTPOS('.',dsn);
n = n+1;
PARSE VAR dsn . =(n) lq;
IF lq = 'TEMP
    THEN PUSH 'DELETE' dsn; /* delete dataset */
```

This code fragment shows how the LASTPOS function can be used to find the last delimiter of a dataset name. The program deletes those datasets which have TEMP as their final qualifier. Compare this solution with that shown for the REVERSE function.

10.2.31 LEFT - Left-Align String

The LEFT function left-aligns a string.

Syntax:

```
►►——LEFT(string,length————————————)——►◄
                        └─,—┬─pad─┬─┘
                            └─' '─┘
```

string
>   The data field to be processed.

length
>   The final length of the aligned **string**.

pad

>   The padding character to be used if the specified **length** is greater than the
>   implicit length of **string**.
>   Default: ' ' (blank).

Example:

```
SAY LEFT("abcde",8); /* 'abcde   ' */
SAY LEFT("abcde",8,'*'); /* 'abcde***' */
```

10.2.32 LENGTH - Determine Length of String

The LENGTH function returns the length of a string. The length includes any blanks
at the start or end of the string.

Syntax:

```
►►——LENGTH(string)——►◄
```

string
>   The data field whose length is to be returned.

Example 1:

```
SAY LENGTH(" alpha "); /* 8 */
```

Example 2:

```
string = '0123abc3458';
inmask = '2468';
outmask = '    ';
temp = TRANSLATE(string,outmask,inmask);
SAY LENGTH(string)-LENGTH(SPACE(temp,0)); /* 3 */
```

This example shows how the LENGTH function (in combination with other functions)
can be used to determine the number of specified characters in a string. In this
particular example, the number of non-zero even digits.

10.2.33 LINESIZE - Return the (Maximum) Width of a Terminal Line

The LINESIZE function returns the maximum width of a terminal line.

Syntax:
```
▶▶──LINESIZE()──▶◀
```

10.2.34 MAX - Determine the Maximum of a Series of Numeric Values

The MAX function returns the largest numeric (signed) value from a series of numbers. The maximum count of the numbers in the TSO implementation is limited to 20. If more values are to be processed, this can be done either by cascading or in a loop.

Cascading the MAX function:
```
      x = MAX(.,.,...);
      x = MAX(x,...);
etc.
```

Using the MAX function for an array of values:
```
      x = -999999999; /* set minimum value */
      DO i = 1 TO n;
        x = MAX(x,a.i);
      END;
```
This example assumes that the data values are in the array a. with n values.

Syntax:
```
▶▶──MAX(──number──┬──)──▶◀
           ▲       │
           └──,────┘19
```

number
      The numeric value that is used as argument.

Example 1:
```
      SAY MAX(1,-4,2); /* 2 */
```

Example 2 (cascading):
```
      x = MAX(1,-4,2);
      x = MAX(x,-3,5,0);
      SAY x; /* 5 */
```

10.2.35 MIN - Determine the Minimum of a Series of Numeric Values

The MIN function returns the smallest numeric (signed) value from a series of numbers. The maximum count of the numbers in the TSO implementation is limited to 20. If more values are to be processed this can be done either by cascading or in a loop.

Cascading the MIN function:
```
x = MIN(.,.,...);
x = MIN(x,...);
```
etc.

Using the MIN function for an array of values:
```
x = 999999999; /* set maximum value */
DO i = 1 TO n;
   x = MIN(x,a.i);
END;
```
This example assumes that the data values are in the array a. with n values.

Syntax:
```
►►──MIN(──number──)──►◄
         └──,──┘19
```

number
>   The numeric value that is used as argument.

Example 1:
```
SAY MIN(1,-4,2); /* -4 */
```

Example 2 (cascading):
```
x = MIN(1,-4,2);
x = MIN(x,-3,5,0);
SAY x; /* -4 */
```

10.2.36 OVERLAY - Overlay Part of a String with a Phrase

The OVERLAY function overlays part of a string with a phrase (substring).

Syntax:

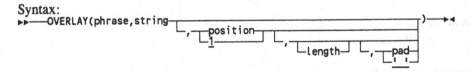

phrase
>   The data field which is to overlay the specified **string**.

string
>   The data field into which the **phrase** is to be overlaid.

position
>   The position in **string** after which **phrase** is to be overlaid.
>   Default: 1 (i.e. **phrase** is overlaid at the start of **string**).

length
> The length of the **phrase** to be overlaid.
> Default: The implicit length of **phrase**.

pad
> The padding character to be used if the specified **length** is greater than the implicit length of phrase.
> Default: ' ' (blank).

Example:
```
x = OVERLAY("snow","The rain in Spain",5); /* The snow in Spain */
x = OVERLAY("snow","The rain in Spain"); /* snowrain in Spain */
```

10.2.37 POS - Search for Substring

The POS function searches for the first occurrence of a substring in a string. POS returns the first position of the substring in the searched string; 0 = substring not found.

Syntax:
```
►►──POS(phrase,string─┬───────────────────┬─)──►◄
                      └─,─┬─startposition─┘
                          └─1─
```

phrase
> The data field being searched for.

string
> The data field being searched.

startposition
> The starting position in **string**.
> Default: 1.

Example:
```
SAY POS("ai","the rain in Spain"); /* 6 */
SAY POS("ai","the rain in Spain",8); /* 15 */
```

10.2.38 QUEUED - Determine the Number of Entries in the Queue (Stack)

The QUEUED function returns the number of entries in the current queue.

Syntax:
```
►►──QUEUED()──►◄
```

Example:

```
"NEWSTACK";
PUSH "alpha";
PUSH "beta";
SAY QUEUED(); /* 2 */
```

10.2.39 RANDOM – Generate a (Pseudo-)Random Number

The RANDOM function generates a pseudo-random number (positive integer). The bounds of the generated number may be specified. A seed value may be specified for the initialisation of the random number generation process; if the same seed value is specified, the same random number will be generated.

Tip
Even if no seed is specified, the same pseudo-random number may, depending on the implementation, always be generated. If this is undesirable, a seed value should be generated using some variable source, e.g. derived from the time-of-day clock (*caution*: the precision of the TIME function is dependent on the timer resolution; see Example 2).

Syntax:

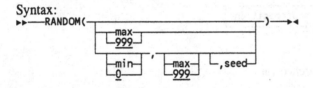

max

A positive integer which specifies the upper limit for the generated value. Default: 999.

min

A positive integer which specifies the lower limit for the generated value. Default: 0.

seed

A positive integer used to initialise the random number generation process. The same random number is always generated if the same seed and bounds are specified.

Example 1:

```
x = RANDOM();

y = RANDOM(,,40);
```

This example returns two random numbers for x and y. The random number generated for y is repeatable, i.e. the same number will always be generated.

Example 2:

```
time = TIME('Long');
PARSE VAR time . '.' seed /* extract microseconds */
SAY RANDOM(1,100,seed);
```

This example shows how the system timer can be used to determine a seed value for the randomisation process. The RANDOM function generates a random number in the range 1 through 100.

10.2.40 REVERSE - Reverse the Sequence of Data

The REVERSE function reverses the sequence of data in a string, i.e. the first byte is returned as the last byte, etc.

Syntax:
```
▶▶──REVERSE(string)──▶◀
```

string

The data being processed.

Example 1:

```
x = REVERSE("the rain"); /* niar eht */
```

Example 2:

```
xdsn = REVERSE(dsn);
PARSE VAR xdsn xlq '.' .;
lq = REVERSE(xlq);
IF lq = 'TEMP'
  THEN PUSH 'DELETE' dsn; /* delete dataset */
```

This code fragment shows a practical application of the REVERSE function. The program deletes those datasets which have TEMP as their final qualifier. Because most REXX parsing instructions and functions process from left to right, there is often no direct way of obtaining the last qualifier. By reversing the sequence, the last element becomes the first element, which can be processed using the standard built-in functions.

Note: This code is demonstrative, in this particular case the LASTPOS function could have been used.

10.2.41 RIGHT - Right-Align String

The RIGHT function right-aligns a string.

Syntax:
```
▶▶──RIGHT(string,length─┬───────┬──)──▶◀
                        └─,─┬pad┬─┘
```

string
> The data field to be processed.

length
> The final length of the aligned **string**.

pad
> The padding character to be used if the specified **length** is greater than the
> implicit length of **string**.
> Default: ' ' (blank).

Example:
```
SAY RIGHT("abcde",8); /* '   abcde' */
SAY RIGHT("abcde",8,'*'); /* '***abcde' */
```

10.2.42 SIGN - Determine Numeric Sign

The SIGN function returns the sign of a number:
- -1, if the number is less than 0
- 0, if the number equals 0
- +1, if the number is greater than 0.

Syntax:
```
►►──SIGN(arg)──►◄
```

arg
> The data field to be processed.

Example:
```
SAY SIGN(-3); /* -1 */
SAY SIGN(0); /* 0 */
SAY SIGN(3); /* 1 */
```

10.2.43 SOURCELINE - Return "Program Line"

The SOURCELINE function can be used in one of two ways:
- return the program (source file) line corresponding to the specified line
  number;
- return the last program line if no line number is specified.

Note: The SIGL special variable contains the source file number of the line from
which a CALL or SIGNAL instruction was invoked.

Syntax:
```
►►──SOURCELINE(─────────────)──►◄
                └─linenumber─┘
```

linenumber
> The line number to be retrieved from the source exec.

Chapter 9 (Debugging) includes an example of the use of the SOURCELINE function.

10.2.44 SPACE – Insert Fill-Character between Words

The SPACE function inserts the specified fill-character between words. The word-string is normalised (leading and trailing blanks are removed, and the string is delimited into its individual words) before the SPACE operation is performed.

Syntax:

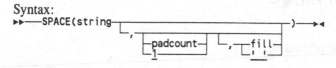

string
> The data field to be processed.

padcount
> The number of padding characters (**fill**) to be placed between each word in the returned string. The pad count can be zero, in which case embedded space characters are removed (see Example 2). Default: 1.

fill
> The fill characters to be placed between each word in the returned string. Default: ' ' (blank).

Example 1:
```
x = SPACE("a bb  c",3,'*'); /* insert 3 asterisks */

y = SPACE(" The  word is   mightier ",2); /* insert 2 spaces */

z = SPACE(" The  word is   mightier ",0); /* insert 0 spaces */
```
This   example   returns   'a***bb***c',   'The   word   is   mightier',   and 'Thewordismightier'.

Example 2:
```
time = TIME('Normal'); /* hh:mm:ss */

inmask = ':';

outmask = ' ';

temp = TRANSLATE(time,outmask,inmask); /* e.g. 01 23 45 */

SAY SPACE(temp,0); /* 012345 */
```
The TRANSLATE function used here replaces colons (:) from the time result with spaces. The SPACE function with zero pad count removes these blanks.

10.2.45 STRIP – Remove Padding-Characters at the Start or End of a String

The STRIP function removes the specified fill-character at the start or end (or start and end) of a string.

If paired, but non-equal, delimiters are to be removed from the string, the STRIP function must be used twice; once on the original string to remove the leading delimiter and once on the intermediate result to remove the trailing delimiter (see Example 2).

Syntax:

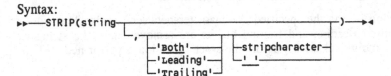

string
> The data field to be processed.

'Both'
> The specified strip-character is to be removed from both the start and end of the **string**. This is the default.

'Leading'
> The specified strip-character is to be removed from the start of the **string**.

'Trailing'
> The specified strip-character is to be removed from the end of the **string**.

stripcharacter
> The character to be removed from the **string**.
> Default: ' ' (blank).

Example 1:
```
SAY STRIP(" abcde ",'L'); /* 'abcde  ' */
SAY STRIP(" abcde ",'T'); /* '  abcde' */
SAY STRIP(" abcde "); /* 'abcde' */
SAY STRIP("(abcde)",,'('); /* 'abcde)' */
```

Example 2:
```
x = STRIP(var,'L',"("); /* remove leading parenthesis */
x = STRIP(x,'T',")"); /* remove trailing parenthesis */
```
This example removes the delimiting parentheses from the contents of var.

10.2.46 SUBSTR – Extract Substring

The SUBSTR function extracts a substring from a data field.

Syntax:

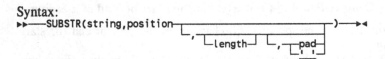

string
> The data field from which the substring is to be extracted.

position
> The position in **string** after which the substring is to be extracted. If the **position** lies outside the **string** limits, a null string is returned.

length
> The length of the substring to be extracted. If omitted, the remaining string.

pad
> The padding character to be used if the specified **length** is not entirely contained in **string**.
> Default: ' ' (blank).

Example:
```
SAY SUBSTR("abcde",3,2); /* 'cd' */
SAY SUBSTR("abcde",3,4); /* 'cde' */
SAY SUBSTR("abcde",3); /* 'cde' */
SAY SUBSTR("abcde",3,4,'*'); /* 'cde*' */
SAY SUBSTR("abcde",6); /* '' (null string) */
```

10.2.47 SUBWORD - Extract Series of Words from Word-String

The SUBWORD function extracts one or more words from a word-string.

Syntax:
```
►►──SUBWORD(string,wordnumber──────────────)──►◄
                           └,wordcount┘
```

string
> The data field to be processed.

wordnumber
> The number of the starting word in **string** from which the words are to be extracted.

wordcount
> The number of words to be extracted.
> Default: All remaining words in string.

Example:
```
x = SUBWORD("the rain in Spain lies mainly",2,3);
```
This statement returns 'rain in Spain' whereas
```
x = SUBWORD("the rain in Spain lies mainly",2);
```
returns 'rain in Spain lies mainly'.

10.2.48 SYMBOL – Determine the Status of a Symbol

The SYMBOL function returns the status of a symbol. This status has one of the values:

- **'VAR'**   The symbol has been assigned a value (and has not been dropped with the DROP function).
- **'LIT'**   The symbol has not been assigned a value or has been dropped with the DROP function or is a literal (numeric or character).
- **'BAD'**   The symbol is not a valid name, although in many cases a REXX error (invalid expression) will be raised.

Syntax:
```
►►──SYMBOL(name)──►◄
```

name
        The symbol to be tested.

Example:
```
alpha = "beta";
SAY SYMBOL("alpha"); /* VAR */
SAY SYMBOL(alpha); /* LIT */
```

10.2.49 TIME – Return the Current Time-of-Day

The TIME function returns the current time-of-day. The time is returned in the specified format.

Syntax:

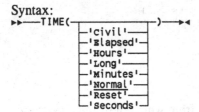

```
►►──TIME(──┬─'Civil'───┬──)──►◄
           ├─'Elapsed'─┤
           ├─'Hours'───┤
           ├─'Long'────┤
           ├─'Minutes'─┤
           ├─'Normal'──┤
           ├─'Reset'───┤
           └─'Seconds'─┘
```

Timeformat
        The time fields have the form:
        · hh is the hour (00 through 23), except for 'civil';
        · mm is the minute (00 through 59);
        · ss is the number of seconds (00 through 59);
        · uuuuuu is the number of microseconds (*Note*: the actual precision will
          depend on the timer resolution).

'Civil'
        Return the time of day in the form: hh:mmxx . hh is the hour (12-hour clock with leading zeros suppressed); xx is either am or pm, depending on whether the time is before midday (am) or after midday (pm). The minute is truncated, e.g. 10 minutes 59 seconds is returned as 10.

'Elapsed'

Return the time which has elapsed since the elapsed-clock was set. This time is returned in the form: sssssss.uuuuuu .

The elapsed-clock is set by either the `Elapsed` or `Reset` operand.

Note: The elapsed time in a multiprogramming environment has only statistical significance, and, because it is influenced by the computer load, it cannot be used for reliable bench-marking (Example 3 shows a better bench-marking method).

'Hours'

Return the number of hours since midnight.

'Long'

Return the time of day in the long form: hh:mm:ss.uuuuuu .

'Minutes'

Return the number of minutes since midnight.

'Normal'

Return the time of day in the default form: hh:mm:ss .

'Reset'

Return the time which has elapsed since the elapsed-clock was set or reset, and resets the elapsed-clock to zero. This time is returned in the form: sssssss.uuuuuu .

The elapsed-clock is set by either the `Elapsed` or `Reset` operand.

'Seconds'

Return the number of seconds since midnight.

Example 1:
```
SAY TIME();
```

Example 2:
```
CALL TIME('R'); /* reset elapsed-time */
 /* start of interval */

    ...

 /* end of interval */
SAY TIME('E'); /* display elapsed time */
```
Note: The elapsed time clock should only be used for statistical purposes. Example 3 shows a better method that can be used for bench-marking.

Example 3:
```
before = SYSVAR('SYSSRV');
/* start benchmark interval */

   ...

/* end benchmark interval */
```

```
after = SYSVAR('SYSSRV');
SAY (after-before) 'service units used';
```

The system service unit, which is a weighted measurement of the system resource usage (e.g. man-storage usage, CPU time, etc.). Service units normally provide a more appropriate indication of the overall computer system loading than just the CPU time usage.

10.2.50 TRACE – Return (and Set) the Current Trace Mode

The TRACE function returns the current trace mode and sets the specified trace mode. Chapter 9 (Debugging) contains a detailed description of the use of the TRACE function. If no argument is specified, the current trace mode remains unchanged.

Note: The TRACE instruction is more commonly used in preference to the TRACE function. Whereas the TRACE instruction is ignored during interactive tracing, the TRACE function is processed.

Syntax:

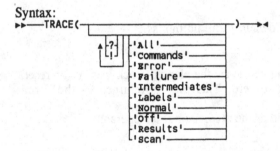

'All'
> All expressions are displayed before being executed.

'Commands'
> Host commands are displayed before being executed.

'Error'
> Host commands which return a non-zero code are displayed after being executed.

'Failure'
> Host commands which return a negative code are displayed after being executed. This is the same as the **Normal** setting.

'Intermediate'
> All expressions (and intermediate results) are displayed before being executed.

'Labels'
> Labels are displayed as they are reached.

'Normal'
> Host commands which return a negative code are displayed after being executed.

'Off'
> Stop trace.

'Results'
> All expressions (and end results) are displayed before being executed.

'Syntax'
> Check the syntax without processing the statements.

?
> Turn on interactive debugging.

!
> Suppress the execution of host commands. The return code is set to zero for each host command which would have been performed.

Note: "?" and "!" are binary switches (toggles), i.e. each setting reverses the current setting of the option.

Example:

```
x = TRACE();

y = TRACE('O');
```

This example returns the current trace mode in x and y, respectively; the first invocation does not alter the trace mode, the second invocation disables tracing (option 'OFF').

10.2.51 TRANSLATE - Translate Characters

The TRANSLATE function transforms the contents of the input data based on translation tables. The translation is performed character by character from left to right.

The TRANSLATE function has two forms:
· translation tables present;
· translation tables not present.

When translation tables are present, the entries in the input table (**inputtable**) are replaced by the corresponding entries in the output table (**outputtable**); entries which are not present remain unchanged. When translation tables are not present, the input is translated from lowercase to uppercase.

Tip
TRANSLATE is a powerful function which can often simplify processing by normalising data. For example, the TRANSLATE function used in Example 3 converts

alphabetic data to uppercase and replaces non-alphabetic characters by an asterisk. The TRANSLATE function could be similarly used to normalise data strings to word-strings, i.e. separate words with blanks, which can then be processed using standard word-parsing functions. TRANSLATE also can be used to format strings; see Example 4.

Syntax:

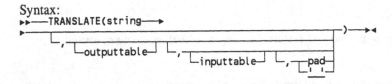

```
▶▶──TRANSLATE(string──▶
▶───────────────────────────────────────────────────)──▶◀
    └─,─┴─outputtable─┘ └─,─┴─inputtable─┘ └─,─┬─pad─┬─┘
                                              └─' '─┘
```

string

> The data to be processed.

outputtable

> The character to be substituted for the character at the same position of **inputtable**.

inputtable

> The characters to be translated. The position of the entries (characters) in this table is used as index to the entries in the **outputtable**, e.g. the first entry in **inputtable** indexes to the first entry in **outputtable**. The first occurrence is used if the same character appears more than once.
> If a character from **string** is not present in the **inputtable**, it is passed unchanged to the function result field.

pad

> The character to be used for padding, if **outputtable** is shorter than **inputtable**.
> Default: ' ' (blank). The null-string cannot be specified as pad character.

Example 1:
```
SAY TRANSLATE("abcde"); /* ABCDE */
```

Example 2:
```
tod = TIME('L'); /* hh:mm:ss.uuuuuu */
SAY TRANSLATE(tod,".,",":."); /* for example, 19.40.27,450000 */
```
Convert the time to a Continental format, replacing colons (:) with periods (.) and the original period with a comma (,).

Example 3:

```
fld = "abcIJK 123  QRS";
UpperCase = "ABCDEFGHIJKLMNOPQRSTUVWXYZ";
AllChars = UpperCase||XRANGE(); /* uppercase + '00'x - 'FF'x */
fld = TRANSLATE(fld); /* convert to uppercase */
fld = TRANSLATE(fld,UpperCase,AllChars,'*');
SAY fld; /* 'ABCIJK******QRS' */
```

Example 4:

```
date = 19941231;
inmask = 'abcdefgh'; /* abcd = yyyy, ef = mm, gh = dd */
outmask = 'ef/gh/cd';
SAY TRANSLATE(outmask,date,inmask); /* 12/31/94 */
time = '01:23:45';
inmask = 'ab:cd:ef';
outmask = 'abcdef';
SAY TRANSLATE(outmask,time,inmask); /* 012345 */
```

This example uses the TRANSLATE function for both inclusive and exclusive formatting. The date string is both reformatted in its order (from year-day-month to the American form month-day-year) and a virgule (/) inserted between the items. The colons are removed from the time string.

10.2.52 TRUNC - Truncate Numeric Value

The TRUNC function formats a number to a have a specified number of decimal places (truncate is a misnomer, as the TRUNC function can also expand). The NUMERIC DIGITS setting takes priority.

Syntax:

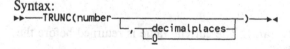

number
>The value to be processed.

decimalplaces
>The number of decimal digits (to the right of the decimal point) to be returned.
>Default: 0.

Example 1:

```
SAY TRUNC("123.45"); /* 123 */
SAY TRUNC("123.45",3); /* 123.450 */
```

Example 2:
```
SAY TRUNC("123.45"); /* 123 */
NUMERIC DIGITS 4;
SAY TRUNC("123.45",3); /* 123.500 - false precision */
```
Note: If the number of digits implied by the TRUNC function is greater than set with the NUMERIC DIGITS instruction (default: 9 digits), a false precision is formed (as in this example).

10.2.53 USERID - Return Userid

The USERID function returns the job identifier. This identifier is dependent on the current environment:
- TSO   userid;
- MVS   the first entry that is present from userid, stepname or jobname.

Syntax:
```
▶▶──USERID()──▶◀
```

10.2.54 VALUE - Return (and Set) the Contents of a Symbol

The VALUE function returns the contents of the specified symbol. This is equivalent to indirect addressing. The VALUE keyword is also used in certain instructions, where it has the same meaning as this function.

Syntax:

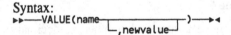

name
> The symbol whose contents are to be returned.

newvalue
> The value to be assigned to **name**. The current value is returned before the new value assignment is made.

Example 1:
```
alpha = "beta";
beta = "gamma";
SAY VALUE(alpha); /* gamma */
SAY VALUE("alpha"); /* beta */
```

Example 2:
```
a = 1;
b = VALUE("A",2);
SAY a b; /* 2 1 */
```

10.2.55 VERIFY – Test Whether Only Characters in a Phrase are Present in String

The VERIFY function verifies the presence of characters in a string against a pattern.

The VERIFY function returns either:
· the first position of a character in a string which is present in the specified pattern (option Match), or
· the first position of a character in a string which is not present in the specified pattern (option Nomatch).

The processing is performed character by character from left to right.

Syntax:

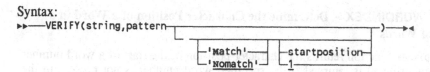

string
> The data to be processed.

pattern
> The data field which contains the test characters.

startposition
> The starting position.
> Default: 1.

'Match'
> The test is to be performed for the first matching character from **string** which also occurs in **pattern**.

'Nomatch'
> The test is to be performed for the first character from **string** which does not occur in **pattern**.
> Default: 'Nomatch'.

Example:
```
SAY VERIFY("beta","ab",'M'); /* 1 */
SAY VERIFY("beta","ab",'N'); /* 2 */
SAY VERIFY("abcabc","abcd",'N'); /* 0 */
```

10.2.56 WORD – Fetch Word

The WORD function fetches a word from a word-string. The null string is returned if the specified word number is not present in the word-string.

Syntax:
```
►►──WORD(string,wordnumber)──►◄
```

string
> The data field to be processed.

wordnumber
> The number of the word in **string** to be fetched.

Example:
```
SAY WORD("the rain in Spain",2); /* rain */
SAY WORD("the rain in Spain",5); /* '' (null string) */
```

10.2.57 WORDINDEX - Determine the Character Position of a Word in a String of Words

The WORDINDEX function returns the character position of the start of a word number in a word-string. 0 is returned if the specified word number is not present in the word-string.

Syntax:
```
►►──WORDINDEX(string,wordnumber)──►◄
```

string
> The word-string to be processed.

wordnumber
> The number of the word in **string** whose position is to be determined.

Example:
```
SAY WORDINDEX("the rain in Spain",3); /* 10 */
SAY WORDINDEX("the rain in Spain",5); /* 0 */
```

10.2.58 WORDLENGTH - Determine Word Length

The WORDLENGTH function returns the length of a word·in a word-string. 0 is returned if the specified word number is not present in the word-string.

Syntax:
```
►►──WORDLENGTH(string,wordnumber)──►◄
```

string
> The data field to be processed.

wordnumber
> The number of the word in **string** whose length is to be determined.

Example:
```
SAY WORDLENGTH("the rain in Spain",2); /* 4 */
SAY WORDLENGTH("the rain in Spain",5); /* 0 */
```

10.2.59 WORDPOS - Determine the Word-Number of Word in a Word-String

The WORDPOS function returns the number of the word in the word-string that corresponds to a phrase. 0 is returned if the specified phrase is not present in the word-string.

Tip
The WORDPOS function is wellsuited to checking whether an argument belongs to a set of values (see Example 2).

Syntax:
```
►►──WORDPOS(phrase,string─┬─────────────────────┬─)──►◄
                          └─,─┬─startwordnumber─┬─┘
                              └─1───────────────┘
```

string
    The word-string to be processed.

phrase
    The phrase to be used to search **string**.

startwordnumber
    The number of the word in **string** at which the search is start.
    Default: 1.

Example 1:
```
SAY WORDPOS("in","the rain in Spain"); /* 3 */
SAY WORDPOS("in","the rain in Spain",4); /* 0 */
SAY WORDPOS("ain","the rain in Spain"); /* 0 */
```

Example 2:
```
x = WORDPOS(state,"CA NJ NY TX");
IF x > 0 THEN SAY "Valid state";
```

10.2.60 WORDS - Determine the Number of Words in a Word-String

The WORDS function returns the number of words in a word-string.

Syntax:
```
►►──WORDS(string)──►◄
```

string
    The word-string to be processed.

Example:
```
SAY WORDS("the rain in Spain"); /* 4 */
```

10.2.61 XRANGE - Define a Range of Hexadecimal Values

The XRANGE function defines a string of character-codes lying in the range of values (including the bounds).

Syntax:

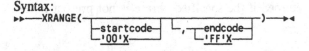

startcode
> The lower bound of the range.
> Default: '00'x.

endcode
> The upper bound of the range.
> Default: 'FF'x.

Note: If **endcode** is less than **startcode**, wrap-around will occur.

Warning
Care should be taken with the definition of code tables if the application is going to be ported to other hardware environments. For example, the table of uppercase characters should be defined by specifying each character:

"ABCDEFGHIJKLMNOPQRSTUVWXYZ".

The shorter definition using the XRANGE function XRANGE('A','Z') is valid only for ASCII codes; the statement

XRANGE('A','I')XRANGE('J','R')XRANGE('S','Z')

would be required to yield the equivalent results in both ASCII and EBCDIC environments.

Example:
```
x = XRANGE('0','9');
```
This example defines 'F0F1F2F3F4F5F6F7F8F9'x (EBCDIC), i.e. 9 characters.

```
x = XRANGE('9','0');
```
This example defines 'F9FAFBFCFDFEFEFF0001'x through 'EEEFF0'x (EBCDIC), i.e. 248 characters.

10.2.62 X2B - Convert Hexadecimal to Binary

The X2B (hexadecimal-to-binary) function converts a string of hexadecimal digits (0 through 9 and A through F) to the equivalent binary data. The data are converted from left to right, with four binary-coded digits being used for each hexadecimal digit. The input hexadecimal string may contain embedded blanks on byte boundaries. A zero will be prefixed to the start of the input string if its length is not even.

Syntax:
```
►►——X2B(hexstring)——►◄
```

hexstring
     The string of hexadecimal digits to be processed.

Example:
```
SAY X2B("C1"); /* 11000001 */
SAY X2B("C"); /* 00001100 (left-pad with "0") */
SAY X2B("1 C2"); /* 0000000111000010 */
```

10.2.63 X2C - Convert Hexadecimal to Character

The X2C (hexadecimal-to-character) function converts a string of hexadecimal digits (0 through 9 and A through F) to the equivalent character data. The data are converted from left to right, with two hexadecimal digits being used for each character. A zero will be padded to the start of the input string if its length is not even.

Syntax:
```
►►——X2C(hexstring)——►◄
```

hexstring
     The string of hexadecimal digits to be processed.

Example:
```
SAY X2C("C1C2"); /* AB */
SAY X2C("F0 F1"); /* 01 */
SAY X2C("1C2"); /* '01C2'x */
```

10.2.64 X2D - Convert Hexadecimal to Decimal

The X2D (hexadecimal-to-decimal) function converts the binary representation of a string of hexadecimal digits (0 through 9 and A through F) to its equivalent decimal value. The sign of the input hexadecimal string (truncated or padded, if necessary) is used for the result.

Syntax:
```
►►——X2D(hexstring——————————)——►◄
                 └—,length—┘
```

hexstring
     The string of hexadecimal digits to be processed.

length
> The length (in hexadecimal digits) of the input data. The input **hexstring** is padded on the left with 0 or truncated to the specified **length**.

Example:
```
SAY X2D("F0"); /* 240 */
SAY X2D("F0",2); /* -16 (signed) */
SAY X2D("F0",4); /* 240 */
```

10.3 EXAMPLES

Because of the importance of REXX functions, two practical examples of their usage are shown. The sample functions illustrate the use of several built-in REXX functions. In addition, the sample LINEIN function makes use of host commands and host command functions.

10.3.1 Example 1

The sample D2P (Decimal to Packed) function shown here converts a decimal argument to packed decimal. A negative input value is prefixed with a '-' character. Section 15.6 shows the same function as a programmed function.

Function code:
```
/* REXX - D2P() */
PARSE ARG val;
sign = SUBSTR(val,1,1); /* extract sign, if present */
y = ''; /* initialise result */
IF sign = '-'
  THEN val = SUBSTR(val,2); /* remove sign character */
  ELSE sign = '';
len = LENGTH(val);
IF len // 2 = 0
  THEN DO; /* even length, prefix '0' */
    val = '0'val; /* prefix '0' */
    len = len+1; /* increment length by 1 */
  END;
DO i = 1 TO len BY 2;
  ho = SUBSTR(val,i,1); /* high-order */
  ho = C2D(BITAND(ho,'0f'x));
  ho = ho*16;
  ho = D2C(ho);
  IF i < len THEN DO;
    lo = SUBSTR(val,i+1,1); /* low-order */
```

```
          lo = BITAND(lo,'0f'x);
       END;
       ELSE DO;
         IF sign = '-'
           THEN lo = '0d'x;
           ELSE lo = '0f'x;
       END;
       y = y || BITOR(ho,lo); /* append to previous result */
     END;
     RETURN y; /* result */
```

Test driver:

```
     /* test driver */
     x = D2P("-1234")
     SAY C2X(x) /* 01234D */
     x = D2P("12345")
     SAY C2X(x) /* 12345F */
```

10.3.2 Example 2

Although the LINEIN function is available for most REXX implementations, it is not
provided with TSO. This sample LINEIN function shows a possible simplified
implementation. The sample code also shows how the specification of a 'standard'
function may need to be modified to suit implementation-specific restrictions; this
implementation allows 0 as line parameter, which causes the file to be closed after
the function call.

Function code:

```
     /* REXX - LINEIN() TSO implementation */
     LINEIN: PROCEDURE;
       PARSE ARG name,line,count;
       IF ARG(1,'O') THEN name = '*'; /* set default */
       /* trap any allocation error messages */
       CALL OUTTRAP 'msg.',,'NOCONCAT';
       ADDRESS TSO "ALLOC F(TEMP) DA("name") SHR REUS";
       DROP msg.; /* release storage */
       CALL OUTTRAP 'OFF'; /* disable message trapping */
       IF ARG(2,'E')
         THEN DO; /* 2nd argument present */
           SELECT
             WHEN line = 1
               THEN finis = '';
             WHEN line = 0
               THEN DO;
                 line = '';
```

```
                finis = 'FINIS';
            END;
          OTHERWISE
            EXIT -3; /* invalid parameter */
      END;
    END;
    ELSE finis = '';
  IF ARG(3,'O')
    THEN count = 1; /* default count */
    ELSE IF (count <> 0 & count <> 1) THEN EXIT -3; /* invalid count */
  "NEWSTACK"; /* create new stack */
  "EXECIO" count "DISKR TEMP" line "(FIFO" finis;
  IF QUEUED() > 0
    THEN PARSE PULL record;
    ELSE record = ''; /* null result */
  "DELSTACK"; /* restore original stack */
  RETURN record;
```

Test driver:

```
/* test driver */
SAY 'prompt for terminal input';
SAY LINEIN(,0,1); /* close after input */
SAY LINEIN('DATA.FILE'); /* read next record */
SAY LINEIN('DATA.FILE',1); /* position at file start */
SAY LINEIN('DATA.FILE',,0); /* read no record */
SAY LINEIN('DATA.FILE',0); /* close after reading record */
```

Sample output:

```
PROMPT FOR TERMINAL INPUT
term in
TERM IN

alpha

alpha


beta
```

The input file DATA.FILE contained the following records:

```
alpha
beta
gamma
delta
```

11

Host REXX Commands
What is pleasanter than the tie of host and guest

The Libation Bearers

Aeschylus

11.1 INTRODUCTION

Each REXX implementation has a number of extensions which do not belong to the SAA definition of the REXX language – these are known as **host REXX commands**. This chapter describes the host REXX commands implemented for TSO.

The result or status of the host REXX command is set in the RC special variable.

11.2 HOST REXX COMMAND DEFINITIONS

TSO REXX provides the following host commands:
- DELSTACK   Delete stack
- DROPBUF   Release buffer
- EXECIO   Perform input/output operation
- EXECUTIL   Specify execution environment for REXX program
- HE   Halt execution
- HI   Halt interpretation
- HT   Halt typing
- MAKEBUF   Create new buffer in the stack
- NEWSTACK   Create a new stack

- · QBUF   Query buffer. Return the number of buffers in the current stack
- · QELEM   Return number of elements in the current buffer
- · QSTACK   Query stack. Return the current number of stacks
- · RT   Resume typing
- · SUBCOM   Confirm the host environment
- · TE   Trace end
- · TS   Trace start.

11.2.1 DELSTACK - Delete Stack

The DELSTACK command deletes the most recently created stack. If no stack has been created (with the NEWSTACK command), all elements from the original stack are deleted.

Syntax:
```
▶▶——DELSTACK——▶◀
```

Example:
```
QUEUE 'line1'
QUEUE 'line2'
SAY QUEUED() /* 2 */
"NEWSTACK"
QUEUE 'line3'
SAY QUEUED() /* 1 */
"DELSTACK"
SAY QUEUED() /* 2 */
```

11.2.2 DROPBUF - Release Buffer

The DROPBUF command deletes the specified buffer (and its elements) from the current stack. Buffers are created with the MAKEBUF command.

The RC special variable is set to contain the return code:
- 0   successful completion;
- 1   the buffer number is invalid;
- 2   the buffer number does not exist.

Syntax:
```
▶▶——DROPBUF—————————————▶◀
            └ buffernumber ┘
```

buffernumber
> The number of the first buffer to be deleted. This buffer and all higher numbered (newer) buffers are deleted.
> Default: The most recently created buffer is deleted.

Example:

    "DROPBUF 4";

Delete buffer number 4 and all newer buffers from the current stack.

11.2.3 EXECIO - Perform Input/Output Operation

The EXECIO command performs the specified input/output operation. One of the following operations may be performed:

· read;
· read for update;
· write.

The EXECIO command is primarily concerned with processing at the file level, although single records or groups of records can also be processed. The processed records are stored or taken from either the current stack or a stem variable.

When records are read into the stack, these records may be placed either at the head (FIFO) or tail (LIFO) of the stack, or ignored (SKIP). Ignored records are read but not stored.

A record which has been read for update (DISKRU option) may be rewritten (updated) by an immediately following write operation (DISKW option). Only a single record may be stored for update. An option is available to close the dataset after the last record has been processed (FINIS parameter).

The dataset to be processed must have been previously allocated, using either the TSO ALLOC command or the JCL DD statement.

The record formats may be either:
· fixed (blocked);
· variable (blocked).

The RC special variable is set to contain the return code:

0	successful completion;
1	data were truncated during the DISKW operation;
2	end of file was reached during a read operation;
20	a severe error occurred.

Syntax:

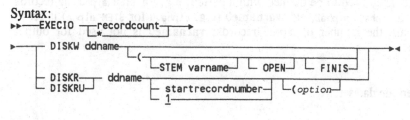

option:

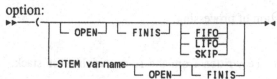

Note: The TSO implementation allows a right-parenthesis (")") at the end of the option list. This delimiter is invalid in other implementations, and should be omitted if compatibility is required.

recordcount

The number of records to be processed. Processing is also terminated by a null entry. A zero **recordcount** with option OPEN opens the dataset without processing any records. A zero **recordcount** with option FINIS closes the dataset without processing any records.

*

Read the complete dataset or write the complete buffer, or process until the first null entry is reached (whichever occurs first).

DISKW

Write the dataset.

DISKR

Read the dataset.

DISKRU

Read the dataset for update. In update mode, only a single record may be read. If this DISKRU operation is followed (without any intervening input/output operations for this file) by a DISKW operation, this dataset record will be updated.

ddname

The DD-name of the dataset to be processed. The **ddname** is the filename previously allocated with a TSO ALLOC statement or the DD-name specified by a JCL DD statement.

STEM varname

The records are written from or read into stem variables, as appropriate. **varname** appended with the entry number contains the record, e.g. for STEM alpha. The records are in alpha.1, alpha.2, etc. **varname** does not necessarily need to be defined with a period, e.g. for STEM alpha the records are in alpha1, alpha2, etc. **varname0** (e.g. alpha.0 for STEM alpha) is set to contain the number of stored records; **varname0** is not used for output files.

OPEN

Open the dataset.

FINIS

Close the dataset on completion of processing.

startrecordnumber

The first record which is to be written from the stem variables or stack. Default: 1.

FIFO

> Store the records at the head of the stack (first-in/first-out). This is the default.

LIFO

> Store the records at the end (tail) of the stack (last-in/first-out).

SKIP

> Skip the specified number of records (**recordcount**), i.e. read but do not store.

Example 1:

```
"EXECIO * DISKR FILEIN (STEM A.)";
```
In this statement the complete dataset with the file name (DD-name) FILEIN is read, the records are stored in A.1, A.2 etc. A.0 is set to contain the number of records read.

Example 2:

```
"EXECIO * DISKR SYSUT1 (STEM r."
DO i = 1 TO r.0
   r.i = TRANSLATE(r.i,' ','05'x)
END
"EXECIO * DISKW SYSUT2 (STEM r."
```
Read the complete dataset with the file name (DD-name) SYSUT1. Change all occurrences of the '05'x character to blanks. Rewrite the converted data to the SYSUT2 file.

11.2.4 EXECUTIL - Specify Execution Environment for REXX Exec

The EXECUTIL command specifies the execution (TSO) environment for the REXX exec. The EXECUTIL command can be:
· used in a REXX exec;
· used from TSO (or CLIST).

The EXECUTIL command can be used to:
· specify whether the system exec library is to be closed after the exec has been loaded;
· specify whether the system exec library is to be searched in addition to the system procedures library;
· specify whether tracing is to be started or stopped;
· specify whether terminal output is to be suppressed or resumed after having been stopped.

The two-character codes (e.g. HT) can be also invoked interactively.

Syntax:

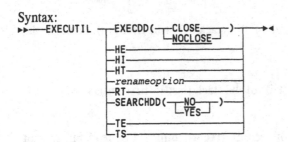

renameoption:
```
▶▶——RENAME NAME(functionname)——▶
▶————————————————————————————————————▶◀
        └ SYSNAME(systemname)┘  └ DD(systemdd)┘
```

EXECDD

The processing to be performed on the system exec library after the exec has been loaded.
CLOSE - close the system exec library.
NOCLOSE - do not close the system exec library.
Default: NOCLOSE.

HE

Halt Execution - terminate the execution of the program that is currently running.

HI

Halt Interpretation - terminate the execution of all execs that are currently running.

HT

Halt Typing - suppress SAY output.

RENAME

Change entries in the function package directory. This is a specialised function normally used only by system administrators, and is not described in this book.

RT

Resume Typing - restart SAY output.

SEARCHDD

Search options for the system exec library.
YES - the system exec library (SYSEXEC) is to be searched before the system procedure library (SYSPROC) is searched.
NO - the system exec library is not to be searched.
Default: NO.

TE

Trace End - terminate tracing.

TS

Trace Start - initiate tracing.

Example:

```
"EXECUTIL SEARCHDD(YES)";
```

This example specifies that the system exec library (SYSEXEC) is to be searched for
the exec.

11.2.5 HE — Halt Execution

The HE command halts the execution of the exec that is currently running. The HE
command is active only in TSO attention mode, which is entered by pressing the
attention interrupt key. The HE command is used to terminate the execution of an
external function or command that is written in a conventional programming
language.

Syntax:
```
▶▶──HE──▶◀
```

Example:

```
ADDRESS LINK "rxpgm";
```
attention interrupt !
```
he
    IRX0929I EXEC EXECUTION HALTED BY USER REQUEST....
    IRX0245I REXX exec execution halted.
    IRX0246I Execution halted while in external function RXPGM.
```
This example shows how the HE command after interruption can be used to
terminate the rxpgm REXX program.

11.2.6 HI — Halt Interpretation

Terminate the execution of all execs that are currently running.

Syntax:
```
▶▶──HI──▶◀
```

11.2.7 HT — Halt Typing

Suppress SAY output.

Syntax:
```
▶▶──HT──▶◀
```

11.2.8 MAKEBUF - Create New Buffer in the Stack

The MAKEBUF command creates a new buffer in the current stack. The stack initially
contains one buffer, buffer 0. Each invocation of MAKEBUF increases the number of
buffers in the current stack. Buffers are removed with the DROPBUF command. New
stacks are created with the NEWSTACK command.

The number of the new buffer is returned in the RC special variable. The QBUF command can be used to obtain the number of buffers in the current stack.

Syntax:
```
►►──MAKEBUF──►◄
```

Example:
```
/* REXX */
"NEWSTACK";
"MAKEBUF";
SAY RC; /* 1 */
"MAKEBUF";
SAY RC; /* 2 */
```

11.2.9 NEWSTACK - Create a New Stack

The NEWSTACK command creates a new stack, which then becomes the current stack. The DELSTACK command deletes the current stack (and all entries in it) and reverts the current stack to being the previous stack. The stack is only available to execs running in the environment which created it. The QSTACK command can be used to obtain the number of entries in the current stack.

Syntax:
```
►►──NEWSTACK──►◄
```

Example:
```
QUEUE 'line1'
QUEUE 'line2'
SAY QUEUED() /* 2 */
"NEWSTACK"
QUEUE 'line3'
SAY QUEUED() /* 1 */
"DELSTACK"
SAY QUEUED() /* 2 */
DO i = 1 TO QUEUED()
   PULL line
   SAY i line
END
```
This displays the two queued elements:
```
1 LINE1
2 LINE2
```

11.2.10 QBUF - Query Buffer

The QBUF command returns the number of buffers created in the current stack with the MAKEBUF command. This number is returned in the RC special variable.

Syntax:
```
▶▶──QBUF──▶◀
```

Example:
```
/* REXX */
"MAKEBUF"
QUEUE 'line1'
QUEUE 'line2'
QUEUE 'line3'
"MAKEBUF"
QUEUE 'line4'
"QBUF"; SAY rc /* 2 */
```

11.2.11 QELEM - Query Elements

The QELEM command returns the number of elements in the buffer most recently created with the MAKEBUF command. This number is returned in the RC special variable.

Syntax:
```
▶▶──QELEM──▶◀
```

Example:
```
/* REXX */
"MAKEBUF"
QUEUE 'line1'
QUEUE 'line2'
QUEUE 'line3'
"QELEM"; SAY RC /* 3 */
"MAKEBUF"
QUEUE 'line4'
"QELEM"; SAY RC /* 1 */
```

11.2.12 QSTACK - Query Stack

The QSTACK command returns the current number of stacks in existence. This number is returned in the RC special variable.

One stack exists when the exec is invoked. Additional stacks are created with the NEWSTACK command. Stacks are deleted with the DELSTACK command.

Syntax:
```
▶▶──QSTACK──▶◀
```

Example:
```
/* REXX */
QUEUE 'line1'
QUEUE 'line2'
```

```
QUEUE 'line3'
"NEWSTACK"
"QSTACK"; SAY RC /* 3 */
```

11.2.13 RT - Resume Typing

Resume SAY output.

Syntax:
```
►►——RT——►◄
```

11.2.14 SUBCOM - Confirm the Host Environment

The SUBCOM command sets the status as to whether the invoking exec is in the specified host environment.

The status is returned in the RC special variable:
        0   the exec is running in the specified environment;
        1   the exec is not running in the specified environment.

Warning
The value returned is not true (1) or false (0) as might be expected.

Syntax:
```
►►——SUBCOM environment——►◄
```

environment
        The environment to be tested, e.g. TSO, ISPEXEC.

Example:
```
"SUBCOM TSO";
IF RC = 0 THEN SAY "TSO active";
```
Display the message "TSO active" if the TSO environment is active.

11.2.15 TE - Trace End

Terminate tracing.

Syntax:
```
►►——TE——►◄
```

11.2.16 TS - Trace Start

Initiate tracing.

Syntax:
```
►►——TS——►◄
```

11.3 EXAMPLE

illustrates the use of the EXECIO host command. The example appends a timestamp
to each record in the USER.DATA file.

```
/* REXX */
ADDRESS TSO;
"ALLOC FILE(IOFILE) DSNAME(USER.DATA) SHR REUS"; /* allocate file */
"EXECIO * DISKR IOFILE (STEM s. FINIS"; /* read file in stem */
/* create timestamp */
tod = TIME('Normal'); /* time-of-day hh:mm:ss */
tod = SUBSTR(tod,1,2)SUBSTR(tod,4,2)SUBSTR(tod,7,2);
timestamp = DATE('Sorted') || tod;
IF RC = 0 THEN DO;
  DO i = 1 TO s.0;
    s.i = s.i || timestamp;
  END;
  "EXECIO * DISKW IOFILE (STEM s. FINIS"; /* rewrite file from stem */
END;
```

12

MVS Command Functions

There is nothing that gives a man consequence, and renders him fit for command, like a support that renders him independent of everybody but the State he serves.

Letter to the president of Congress

George Washington

12.1 INTRODUCTION

Each REXX implementation has a number of functions pertaining to the host environment. The MVS (OS/390) host environment commands described in this chapter are, with the exception of the GETDSN and STORAGE commands, equivalent CLIST statements. Other host environment commands may be invoked in the normal (REXX) way, see Sections 13.2 through 13.4.

MVS command functions are called in the same way as REXX functions. All MVS command functions described in this chapter set a **function return value**, which is returned to the point of invocation. The function return value is either the status code or the data returned by the command, as appropriate.

12.2 MVS COMMAND FUNCTION CALLS

TSO REXX provides the following host command functions:

- GETMSG[*]   Retrieve a console session message;
- LISTDSI[*]   List (obtain) dataset information;
- MSG[*]   Set (interrogate) CLIST CONTROL MSG option;
- MVSVAR   Obtain information MVS, TSO, and the current session;
- OUTTRAP[*]   Trap TSO display output;

- · PROMPT*   Set (interrogate) CLIST CONTROL PROMPT option;
- · SETLANG   Set (interrogate) current language;
- · STORAGE*   Set (interrogate) main-storage contents;
- · SYSCPUS*   Request CPU information;
- · SYSDSN*   Request dataset status;
- · SYSVAR*   Fetch TSO system variable;
- · Invocation of other TSO commands.

* indicates that the MVS command function can only be used in the TSO environment.

Table 12.1 shows the equivalent TSO CLIST component.

Table 12.1 – Equivalent TSO CLIST components

LISTDSI		LISTDSI
MSG		CONTROL [NO]MSG
OUTTRAP	variable	&SYSOUTTRAP, &SYSOUTMAX
PROMPT		CONTROL [NO]PROMPT
SYSDSN	variable	&SYSDSN
SYSVAR	variable	see command description

[ ] indicates an optional item

Several MVS command functions used in the TSO environment require a dataset name. A dataset name in TSO has two possible forms:
- · fully qualified, enclosed within quotes;
- · user dataset, to which the user's prefix is appended as first qualifier.

To avoid fully qualified dataset names being processed as REXX literals, such dataset names must be enclosed within either paired single quotes (') or double quotes ("). This is illustrated in the following example:

```
    x = SYSDSN("'sys1.maclib'");
```
specifies the fully qualified dataset name 'SYS1.MACLIB',
whereas
```
    x = SYSDSN('sys1.maclib');
```
specifies the user's SYS1.MACLIB dataset. For example, if the user has TUSER01 as userid this call is equivalent to
```
    x = SYSDSN("'tuser01.sys1.maclib'");
```

Similarly, certain MVS command functions have parameters with subparameters contained within parentheses. Such terms must be defined as a REXX literal so that

they themselves are not processed as a (non-existent) function. This is illustrated in
the following example:

```
x = LISTDSI(datafile 'VOLUME(DISK00)')
```
If VOLUME(DISK00) were specified without the enclosing quotes, it would be
interpreted as being the invocation of the function VOLUME with argument DISK00.

The arguments passed to MVS command functions are subject to the usual REXX
syntax rules, e.g. terms not enclosed within quotes are processed as symbols. In
the following example, the dataset name passed to the LISTDSI command function
is the contents of the variable dsnvar, i.e. DATA.FILE.

```
dsnvar = 'DATA.FILE';
x = LISTDSI(dsnvar);
```

The following statement is required to pass the dataset name DSNVAR to the LISTDSI
command function:
```
x = LISTDSI('DSNVAR');
```

12.2.1 GETMSG - Retrieve a Console Session Message

The GETMSG command function retrieves a console session message. The GETMSG
command function is designed to be used in MVS operator procedures.

Syntax:

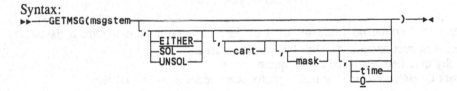

msgstem
> The stem into which GETMSG is to place the list of messages (**msgstem1**,
> **msgstem2**, etc.; **msgstem0** is set to contain the number of messages
> returned).

msgtype
> The type of message to be retrieved:
>
> SOL   A solicited message, which is the response to an MVS system
>   or subsystem command.
>
> UNSOL   An unsolicited message, which is not issued in response to an
>   MVS system or subsystem command.
>
> EITHER   Either SOL or UNSOL. EITHER is the default **msgtype**.

cart

The Command And Response Token. The **cart** is a token used to associate MVS system or subsystem commands with their responses.

mask

The optional search argument to be used as mask for the **cart** to obtain a message. If omitted, no masking is performed.

time

The time in seconds that GETMSG waits if the requested message has not been routed to the user's console. If this interval elapses before the message can be routed, GETMSG does not retrieve the message. Default: 0 seconds.

One of the following function codes is returned:

    0   Successful completion.
    4   Successful processing, although no message was retrieved.
    8   Successful processing, but the ATTN key was pressed during processing. No message was retrieved.
  12   Unsuccessful processing. No console session is active.
  16   Unsuccessful processing. The console session is being deactivated.

Note: The use of GETMSG is subject to the following restrictions:
·   The user must have console authority.
·   Console messages must have been stored rather than displayed.

Example 1:

```
CALL GETMSG msg.,'SOL';
IF RESULT = 0 THEN DO i = 1 TO msg.0;
    SAY msg.i;
    END;
```
Display the solicited messages.

Example 2:

```
ARG uid . /* get TSO userid */
IF uid = '' THEN uid = USERID()
/* activate MVS-Console */
ADDRESS TSO "CONSOLE ACTIVATE "
ADDRESS TSO "CONSPROF SOLDISPLAY(NO) UNSOLDISPLAY(NO)"
lu = '' /* initialise */
/* VTAM display to TSO user */
ADDRESS CONSOLE "D net,u,id="uid
/* first message from display = accept or not (logon or not) */
IF GETMSG('msg.',,,,10) = 0 THEN DO
  IF WORD(msg.1,1) <> 'IST453I' THEN DO /* next messages for accept only
*/
    CALL GETMSG 'msg.',,,,10
```

```
              /* search LUNAME = terminal-id */
              DO i=1 TO msg.0
                PARSE VAR msg.i 'LUNAME = ' lu ',' .
                IF lu <> '' THEN LEAVE i
              END
            END
          END
          ADDRESS TSO "CONSOLE DEACTIVATE"
          IF lu = ''
            THEN lu = 'not Logon'
            ELSE lu = 'Logon on Terminal 'lu
          SAY 'User 'uid' is 'lu
```
Display the terminal-ID for the TSO-user specified as invocation argument.

12.2.2 LISTDSI - List (Obtain) Dataset Information

The LISTDSI command function returns information pertaining to a dataset as REXX variables. The LISTDSI command function can be used in one of two ways:
·   using the dataset name;
·   using the file (DD) name.

Syntax:

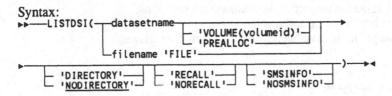

datasetname
The name of the dataset to be processed. The form of **datasetname** conforms to the usual TSO conventions, i.e. a dataset name written without enclosing quotes has the user's TSO prefix appended.

'VOLUME(volumeid)'
This operand is only required for datasets which are not catalogued; **volumeid** is the name of the volume on which the dataset resides.

'PREALLOC'
A preallocation of the dataset is to be used if possible.

filename
The name of the file to be processed. File in this context is the DD statement. This **filename** must have been previously allocated.

'FILE'
This keyword denotes that the previous operand is the name of a file.

'DIRECTORY'

The directory of a partitioned dataset is to be read in order that directory information (SYSADIRBLK, SYSUDIRBLK and SYSMEMBERS) can be obtained.

Note: This processing can be relatively time-consuming for large directories, and so should be specified only when the directory information is required.

'NODIRECTORY'

No directory information is to be returned.

Default: NODIRECTORY.

'RECALL'

A dataset migrated with DFHSM (Data Facility Hierarchical Storage Manager) is to be restored.

'NORECALL'

A dataset migrated with DFHSM is to not be restored.

If neither RECALL nor NORECALL is specified, a dataset is restored only if it has been migrated to a direct access storage device.

The LISTDSI command function sets the following variables:

SYSDSNAME	Dataset name.
SYSVOLUME	Volume serial number.
SYSUNIT	Unit name.
SYSDSORG	Dataset organisation: PS, PSU, DA, DAU, IS, ISU, PO, POU, VS(am), ??? (=unknown).
SYSRECFM	Record format: U, F[B][A|M], V[B][A|M], ? (=unknown). [] = optional, | = or.
SYSLRECL	Record length.
SYSBLKSIZE	Block length.
SYSKEYLEN	Key length.
SYSALLOC	Allocation (in space units).
SYSUSED	Space used (in space units); N/A for PDSE.
SYSUSEDPAGES	Number of used pages for PDSE if SMSINFO is specified.
SYSPRIMARY	Primary allocation (in space units).
SYSSECONDS	Secondary allocation (in space units).
SYSUNITS	Space unit: CYLINDER, TRACK, BLOCK, ? (=unknown).
SYSEXTENTS	Number of extents.
SYSCREATE	Date created (yyyy/ddd).
SYSREFDATE	Date last referenced (yyyy/ddd).
SYSEXDATE	Expiry date (yyyy/ddd).
SYSPASSWORD	Password indicator: NONE, READ (read password required), WRITE (write password required).
SYSRACF	RACF indicator: NONE, GENERIC (generic profile for dataset), DISCRETE (discrete profile for dataset).
SYSUPDATED	Dataset updated: YES or NO.

SYSTRKSCYL	Number tracks per cylinder.
SYSBLKSTRK	Number blocks per track; N/A for PDSE.
SYSADIRBLK	Number of allocated directory blocks; NO_LIM for PDSE.
SYSUDIRBLK	Number of used directory blocks; N/A for PDSE.
SYSMEMBERS	Number of directory members.
SYSREASON	LISTDSI reason code.
SYSMSGLVL1	First level error message.
SYSMSGLVL2	Second level error message.
SYSDSSMS	Dataset type: SEQ, PDS, PDSE. LIBRARY (empty PDSE), PROGRAM_LIBRARY (program library), DATA_LIBRARY (data library) if SMSINFO is specified.
SYSDATACLASS	SMS data class name if SMSINFO is specified.
SYSSTORCLASS	SMS storage class name if SMSINFO is specified.
SYSMGMTCLASS	SMS management class name if SMSINFO is specified.

Note:
·   The directory information is returned only when the DIRECTORY parameter is specified.
·   Only limited information is returned for VSAM datasets (the TSO LISTC command, invoked in REXX by the instruction ADDRESS TSO "LISTC", returns comprehensive information).
·   SYSDSSMS returns X_LIBRARY only for an SMS-managed PDSE.

SYSREASON values:

0	Normal completion
1	Parsing error
2	Dynamic allocation processing error
3	Unsupported dataset type
4	UNIT name error
5	Dataset not catalogued
6	Dataset name cannot be found
7	Device type cannot be found
8	Non-DASD dataset
9	Migrated dataset (NORECALL specified)
11	No authorisation to obtain directory information; no authorisation to access the data set
12	VSAM dataset not supported
13	Dataset open error
14	Device type not found
17	Internal error
18	Dataset information incomplete
19	Dataset resides on multiple volumes (only in information for first volume returned)
20	Device type not found
21	Catalog error

22	Volume not mounted
23	Permanent I/O error on volume
24	Dataset not found
25	Dataset migrated to non-DASD device
26	Dataset on mass-storage device
27	No volume serial allocated to the dataset
28	DD-name length error
29	Neither dataset name nor DD-name specified
30	Dataset is not SMS-managed
31	Internal error
32	SMS level error
33	SMS not active
34	SMS OPEN error
35	SMS internal service error
36	SMS internal service error

One of the following function codes is returned:

0	successful completion;
4	some dataset (directory) information is not available;
16	severe error (refer to SYSREASON).

Example 1:

```
cmdrc = LISTDSI('EX.ISPCLIB' 'DIRECTORY');
IF cmdrc = 0 THEN SAY "number of members" SYSMEMBERS;
```

This example displays the number of members stored in the directory of the user's EX.ISPCLIB partitioned dataset; cmdrc is assigned the LISTDSI return code.

Note the use of quotes in the above example. The quotes for 'EX.ISPCLIB' and 'DIRECTORY' are used by REXX to denote alphanumeric literals. If an explicit dataset name, i.e. a dataset name which is not to be prefixed with the user's TSO prefix, two levels of quotes are required. This is shown in the following example.

```
rc = LISTDSI("'SYS1.MACLIB'");
```

or

```
rc = LISTDSI('''SYS1.MACLIB''');
```

Example 2:

```
rc = LISTDSI("NOFILE SMSINFO")
IF rc > 0 THEN DO
  SAY rc SYSREASON
  SAY SYSMSGLVL1
  SAY SYSMSGLVL2
END
```

This example tries to reference a file that does not exist. The following display results:
```
16 0005
IKJ58400I LISTDSI FAILED.  SEE REASON CODE IN VARIABLE SYSREASON.
IKJ58405I DATA SET NOT CATALOGUED. THE LOCATE MACRO RETURN CODE IS 0008
```

12.2.3 MSG - Set (Interrogate) CLIST CONTROL MSG Option

The MSG command function can be used in one of two ways:
- Return the current CONTROL MSG status (as function code).
- Set the CONTROL MSG status (optional).

Syntax:

'OFF'

Set the MSG status OFF, i.e. messages issued from TSO commands will be suppressed.

'ON'

Set the MSG status ON, i.e. any messages issued by TSO commands will be displayed.

If no argument is specified, the current MSG setting remains unchanged. The function code is returned with the current MSG setting.

Example:
```
rc = MSG('ON');
```
rc is assigned the current MSG status, and MSG is set ON (irrespective of the previous status).

12.2.4 MVSVAR - Obtain Information MVS, TSO, and the Current Session

The MVSVAR command function obtains information about MVS (OS/390), TSO (TSO/E), and the current session. The argument specifies the information to be returned. The TSOVAR command function returns TSO-related information.

Syntax:
```
►►——MVSVAR(argument)——►◄
```

argument can have the following values:

SYSAPPCLU	The APPC/MVS logical unit name
SYSDFP	The Data Facility Product component level
SYSMVS	The OS/390 base control program component level
SYSNAME	The name of the system where this REXX exec is running
SYSOPSYS	The OS/390 name, version, etc.
SYSSECLAB	The security label name of the TSO session

SYSSMFID   The identification of the system on which System
            Management Facilities (SMF) is running
SYSSMS   Flag whether DFSMS/MVS is available
SYSCLONE   MVS system symbol
SYSPLEX   MVS sysplex name
SYMDEF,varname   OS/390 symbolic variable (the entry from SYS1.PARMLIB).

Example 1:
```
SAY SYSVAR('SYSCPU')       /* 2.67 */
SAY SYSVAR('SYSHSM')       /* */
SAY SYSVAR('SYSJES')       /* JES2 OS 2.5.0 */
SAY SYSVAR('SYSLRACF')     /* 2060 */
SAY SYSVAR('SYSNODE')      /* E1 */
SAY SYSVAR('SYSRACF')      /* AVAILABLE */
SAY SYSVAR('SYSSRV')       /* 742803 */
SAY SYSVAR('SYSTERMID')    /* X0607701 */
SAY SYSVAR('SYSTSOE')      /* 2060 */
SAY MVSVAR('SYSAPPCLU')    /* */
SAY MVSVAR('SYSDFP')       /* 01.01.04.00 */
SAY MVSVAR('SYSMVS')       /* SP6.0.6 */
SAY MVSVAR('SYSNAME')      /* E001 */
SAY MVSVAR('SYSOPSYS')     /* OS/390 02.06.00 HBB6606 */
SAY MVSVAR('SYSSECLAB')    /* */
SAY MVSVAR('SYSSMFID')     /* E001 */
SAY MVSVAR('SYSSMS')       /* ACTIVE */
SAY MVSVAR('SYSCLONE')     /* E1 */
```

Example 2:
```
/* REXX */
SAY MVSVAR('SYMDEF','SYSNAME')    /* E001 */
SAY MVSVAR('SYMDEF','SYSCLONE')   /* E1 */
SAY MVSVAR('SYMDEF','DENVI')      /* TEST */
SAY MVSVAR('SYMDEF','DENVIS')     /* T */
SAY MVSVAR('SYMDEF','MIMENVI')    /* E1 */
SAY MVSVAR('SYMDEF','LOGCLS')     /* 2 */
SAY MVSVAR('SYMDEF','MDLIB')      /* DS39A7 */
SAY MVSVAR('SYMDEF','MDLB2')      /* DS39B7 */
SAY MVSVAR('SYMDEF','SYSR2')      /* TRESB2 */
SAY MVSVAR('SYMDEF','OS390REL')   /* 6 */
```

SYS1.PARMLIB member:
```
SYSDEF SYSNAME(E001)
       SYSCLONE(E1)
       SYMDEF(&DENVI='TEST')
```

```
SYMDEF(&DENVIS='T')
SYMDEF(&MIMENVI='&SYSCLONE')
SYMDEF(&LOGCLS='2')
SYMDEF(&MDLIB='DS39A7')
SYMDEF(&MDLB2='&MDLIB(1:4).B&MDLIB(6:1)')
SYMDEF(&SYSR2='&SYSR1(1:4).B&SYSR1(6:1)')
SYMDEF(&OS390REL='6')
```

12.2.5 OUTTRAP - Trap TSO Display Output

The OUTTRAP command function is used to trap the TSO output that would normally be displayed on the terminal.

The OUTTRAP command function can be used in one of three ways:
·   Return the name of the stem variable in which the trapped output is to be stored (no arguments).
·   Disable trapping (OFF option), i.e. subsequent TSO output will be displayed normally.
·   Set the trapping options.

Note: Only TSO output issued with the PUTLINE service using the OUTPUT keyword can be trapped.

Syntax:

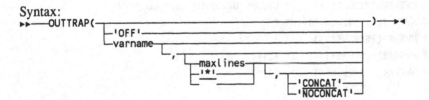

'OFF'
        The trapping of TSO display output is to be disabled, i.e. TSO display output is to be displayed normally.

varname
        The name of the stem variable which is to contain the trapped TSO display output. The form of **varname** determines how the trapped data is accessed.

maxlines
        The maximum number of lines which can be trapped, any additional TSO output will be ignored.

'*' or blank
        The complete TSO output will be trapped. This is the default.

'CONCAT'

The trapped output will be appended to the end of any output which has been previously trapped.

'NOCONCAT'

The trapped output will overwrite any output which has been previously trapped, i.e. the first line of trapped output from each TSO command will be stored in the first stem variable, etc.
Default: CONCAT

The OUTTRAP command function sets the following variables:

varname0   The number of lines that have been actually trapped.

varnameMAX   The maximum number of lines which can be trapped - this is a parameter passed to the OUTTRAP command function.

varnameTRAPPED The number of lines which have been intercepted. The difference between **varnameTRAPPED** and **varname0** is the number of output lines which have been lost.

varnameCON   The status of the concatenation option, either CONCAT or NOCONCAT.

Example 1:
```
rc = OUTTRAP('a.',,'NOCONCAT');
ADDRESS TSO "TIME";
SAY a.0 a.1;
```
> 1st output line
> actual number of trapped output lines

Example 2:
```
rc = OUTTRAP();
```
This statement returns the name of the stem variable to be used for trapping TSO display output; in the previous example this is a., the variable a.CON contains NOCONCAT.

Example 3:
```
x = OUTTRAP('OFF');
```
This statement disables the trapping of TSO display output.

Example 4:

```
CALL OUTTRAP 'a.',,'NOCONCAT';
ADDRESS TSO "LISTC L(TUSER01)";
IF RC = 0 THEN DO i = 1 TO a.0;
  SAY i a.i;
END;
```

This example uses the TSO LISTC command to list the TUSER01 catalogue entries, which the OUTTRAP command function traps and stores as the stem variables a.1,.... The VSAM file entries are listed subsequently.

12.2.6 PROMPT - Set (Interrogate) CLIST CONTROL PROMPT Option

The PROMPT command function can be used in two ways:
· Return the current CONTROL PROMPT status (as function code).
· Set the CONTROL PROMPT status (optional).

Syntax:

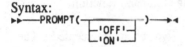

'OFF'

Set the PROMPT status OFF, i.e. TSO commands cannot prompt for any missing information, a TSO command which needs additional information will fail.

'ON'

Set the PROMPT status ON, i.e. TSO commands can prompt for any missing information.

If no argument is specified, the current PROMPT setting remains unchanged. The function code is returned with the current PROMPT setting.

Example:

```
rc = PROMPT('ON');
ADDRESS TSO "LISTC";
```

This example will prompt for the name of the dataset to be processed by the TSO LISTC command.

12.2.7 SETLANG - Set (Interrogate) Current Language

The SETLANG command function is used to interrogate (return) the language in which REXX displays its messages. The current language is returned.

Syntax:

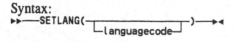

languagecode
> The language code in which REXX displays its messages:

> CHS simplified Chinese
> CHT traditional Chinese
> DAN Danish
> DEU German
> ENP English (uppercase)
> ENU English (mixed case)
> ESP Spanish
> FRA French
> JPN Japanese
> KOR Korean
> PTB Portuguese (Brazilian).
> If omitted, the current language remains unchanged.

Note: The installation parameters determine the default language and the supported languages; if necessary, consult the system support staff for details.

Example:
```
rc = SETLANG('ENP');
```

12.2.8 STORAGE – Set (Interrogate) Main-Storage Contents

The STORAGE command function is used to interrogate (return) the contents of the specified absolute main-storage address and to optionally change the contents.

In the MVS environment, there are few absolute addresses — the CVT (Communications Vector Table) is one control block frequently used by systems specialists (see the example).

Syntax:

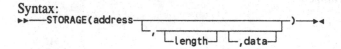

address
> The hexadecimal address of the storage area.

length
> The length (in bytes) of the storage area.

data
> The new contents of the storage area. If present, this data will be set in the specified storage area, otherwise the contents of the specified storage area will be returned as the function return value.

Note: Whereas a hexadecimal address is used in the STORAGE function, decimal addresses are used in REXX address arithmetic (see examples).

Example 1:

```
acvt = STORAGE(10,4) /* decimal address 16 = hex address 10 */
cvt = C2D(acvt,4) /* convert to decimal */
cvtsname = cvt+340 /* displacement X'0154'=340 */
cvtsnamex = D2X(cvtsname) /* hex address */
SAY STORAGE(cvtsnamex,8) /* display system name */
```

This example gets (and displays) the system identification. The word at absolute address 16 (decimal) contains the address of the CVT.

Example 2:

```
acvt = STORAGE(10,4)
cvt = C2D(acvt)
cvtllta = C2X(D2C(cvt+1244,4)) /* Link List Table Address */
addr = C2X(STORAGE(cvtllta,4))
llthead = STORAGE(addr,8) /* LLT header */
lltcount = C2D(SUBSTR(llthead,5,4)) /* number of entries */
len = (lltcount * 45) + 8 /* length of LLT */
llt = STORAGE(addr,len) /* copy the LLT */
start = 10 /* first entry */
SAY "LINKLIST libraries "
DO i = 1 TO lltcount
   dsn = SUBSTR(llt,start,44)
   start = start + 45 /* displacement of next entry */
   SAY dsn /* display dataset name */
END
SAY lltcount /* display count */
```

This example, which lists the operating system link list libraries, also illustrates the use of hexadecimal arithmetic.

Sample output:

```
LINKLIST LIBRARIES
SYS1.LINKLIB
SYS1.MIGLIB
MVS.LINKLIB
SYS1.SCEERUN
4
```

12.2.9 SYSCPUS - Obtain CPU Information

The SYSCPUS command function obtains information about the online CPUs.

Syntax:
```
▶▶──SYSCPUS(stem)──▶◀
```

stem
>   The stem variable for the compound variables that contain the serial
>   numbers. stem.0 contains the number of online CPUs.

Example:
```
rc = SYSCPUS(cpu.)
IF rc = 0 THEN DO i = 1 TO cpu.0
  SAY i cpu.i
END
```

Sample output (four online CPUs):
```
1 980395289672
2 981395289672
3 982395289672
4 983395289672
```

12.2.10 SYSDSN - Request Dataset Status

The SYSDSN command function obtains the status of a catalogued dataset (or
member).

Syntax:

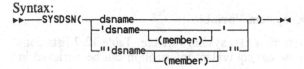

dsname
>   The name of the dataset to be processed.

member
>   The name of the member of the partitioned dataset (**dsname**) to be
>   processed.

If the dataset name is fully qualified, it must be written in the form shown in the
following example:
```
x = SYSDSN("'sys1.maclib(alpha)'");
```
This statement tests whether the member ALPHA is present in the 'SYS1.MACLIB'
partitioned dataset.

The function code is returned with text describing the status of the dataset (and
member, if specified). The following text can be returned:

OK	**Dsname** (and **member**, if specified) are present.
DATASET NOT FOUND	Dataset **dsname** is not present.
MEMBER NOT FOUND	**Member** is not present in **dsname**.

MEMBER SPECIFIED BUT DATASET IS NOT PARTITIONED

A member name may not be specified for a non-partitioned dataset.

ERROR PROCESSING REQUESTED DATASET — An error was detected during the processing of **dsname**.

PROTECTED DATASET — The user is not authorised to process **dsname** (RACF protection).

VOLUME NOT ON SYSTEM — The volume containing the catalogued dataset is not currently mounted.

INVALID DATASET NAME — The form of **dsname** is invalid.

MISSING DATASET NAME — No dataset name has been specified.

UNAVAILABLE DATASET — Another user is currently processing **dsname**.

Example:

```
dsn = 'jcl.cntl';
status = SYSDSN(dsn);
IF status <> 'OK' THEN SAY 'Dataset:' dsn 'error:' status;
```

This example assigns status the text describing the status of the user's dataset jcl.cntl (e.g. OK, DATASET NOT FOUND).

12.2.11 SYSVAR - Fetch TSO System Variable

The SYSVAR command function returns a TSO system variable. Table 12.2 lists non-supported CLIST variables and how the equivalent information can be retrieved in REXX.

Table 12.2 - Non-supported CLIST variables

&SYSDATE	DATE('usa')
&SYSDLM	-
&SYSJDATE	DATE('julian')
&SYSSDATE	DATE('ordered')
&SYSSTIME	SUBSTR(TIME('normal'),1,5)
&SYSTIME	TIME()

Syntax:

```
▶▶──SYSVAR(sysvarname)──▶◀
```

sysvarname

The name of the TSO system variable to be retrieved. Table 12.3 lists the available TSO system variable names together with their equivalent CLIST variable name and a brief description.

Example:

```
SAY SYSVAR('SYSSRV');
```

Display the number of service units currently used. The service units give a weighted system resource usage; the before and after values can be used to form an estimate of the resource usage (benchmarking).

For example:
```
before = SYSVAR('SYSSRV');
CALL userproc;
after = SYSVAR('SYSSRV');
SAY (after-before) 'service units used';
```

Table 12.3 - TSO system variables

SYSCPU	&SYSCPU	Number of CPU (processor) seconds currrently used during the session (sss.hh)
SYSDTERM	-	DBCS support
SYSENV	&SYSENV	Execution environment (FORE = foreground, BACK = background)
SYSHSM	&SYSHSM	HSM version
SYSICMD	&SYSICMD	Name with which the user implicitly invoked the exec
SYSISPF	&SYSISPF	ISPF services available (ACTIVE, NOT ACTIVE)
SYSJES	&SYSJES	JES version
SYSKTERM	-	Katakana support
SYSLRACF	&SYSLRACF	RACF version
SYSLTERM	&SYSLTERM	Number of lines on the terminal (0 for background)
SYSNEST	&SYSNEST	Exec nested (YES, NO)
SYSNODE	&SYSNODE	JES network node name
SYSPCMD	&SYSPCMD	The name of the TSO command that the exec most recently executed
SYSPLANG	-	Primary language
SYSPREF	&SYSPREF	Dataset name prefix used for non-fully qualified dataset names
SYSPROC	&SYSPROC	Logon procedure name
SYSRACF	&SYSRACF	RACF status (text message)
SYSSCMD	&SYSSCMD	The name of the subcommand
SYSSLANG	-	Secondary language
SYSSRV	&SYSSRV	Number of service units used during the session)
SYSTERMID	&SYSTERMID	Terminal identity where the exec was started
SYSTSOE	&SYSTSOE	TSO/E level
SYSUID	&SYSUID	Userid identification used at login
SYSWTERM	&SYSWTERM	Width of the terminal (0 for background)

12.3 INVOCATION OF OTHER TSO COMMANDS

Other TSO commands can be invoked from the TSO environment using the ADDRESS TSO instruction.

Syntax:
```
►►──ADDRESS TSO "tsocommand"──►◄
```

The RC special variable is set to contain the command return code (equivalent to the CLIST &LASTCC variable); -3 is returned if the command cannot be invoked.

Example 1:
```
ADDRESS TSO "LISTDS (USER.CLIST) MEMBERS";
```
This example invokes the TSO LISTDS command to return the members of the user's USER.CLIST dataset.

Example 2:
```
ADDRESS TSO "LISTDS ('TUSER01.USER.CLIST) MEMBERS'";
```
This example invokes the TSO LISTDS command to return the members of the TUSER01.USER.CLIST dataset.

12.4 EXAMPLE

An important use of REXX is to create applications from existing components (such a use is often known as a glue module). For example, selected output from the TSO LISTC command can be processed; in the following example, the number of records and the byte-size of a VSAM file is displayed. The REXX variables so obtained could be processed further, for example, passed to an ISPF dialogue.

```
/* REXX */
CALL OUTTRAP 's.','*','NOCONCAT';
"LISTC ENTRIES(test.esds) ALL";
IF RC = 0 THEN DO i = 1 TO s.0;
  PARSE VAR s.i . 'REC-TOTAL-' n .;
  IF n <> '' THEN SAY 'Recs:' STRIP(n,'L','-');
  PARSE VAR s.i . 'HI-U-RBA-' n .;
  IF n <> '' THEN SAY 'Size:' STRIP(n,'L','-');
END;
```

Sample output:
```
Recs: 16
Size: 8192
```

Note: Such programs that process report output are obviously very sensitive to change to the report layout. For example, whereas the LISTC current at the time of the previous edition of this book used the expression 'HI-USED-RBA-', the latest LISTC version uses 'HI-U-RBA-'.

13

REXX Invocation
I invoke the genius of the Constitution

Speech [November 18, 1777]
William Pitt, Earl of Chatham

13.1 INTRODUCTION

The TSO/E implementation allows a REXX exec to run in several environments, both dialogue and batch. From within this invoking environment, the ADDRESS instruction is used to select a sub-environment for non-REXX statements. This sub-environment forms the interface to other components, for example, the ISPEXEC sub-environment for ISPF Dialog Manager services.

REXX execs must have a commentary containing the word REXX in the first line to distinguish them from normal command procedures (CLISTs).

REXX execs can invoke non-REXX programs; there are several forms with which parameters can be passed to such programs.

A REXX exec can be invoked from:
· TSO/ISPF dialogue
· TSO batch
· OS/390 (MVS) batch.

Although a REXX exec can be a sequential dataset, it is more usually a member of a partitioned dataset (library). The name of this dataset must be made available to the REXX interpreter.

13.2 INVOCATION FROM TSO/ISPF

REXX execs can be invoked from either TSO native mode or ISPF.

Syntax:

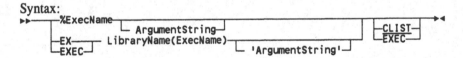

EX or EXEC
The dataset containing the REXX exec to be invoked is specified explicitly.
If EX is not specified, the REXX exec is loaded from a standard file. This file
is specified in the REXX customisation process; by default, REXX execs are
loaded from either the SYSEXEC or the SYSPROC file — SYSEXEC takes
precedence. Because the SYSEXEC file can contain both REXX execs and
CLISTs, REXX execs must be written with a REXX comment in the first line
to distinguish them from CLISTs.
The TSO ALTLIB command can be used to allocate an alternative REXX library
(see Example 2).

LibraryName
The dataset name of the library that contains the REXX exec. If the dataset
name is not fully qualified (i.e. not enclosed within quotes), the user's TSO
prefix is set as first qualifier in front of the specified **LibraryName**, and
the final option (CLIST (default) or EXEC) is set as final qualifier.

ExecName
The name of the exec to be executed.

ArgumentString
The arguments to be passed to the program.

CLIST or EXEC
The type of procedure (CLIST or REXX exec). This option is also used as
low-level qualifier for a non-explicit library name.

Example 1:

        "%BETA 12 4"

The REXX exec BETA is invoked from the library assigned to SYSEXEC or SYSPROC,
and is passed the parameter "12 4".

Example 2:

        ADDRESS TSO
        "ALLOC F(SYSUEXEC) DATASET(rexx.lib) SHR REUS"
        "ALTLIB ACTIVATE USER(EXEC)"
        "BETA 12 4"

The REXX exec BETA is invoked from the REXX.LIB library. This example shows one form of the ALTLIB command; there are other forms that, for example, do not require that the library dataset be preallocated.

13.3 INVOCATION FROM BATCH TSO

The TSO terminal monitor program (IKJEFT01) can be invoked as a batch job. REXX execs can then be invoked in the normal manner. Terminal input and output is made from or to a file, respectively.

IKJEFT01 requires the following control statements:
- SYSEXEC or SYSPROC file (DDname) is the library containing the REXX exec to be executed.
- SYSTSPRT file (DDname) is the dataset to contain TSO terminal output and output produced with the SAY instruction.
- SYSTSIN file (DDname) is the dataset which contains command input for batch TSO and the (terminal) input required by the PULL instruction. The command to invoke the REXX exec is contained in this dataset.

Syntax:
```
►►──//──┬──────────┬── EXEC PGM=IKJEFT01,DYNAMNBR=Number──►◄
        └Stepname──┘
```

Stepname
> The job step name (optional).

Number
> The maximum number of dynamically allocated files which can be open at any one time. The number depends on the REXX exec being executed; 20 will usually be sufficient.

Sample JCL statements:
```
//          EXEC PGM=IKJEFT01,DYNAMNBR=20
//SYSEXEC  DD   DSN=TUSER01.ALPHA.EXEC,DISP=SHR
//SYSTSPRT DD   SYSOUT=A
//SYSTSIN  DD   DSN=TUSER01.ALPHA.INPUT,DISP=SHR
```

The TUSER01.ALPHA.EXEC dataset contains member BETA.

The TUSER01.ALPHA.INPUT dataset contains:
```
EXECUTIL SEARCHDD(YES)
%BETA 12 4
6
```

The TSO commands are read from the SYSTSIN file (TUSER01.ALPHA.INPUT dataset). The first command, EXECUTIL SEARCHDD(YES), specifies that the SYSEXEC file is to be searched for REXX execs.

The REXX source program BETA is loaded from the SYSEXEC file
(TUSER01.ALPHA.EXEC dataset). Two parameters, 12 and 4, are passed to BETA. BETA
fetches one data item with the PARSE PULL instruction, which reads the SYSTSIN file.
The result of dividing the product of the two invocation parameters (operand1 and
operand2) by the pulled operand (operand3) is displayed with the SAY instruction on
the SYSTSPRT file (here assigned to the printer, SYSOUT=A).

13.4 INVOCATION FROM BATCH

REXX execs running in batch can use the IRXJCL interpreter, unless TSO (or ISPF)
facilities are required.

IRXJCL requires the following input:
· EXEC-parameter, the name of the member to be executed; additional parameters
  are passed to the REXX exec when it is invoked, i.e. parameters fetched with
  the PARSE ARG instruction.
· SYSEXEC file (DDname), the library containing the REXX exec to be executed.
· SYSTSPRT file (DDname), the dataset to contain output produced with the SAY
  instruction.
· SYSTSIN file (DDname), the dataset which contains (terminal) input required by
  the PULL instruction.

Syntax:

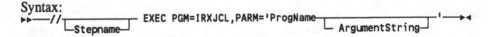

Stepname
    The job step name (optional).

ProgName
    The name of the exec to be executed.

ArgumentString
    The arguments to be passed to the program.

Sample JCL statements:

```
//          EXEC PGM=IRXJCL,PARM='BETA 12 4'
//SYSEXEC  DD   DSN=TUSER01.ALPHA.EXEC,DISP=SHR
//SYSTSPRT DD   SYSOUT=A
//SYSTSIN  DD   DSN=TUSER01.ALPHA.INPUT,DISP=SHR
```

The TUSER01.ALPHA.EXEC dataset contains member BETA.

The TUSER01.ALPHA.INPUT dataset contains:
    6

The REXX source program BETA is loaded from the TUSER01.ALPHA.EXEC dataset. Two parameters, 12 and 4, are passed to BETA. BETA fetches one data item with the PARSE PULL instruction, which reads the SYSTSIN file (TUSER01.ALPHA.INPUT dataset). The result of dividing the product of the two invocation parameters (operand1 and operand2) by the pulled operand (operand3) is displayed with the SAY instruction on the SYSTSPRT file (here assigned to the printer, SYSOUT=A).

BETA program code:
```
/* REXX */
PARSE ARG operand1 operand2;
PARSE PULL operand3;
SAY operand1*operand2/operand3;
```

13.5 LINKAGE TO THE HOST ENVIRONMENT

A REXX exec can link to components from the host environment. The ADDRESS instruction is used to set the host environment.

Example:
```
ADDRESS TSO "TIME";
```
This example invokes the TSO TIME command.

13.6 LINKAGE TO PROGRAMS

REXX provides commands to enable a REXX exec to pass control to a program written in a conventional programming language, such as PL/I or COBOL.

TSO REXX provides three basic commands to invoke a program:
·   LINK (ATTACH)
·   LINKMVS (ATTACHMVS)
·   LINKPGM (ATTACHPGM)

Whereas the LINK command family invokes a program synchronously, the ATTACH command family invokes a program asynchronously (i.e. as a separate task). The program is loaded from the program (load) library assigned to the environment.

Within each command group, the individual commands differ only in the form with which they pass parameters to the invoked program. In all cases, register 1 contains the address of the parameter list. The last address in the parameter list has its high-order bit set.

The program libraries are searched in the following order:
·   the job pack area
·   ISPLLIB (load library concatenation)
·   the task library
·   the step library (or the job library, if no step library exists)

· the link pack area
· the link library.

13.6.1 LINK (ATTACH)

The program may be passed a single parameter, which may contain subparameters. The invoked program always receives two parameters on entry:
· the address of the parameter string;
· the length of the parameter string (fullword).

The length parameter may contain zero, which means no parameters were passed to the invoked program.

Example:
```
ADDRESS LINK "PGM1 12 4";
```

This example (shown in Figure 13.1) links to the program PGM1 to which the parameter "12 4" is passed. A sample PL/I program to process the parameter follows ↑ = pointer. This program displays the parameter and its length following the text "REXX PARAMETER:".

Note: The maximum length of the parameter passed to a program is 100 characters.

```
PGM1: PROC(PARMADDR,PARMLEN) OPTIONS(MAIN);
DCL PARMADDR POINTER;
DCL REXXPARM CHAR(100) BASED(PARMADDR);
DCL PARMLEN FIXED BIN(31);
PUT SKIP LIST ('REXX PARAMETER:',SUBSTR(REXXPARM,1,PARMLEN),PARMLEN);
END PGM1;
```

This program would display:
```
REXX PARAMETER:              12 4                              4
```

Note: If the parameter list is to contain variable (parameterised) data, such variables must be placed outside the delimiting quotes. For example,
```
parm1 = '12 4';
ADDRESS LINK "PGM1" parm1;
```

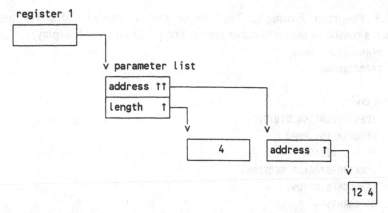

Figure 13.1 — LINK (ATTACH) parameter format (example)

13.6.2 LINKMVS (ATTACHMVS)

The program may be passed zero or more parameters. Each of these parameters may themselves contain subparameters. The invoked program receives an address-list as parameter; each address points to the corresponding argument, each of which is prefixed by a halfword containing the argument length.

The arguments specified in the LINKMVS argument list differ from the usual REXX syntax; although the arguments are specified within quotes, they are treated as variables.

Example:
```
PARM1 = 'alpha beta'
PARM2 = 'gamma'
ADDRESS LINKMVS 'PGM2 parm1 parm2'
```
Figure 13.2 shows the form of the parameters.

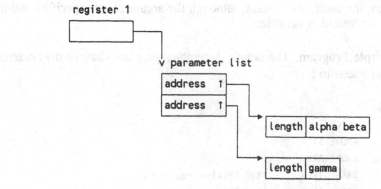

Figure 13.2 — LINKMVS (ATTACHMVS) parameter format (example)

13.6.2.1 Program Example. The sample COBOL program displays the two arguments passed in the previous example. The program would display:

```
PARM1:alpha beta
PARM2:gamma
```

Program code:

```
IDENTIFICATION DIVISION.
PROGRAM-ID. PGM2.
DATA DIVISION.
WORKING-STORAGE SECTION.
LINKAGE SECTION.
01 PARM1. ·
 02 PARM1LEN PIC 9(4) COMP.
 02 PARM1DATA PIC X(16).
01 PARM2.
 02 PARM2LEN PIC 9(4) COMP.
 02 PARM2DATA PIC X(16).
PROCEDURE DIVISION
    USING PARM1 PARM2.
    DISPLAY 'PARM1:' PARM1DATA
    DISPLAY 'PARM2:' PARM2DATA
    STOP RUN.
```

13.6.3 LINKPGM (ATTACHPGM)

The LINKPGM (ATTACHPGM) command can pass zero or more arguments to the program. The invoked program receives an address-list as parameter; each address points to an address, which contains the address of the argument. The invoked program can change the contents of these arguments, provided that the original length is not exceeded. This is a simple (but restricted) method for a program to set REXX variables.

As with the LINKMVS command, the arguments specified in the LINKPGM argument list differ from the usual REXX syntax; although the arguments are specified within quotes, they are treated as variables.

13.6.3.1 Sample Program. The sample Assembler program changes the contents of the first parameter to DELTA.

Program code:

```
PGM3     CSECT
PGM3     AMODE 31
PGM3     RMODE ANY
         BAKR  14,0      save calling registers
         BASR  11,0      load base register
         USING *,11      use base register
```

```
LM    2,3,0(1)  load pointers to parameters
MVC   0(5,2),=C'DELTA'
LA    15,0      set program return code
PR    ,         return
END
```

Invocation exec:

```
PARM1 = 'alpha beta'
PARM2 = 'gamma'
ADDRESS LINKPGM 'PGM3 parm1 parm2'
SAY parm1 /* DELTA beta */
SAY parm2 /* gamma */
```

The PARM1 variable has been changed to 'DELTA beta'. Figure 13.3 shows the form of the parameters.

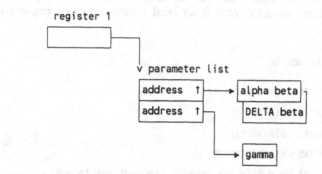

Figure 13.3 — LINKPGM (ATTACHPGM) parameter format (example)

13.7 INTERFACE WITH ISPEXEC (ISPF DIALOG MANAGER)

REXX execs invoked from the TSO/ISPF environment can use the ADDRESS ISPEXEC instruction to access ISPEXEC (ISPF Dialog Manager) services. The parameters for the ISPEXEC service are passed as a normal REXX string, i.e. may be a literal, symbol or mixture. The return code from the ISPEXEC service is set into the RC special variable.

REXX execs and ISPF Dialog Manager share the same function pool, with two restrictions:
· variable names longer than 8 characters cannot be used in ISPF;
· the VGET and VPUT services cannot be used with compound symbols.

Example:

```
panname = "PAN1";
ADDRESS ISPEXEC "DISPLAY PANEL("panname")";
SAY RC;
```

This example uses ISPEXEC to display panel PAN1; the return code from the service
is displayed.

13.8 INTERFACE WITH ISREDIT (ISPF/PDF EDIT MACRO)

The ISPF/PDF Editor can invoke a procedure to perform processing on a dataset —
this procedure is called an Edit macro and can be a REXX exec. The ADDRESS
ISREDIT instruction invokes Edit macro services. The parameters for the ISREDIT
service are passed as a normal REXX string, i.e. may be a literal, symbol or
mixture. The return code from the ISREDIT service is set into the RC special
variable.

Edit macros can make full use of REXX facilities. The powerful string
processing features of REXX make it an ideal language for the implementation of
Edit macros.

13.8.1 Macro Example

```
1       /* REXX Edit macro */
2       ADDRESS ISREDIT;
3       MACRO (STRING)";
4       "FIND" string "NEXT";
5       IF RC /= 0 THEN SAY "search argument not found";
6       "END";
7       EXIT 0;
```

The line number preceding the REXX statement is not actually part of the Edit
macro, and serves only as identification for the following explanation.

2   Set ISREDIT as the default address environment. This saves prefixing ISREDIT
        to each command.

3   Macro header. The ISREDIT variable STRING is passed to the macro.

4   Invoke the ISREDIT FIND command, string is passed as data.

5   Display the message "search argument not found" if a non-zero return code
        is passed back from ISREDIT.

6   Terminate ISREDIT. For edit macros (such as this example) that operate
        interactively, the END statement should not be present.

7   Terminate the REXX exec. This statement is optional.

13.9 INTERFACE WITH DB2 (DATABASE 2)

The TSO DSN command is used to initiate a DB2 session. The DB2 RUN subcommand is used to invoke a program which is to run in the DB2 environment.

The DB2 subcommands to invoke the program, and to terminate the DB2 session, RUN and END, respectively, are set into the stack in the required order before the DB2 session is initiated.

Note: The subcommands cannot be passed directly, as is the case with CLISTs.

13.9.1 DB2 Invocation Example

```
1      QUEUE "RUN PROGRAM(TDB2PGM) PLAN(TDB2PLN)

       LIB('TUSER01.RUNLIB.LOAD')"; /* set initial parms for DB2 */

2      QUEUE "END"; /* set final (termination) parameter for DB2 */

    3   ADDRESS TSO "%DSN"; /* invoke DB2 */
```

1   Set the RUN subcommand at the head of the stack. The subcommand specifies the parameters required to invoke the program.

2   Set the END subcommand as second element in the stack. This subcommand is required to terminate the DB2 session.

3   Invoke the DB2 session — the subcommands are taken from the stack. If the invoked DB2 program makes use of ISPF services, the DSN command should be invoked from the ISPF environment rather from TSO, for example with the statement: ADDRESS ISPEXEC "SELECT CMD(%DSN)";

13.10 INTERFACE WITH QMF (QUERY MANAGEMENT FACILITY)

The invocation of QMF is more involved than invoking DB2 directly. There are two methods of invoking QMF:
·   QMF Callable Interface (DSQCIX)
·   QMF Command Interface (CI, program DSQCCI).

13.10.1 DSQCIX - QMF Callable Interface

The QMF Callable Interface passes the specified command to QMF, which then performs the command.

The QMF START command is normally invoked to set the QMF operating environment. The most important START parameters (each parameter is specified as keyword=operand) follow:

DSQSCMD   The REXX exec that sets the QMF program parameters, i.e. set installation-defaults. This exec must be in the SYSEXEC concatenation.
Default: DSQSCMDE

DSQSMODE   The QMF processing mode:
B = batch (default)
I = interactive.
Panel display is inhibited in batch mode.

DSQSRUN   The name of the initial QMF procedure to be executed.
Default: NULL (no procedure).

DSQSSUBS   The DB2 subsystem identifier.
Default: DSN

13.10.1.1 DSQCIX Invocation Example

```
        /* REXX - QMF Callable Interface */
1       ADDRESS TSO;
2       "ALLOC F(DSQDEBUG) DUMMY REUS"
3       fn = "DB2OUT.LIST";
4       "ALLOC F(DSQPRINT) DA("fn") SP(15,2) TR UNIT(WKSP)
          RECFM(V B) LRECL(300) BLKSIZE(23404) DSORG(PS)"
5       "ALLOC F(ADMGGMAP) DSN('QMF.TEST.DSQMAPE') SHR REUS"
6       CALL DSQCIX "START",
        "(DSQSDBUG=ALL,DSQSMODE=BATCH,DSQSSUBS=DB2T"
7       SAY dsq_return_code;
8       CALL DSQCIX "SET GLOBAL(PNUM=3001"
9       CALL DSQCIX "RUN QUERY S6Q"
10      CALL DSQCIX "PRINT REPORT(L=CONT"
11      CALL DSQCIX "EXIT"
12      ADDRESS ISPEXEC "BROWSE DATASET("fn")";
```

1   .Set TSO as the default command environment.

2-5   Use TSO to allocate the files that QMF and the command need, DSQDEBUG and ADMGGMAP, and DSQPRINT, respectively. Because the dataset name of the print file (DSQPRINT) is used more than once, it is specified as a variable (FN); line 2.

6   Invoke the QMF Callable Interface in batch (non-interactive) mode.

7   Display the QMF Callable Interface return code (DSQ_RETURN_CODE).

8   Set the PNUM parameter as 3001.

9   Run the S6Q QMF query. *Note*: Queries that do not require any parameters can be started directly in the START command (DSQSRUN parameter).

10   Print the query report to the DSQPRINT file.

11   Terminate the QMF Callable Interface.

12   Invoke the ISPEXEC BROWSE service to display the report.

QMF query (S6Q):
```
SELECT * FROM PERS WHERE PNO = &PNUM
```

13.10.2 DSQCCI – QMF Command Interface

As with the invocation of QMF from a CLIST, two steps are required to invoke the QMF Command Interface:
- initiate the QMF session (program DSQQMFE), and execute a QMF procedure;
- this QMF procedure passes control to a REXX exec, which in turn uses the QMF Command Interface (CI, program DSQCCI) to process a QMF command.

A full description of the QMF interfaces is beyond the scope of this book. The appropriate manual or reference book should be consulted for further details.

Note: The general processing is the same as for CLISTs, with the exception that variable names (and values) cannot be passed with the QMF RUN command. The QMF SET GLOBAL command can be used to assign values for variables.

The following example uses QMF to run a query, the results of which are displayed using the ISPF BROWSE service. Dataset names may have to be altered to suit the requirements of your installation.

13.10.2.1 DSQCCI Invocation Example

```
      /* REXX - QMF Command Interface */
1     ADDRESS TSO;
2     "ALLOC F(DSQDEBUG) DUMMY";
3     "ALLOC F(DSQPRINT) DA(QMFOUT.LIST) RECFM(V B) NEW
      BLKSIZE(10000)";
4     "ALLOC F(ADMGGMAP) DSN('QMF.TEST.DSQMAPE') SHR";
5     "SELECT PGM(DSQQMFE) NEWAPPL(DSQE) PARM(S=DB2,I=TUSER01.S6)";
```

1   Set TSO as the default command environment.

2-4   Use TSO to allocate the files needed by QMF (DSQDEBUG and ADMGGMAP), and the file needed by the command (DSQPRINT).

5 Invoke QMF (DSQQMFE) as sub-environment of ISPF. The QMF procedure TUSER01.S6 is to be processed.

QMF procedure S6:
```
TSO %S6X
```
This procedure passes control to the TSO command (REXX exec) S6X.

REXX exec S6X:
```
    /* REXX - S6X Procedure */
1   ADDRESS ISPEXEC;
2   "SELECT PGM(DSQCCI) PARM(SET GLOBAL (PNUM=3001)";
3   "SELECT PGM(DSQCCI) PARM(RUN S6Q)";
4   "SELECT PGM(DSQCCI) PARM(PRINT REPORT(L=CONT))";
5   "BROWSE DATASET(DB2OUT.LIST)";
6   "SELECT PGM(DSQCCI) PARM(EXIT)";
7   "CONTROL DISPLAY REFRESH";
8   EXIT;
```

1 Set ISPEXEC as the default command environment.

2 Use the CI to assign the value 3001 to the QMF variable PNUM.

3 Use the CI to invoke the QMF query S6Q.

4 Use the CI to write the report produced by running the query onto the DSQPRINT file, which has been assigned to the DB2OUT.LIST dataset.

5 Use the ISPF BROWSE service to display the contents of the report dataset.

6 Use the CI to terminate QMF session (EXIT command).

7 Restore the display.

8 Terminate the REXX exec.

QMF query S6Q:
```
SELECT * FROM PERS WHERE PNO = &PNUM
```

13.11 INTERFACE FROM PROGRAMS WITH REXX

Not only can REXX execs interface with other components, but programs can also make use of REXX services. These service interfaces are described in Chapter 14.

14

System Interfaces

We owe it, therefore, to candor, and to the amicable relations existing between the United States and those powers to declare that we should consider any attempt on their part to extend their system to any portion of this hemisphere as dangerous to our peace and safety.

Annual Message to Congress

James Munroe

14.1 INTRODUCTION

The REXX system interfaces described in this chapter are the standard interfaces provided in the REXX implementation for what I call **REXX interface programs**. A REXX interface program (more simply, a REXX program) is a program written in a conventional programming language (e.g. Assembler, C, C++, COBOL, PL/I) which makes use of the REXX system interfaces.

There are two general ways in which a REXX program can use the REXX system interfaces:

· A program running in the REXX environment (i.e. invoked by the REXX interpreter) can access REXX data (variable pool, stack, etc.).
· A program running outside the REXX environment (i.e. in batch or TSO) has no direct access to the REXX environment, but can invoke the REXX interpreter to process a REXX exec (either program-internal or an external dataset).

Chapter 13 describes how REXX execs can invoke conventional (non-REXX) programs.

The first program type can have three forms:
·   a function;
·   a command;
·   an explicitly invoked program.

In particular, the first two forms can be used for REXX extensions (e.g. installation-specific functions, access methods).

The second method is used less often. It is typically used to invoke an existent REXX exec or to allow a conventional program to make use of high-level REXX services (e.g. parsing).

This book describes only those interfaces of interest to the applications developer — there are a number of other interfaces which can be used by systems specialists to customise the system.

The interfaces can be grouped into the following categories:
·   program invocation of a REXX exec;
·   program access to REXX variables;
·   stack operations;
·   programs as REXX functions (and the grouping of such programs into function packages);
·   general service routines.

14.2 GENERAL CONDITIONS

The interfaces are subject to the following conditions:
·   Programs using REXX services must execute in 31-bit addressing mode (AMODE 31).
·   Numeric fields are in binary format, either fullword (4 bytes) or halfword (2 bytes).
·   Standard calling conventions are used:
    ·   register 15 — entry point address;
    ·   register 14 — return address;
    ·   register 13 — address of save-area.
·   The return code is passed back in register 15 (PLIRETV PL/I variable, RETURN-CODE COBOL special register, function return value in C or C++), and, optionally in many functions, as a parameter field. Many routines also set an error message in the Environment Block.
·   Parameter address lists passed in register 1 must have the high-order bit set in the last address word; Assembler programs use the VL keyword.
·   Standard macros (in the SYS1.MACLIB system macro library) are available for use by Assembler programs to map the more important control blocks. Programs can be written in high-level programming languages (e.g. COBOL, PL/I); however, such programs must themselves define the control block structures — Figure 14.1 shows the equivalent field types in various programming languages; - indicates that there is no exact equivalent. Not all high-level programming languages provide full support for all the required facilities.

Type	Assembler	C, C++	PL/I	COBOL VS II
Address	A	*	PTR	POINTER
Character string	CLn	char[n+1]	CHAR(n)	PIC X(n)
Fullword	F	long	FIXED BIN(31)	PIC S9(9) COMP
Halfword	H	short	FIXED BIN(15)	PIC S9(4) COMP
Hexadecimal	X	:8	BIT(8)	-

Figure 14.1 — Equivalent field types

Notes:
1. Only the most important information for the interfaces is described in this chapter — the appropriate manual should be consulted if a more detailed description is required.
2. The <symbol> entry in diagrams denotes that *symbol* is used as prefix to the field names in the corresponding block. The diagrams show only the significant fields. Any fillers at the end of field layout figures are omitted.

14.2.1 C, C++ Restrictions

REXX functions (and command processors) written in C and C++ are subject to several restrictions:
- The SPC (System Programming for C) environment is needed to access the entry parameters (register 1 has the address of the parameter address list). The edcxregs() function returns the entry contents of the specified register.
- The REXX service routines (e.g. IRXEXCOM that is used to set a REXX variable) are contained usually in the Link Pack Area or link libraries; as such they will be loaded dynamically at execution-time rather than being linked statically to the program. The fetch() function, normally used to obtain the address of or load the module, is not available in the SPC environment. The Environment Block passed to REXX functions and environment processing routines contains the address of the IRXEXTE block, which is a vector of the addresses of the REXX service routines. Another solution is to write a user-specific load function to provide equivalent processing; the sample PGMLOAD function loads the specified program function.
- REXX strings are not the same as C language strings; they are not terminated with a null character and may contain embedded null characters.

14.2.2 Other Program Language Restrictions

The IBM high-level languages are being frequently extended to make them more suitable as Assembler replacements; for example, the SPC environment for C. In the course of time, some of the methods described here may be replaced by more elegant solutions.

14.3 INVOCATION OF A REXX EXEC

There are three ways of invoking a REXX exec:
· using the IRXJCL service routine;
· using the TSO Service Facility (IJKEFTSR program);
· using the IRXEXEC service routine.

These three methods are listed in order of ease of use. This is also the order of increasing flexibility, e.g. the IRXEXEC program interface offers more flexibility than the IRXJCL program interface but is more difficult to invoke. Because of its importance, the IRXEXEC service is described in detail in the next section.

14.3.1 Interface from Programs to Batch REXX (IRXJCL)

Programs written in a conventional language (PL/I, etc.) can use IRXJCL to invoke a REXX exec. Figure 14.2 shows the form of the parameter as passed from the invoking program.

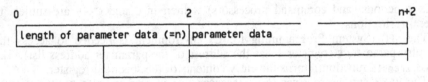

Figure 14.2 — Format of parameter passed to IRXJCL

14.3.1.1 Sample Program. This sample PL/I program uses IRXJCL to invoke the REXX exec BETA; two parameters, 12 and 4, are passed to the exec.

```
RXPPGM1: PROC OPTIONS(MAIN);
DCL IRXJCL EXTERNAL OPTIONS(RETCODE,ASSEMBLER,INTER);
DCL PLIRETV BUILTIN; /* return code */
DCL 1 PARM,
      2 PARM_LEN FIXED BIN(15) INIT(9),
      2 PARM_DATA CHAR(9) INIT('BETA 12 4');
FETCH IRXJCL; /* load address of entry point */
CALL IRXJCL(PARM); /* invoke IRXJCL with parameter */
PUT SKIP LIST ('IRXJCL return code:',PLIRETV);
END;
```

14.3.2 Invocation of a REXX Exec Using the TSO Service Facility (IJKEFTSR)

REXX execs can also be invoked from the TSO environment (either dialogue or batch) with the TSO Service Facility (IJKEFTSR program) — the TSO Service Facility has the alias TSOLNK.

Assembler calling sequence:

```
CALL IJKEFTSR,(Flags,FunctionBuffer,FunctionBufferLength,FunctionRC,
    ReasonCode,AbendCode[,FunctionParmList[,cppl]]),VL
```

[ ] indicates an optional entry

Flags

A fullword containing four hexadecimal flag bytes:

Byte 0 — X'00'.

Byte 1 — internal processing options flag.

· X'00' — invoke function from authorised environment.

· X'01' — invoke function from unauthorised environment (the usual
          setting).

Byte 2 — error processing flag.

· X'00' — force dump if the invoked function aborts.

· X'01' — produce no dump.

Byte 3 — function type flag.

· X'01' — TSO/E command, REXX exec or CLIST is to be invoked.

· X'02' — program is to be invoked.

Note: High-level languages can set the required flag bits by defining the
appropriate binary value: Byte1*65536+Byte2*256+Byte3.

FunctionBuffer

Buffer containing the name of the program, command, REXX exec or CLIST
to be invoked. The buffer can contain parameters to be passed to a
command, REXX exec or CLIST.

FunctionBufferLength

A fullword containing the length of data in **FunctionBuffer**.

FunctionRC

A fullword which is set to contain the return code from the invoked
function.

ReasonCode

A fullword which is set to contain the service routine reason code.

AbendCode

A fullword which is set to contain the abend code if the invoked function
ends abnormally.

The last two parameters are optional, and are not required for the invocation of a
REXX exec.

14.3.1.1 Sample Program Using TSOLNK. This sample PL/I program uses the
TSO Service Facility (TSOLNK) to invoke the REXX exec BETA, which is called with
the parameter "12 4". Assembler programs can also get the address of the TSO

Service Facility (IKJEFTSR) from the CVT (Communications Vector Table). The following Assembler program illustrates the use of the TSO Service Facility.

```
RXPPGM2: PROC OPTIONS(MAIN);
 DCL 1 PARM1,
        2 PARM11 BIT(8) INIT('00000000'B),  /* reserved */
        2 PARM12 BIT(8) INIT('00000001'B),  /* unauthorised */
        2 PARM13 BIT(8) INIT('00000000'B),  /* no dump */
        2 PARM14 BIT(8) INIT('00000001'B);  /* REXX exec */
 DCL 1 PARM2 CHAR(9) INIT('BETA 12 4');  /* command and parameter */
 DCL 1 PARM3 FIXED BIN(31) INIT(9);  /* length of command (PARM2) */
 DCL 1 PARM4 FIXED BIN(31);  /* command return code */
 DCL 1 PARM5 FIXED BIN(31);  /* TSF reason code */
 DCL 1 PARM6 FIXED BIN(31);  /* command abend code */
 DCL TSOLNK ENTRY
     (1,
        2 BIT(8),  /* reserved */
        2 BIT(8),  /* authorised/unauthorised flag */
        2 BIT(8),  /* dump/no dump flag */
        2 BIT(8),  /* function type flag */
      1 CHAR(*),         /* command and parameter */
      1 FIXED BIN(31),  /* length of command (PARM2) */
      1 FIXED BIN(31),  /* command return code */
      1 FIXED BIN(31),  /* TSF reason code */
      1 FIXED BIN(31)   /* command abend code */
      ) EXTERNAL OPTIONS(RETCODE,ASSEMBLER,INTER);
 FETCH TSOLNK;
 CALL TSOLNK(PARM1,PARM2,PARM3,PARM4,PARM5,PARM6);
 END;
```

14.3.1.2 Sample Assembler Program Using IKJEFTSR. This sample program performs the same processing as the previous PL/I sample program.

```
          TITLE 'USE IKJEFTSR TO INVOKE A REXX EXEC'
RXAPGM1 CSECT
* initialise addressing
          BAKR  14,0               save caller's registers
          BASR  12,0               set base register
          USING *,12
          LA    13,SA              internal save area
          L     15,CVTPTR          A(CVT)
          USING CVT,15             address CVT
          L     15,CVTTVT          A(TSO Vector Table)
```

```
          L      15,TSVTASF-TSVT(15)    A(TSO Service Facility)
          CALL   (15),(PARM1,PARM2,PARM3,PARM4,PARM5,PARM6),VL
* R15: TSF return code
          PR     ,                      terminate with return code
SA        DS     18F                    internal save area
* parameter definition
PARM1     DS     0XL4
          DC     X'00'                  reserved
          DC     X'01'                  unauthorised
          DC     X'00'                  no dump
          DC     X'01'                  REXX exec
PARM2     DC     C'BETA 12 4'           command and parameter
PARM3     DC     A(L'PARM2)             length of command (PARM2)
PARM4     DS     F                      command return code
PARM5     DS     F                      TSF reason code
PARM6     DS     F                      command abend code
* DSECT definitions
          IKJTSVT
          CVT    DSECT=YES
          END
```

14.4 INTERFACE FROM PROGRAMS TO REXX PROCESSOR (IRXEXEC)

The IRXEXEC routine is the most flexible method of invoking a REXX exec, for example, it is not restricted to passing a single parameter. Figure 14.3 illustrates the IRXEXEC service. Non-REXX programs can use the IRXEXEC service routine to invoke a REXX exec; this exec may be either stored in a file or contained in the invoking program. The latter method is an in-store exec, and is a simple and efficient means of making a normal program REXX-aware (for example, allow a COBOL program to use REXX parsing services).

Assembler calling sequence:

```
CALL IRXEXEC,(AddrExecblk,AddrArglist,Flags,AddrInstblk,AddrCppl,

AddrEvalBlk,AddrWorkareaDescr,AddrUser[,AddrEnvBlk[,ReturnCode]]),VL
```

Note: Register 0 may contain the address of an Environment Block. If register 0 does not point to a valid Environment Block, the Environment Block created for the environment is used.

AddrExecblk

A fullword containing the address of the Exec Block (EXECBLK).
0 if the exec has been preloaded, i.e. **AddrInstblk** contains the address of the INSTBLK which describes the exec.

AddrArglist

A fullword containing the address of the Argument List.

Flags

A fullword that specifies the form of the exec being invoked:

X'80000000' — The exec is being invoked as command. The invoked exec can return a numeric return code.

X'40000000' — The exec is being invoked as an external function. The invoked exec must return a result.

X'20000000' — The exec is being invoked as a subroutine. The invoked exec can return a result.

AddrInstblk

A fullword containing the address of the In-storage Control Block (INSTBLK).

0 if the exec has not been preloaded, i.e. the exec will be loaded using information contained in the EXECBLK.

AddrCppl

A fullword containing the address of the TSO CPPL. This parameter is only required for invocation from a TSO address space, and must be 0 for invocation from non-TSO address spaces.

AddrEvalblock

A fullword containing the address of the Evaluation Block (EVALBLOCK) which is to contain the result returned by the exec.

0 indicates that no EVALBLOCK is required.

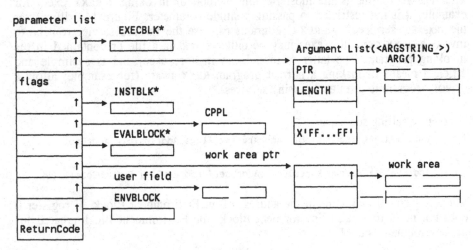

* Detailed diagram follows

Figure 14.3 — IRXEXEC interface (part 1 of 2)

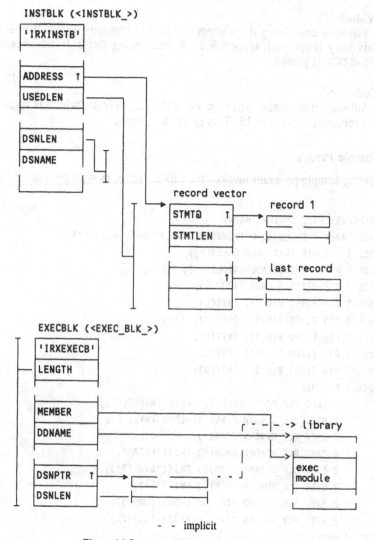

Figure 14.3 — IRXEXEC interface (part 2 of 2)

AddrWorkareaDescr

A fullword containing the address of an 8-byte field which describes a work area to be used by the IRXEXEC routine.

0 indicates that IRXEXEC is to create its own work area.

AddrUser

A fullword containing the address of a user field. IRXEXEC does not use this field.

0 indicates that no user field is passed.

AddrEnvblock

A fullword containing the address of the Environment Block (ENVBLOCK). This entry is optional, if specified it overrides register 0. 0 indicates that no ENVBLOCK is passed.

ReturnCode

A fullword that IRXEXEC sets to contain the return code, which is identical to that returned in register 15. This entry is optional.

14.4.1 Sample Program

The following sample program invokes the REXX exec BETA with parameter "12 4".

```
RXPPGM3: PROC OPTIONS(MAIN);
DCL IRXEXEC EXTERNAL OPTIONS(RETCODE,ASSEMBLER,INTER);
DCL 1 P11 PTR INIT(ADDR(EXECBLK));
DCL 1 P12 PTR INIT(ADDR(ARGLIST));
DCL 1 P13 BIT(32) INIT('1000'B);
DCL 1 P14 FIXED BIN(31) INIT(0);
DCL 1 P15 FIXED BIN(31) INIT(0);
DCL 1 P16 FIXED BIN(31) INIT(0);
DCL 1 P17 FIXED BIN(31) INIT(0);
DCL 1 P18 FIXED BIN(31) INIT(0);
DCL 1 EXECBLK,
      2 EXEC_BLK_ACRYN CHAR(8) INIT('IRXEXECB'),
      2 EXEC_BLK_LENGTH FIXED BIN(31) INIT(48),
      2 EXEC_BLK_RESERV CHAR(4),
      2 EXEC_BLK_MEMBER CHAR(8) INIT('BETA'),
      2 EXEC_BLK_DDNAME CHAR(8) INIT('SYSLIB'),
      2 EXEC_BLK_SUBCOM CHAR(8) INIT(' '),
      2 EXEC_BLK_DSNPTR PTR INIT(ADDR(DUMMY)),
      2 EXEC_BLK_DSNLEN FIXED BIN(31) INIT(0);
DCL 1 ARGLIST,
      2 ARGLIST_ENTRY(2),
        3 ARGSTRING_PTR PTR,
        3 ARGSTRING_LENGTH FIXED BIN(31);
DCL 1 ARG CHAR(4) INIT('12 4'); /* argument for command */
ARGSTRING_PTR(1) = ADDR(ARG);
ARGSTRING_LENGTH(1) = LENGTH(ARG);
ARGSTRING_LENGTH(2) = -1; /* set end-of-list marker */
FETCH IRXEXEC; /* load address of entry point */
CALL IRXEXEC(P11,P12,P13,P14,P15,P16,P17,P18);
END;
```

14.4.2 Invocation of an In-Store Exec

The sample programs each pass two arguments (alpha and beta) to an in-store exec which returns the concatenated parameters (alphabeta). The invoking program displays the returned result. This example illustrates the method of passing arguments and returning a result. In practice, an in-store exec can make full use of REXX services.

14.4.2.1 Sample Assembler Program. *Note*: For simplicity, the sample Assembler program uses the TPUT service to display the result. The program residency mode (RMODE) must be set to 24 because TPUT operands must be below the 16MB limit. The TPUT service is available only under TSO, the WTO service (with routing code 11) operates in both TSO and OS/390 batch.

```
AEXEXC    CSECT
AEXEXC    AMODE 31                    required for REXX
AEXEXC    RMODE 24                    RMODE 24 required for TPUT
          BAKR  14,0                  save registers and return address
          BASR  12,0                  set base register
          USING *,12
          LA    13,SA                 internal save area
* process
          LOAD  EP=IRXEXEC
          LR    15,0                  entry-point address
          CALL  (15),(PO,AARGLIST,FLAGS,AINSTBLK,PO,AEVALBLK,PO,PO),VL
          L     0,EVLEN               length of result
          TPUT  EVDATA,(0)            display result
          PR    ,                     return (restore registers)
SA        DS    18F
PO        DC    A(0)
AARGLIST  DC    A(ARGLIST)
ARGLIST   DS    0A
          DC    A(ARG1,L'ARG1)
          DC    A(ARG2,L'ARG2)
          DC    2F'-1'
ARG1      DC    C'alpha'
ARG2      DC    C'beta'
FLAGS     DC    X'40000000'           invoke as function
AINSTBLK  DC    A(INSTBLK)
AEVALBLK  DC    A(EVALBLK)
EVALBLK   DS    0F      align
          DS    F                     reserved
EVSIZE    DC    A((EVDATAE-EVALBLK)/8)
EVLEN     DC    XL4'80000000'         L(data)
          DS    F                     reserved
```

```
        EVDATA    DS    CL64              data
        EVDATAE   EQU   *
                  DS    OF    align
        INSTBLK   DC    CL8'IRXINSTB'
                  DC    F'128'            L(INSTBLK header)
                  DS    F                 reserved
                  DC    A(INSTPGM)
        NINSTPGM  DC    A(INSTPGML/8)     N(INSTBLK entries)
                  DC    CL8' '            member name (unused)
                  DC    CL8' '            DD name (unused)
                  DC    CL8'MVS'          subcom
                  DS    F                 reserved
                  DC    F'0'              L(DSN), unused
                  DC    CL54' '           DSN, unused
                  ORG   INSTBLK+128
        * INSTPGM entries
        INSTPGM   DC    A(STMT1,L'STMT1)
                  DC    A(STMT2,L'STMT2)
        INSTPGML  EQU   *-INSTPGM
        STMT1     DC    C' PARSE ARG P1,P2'
        STMT2     DC    C' RETURN p1||p2'
                  END
```

14.4.2.2 Sample COBOL Program.

```
        IDENTIFICATION DIVISION.
        PROGRAM-ID. BEXEXC.
        * Invoke an in-store exec
        DATA DIVISION.
        WORKING-STORAGE SECTION.
        01 INSTBLK.
                02 INSTBLK-ACRONYM PIC X(8) VALUE 'IRXINSTB'.
                02 INSTBLK-HDRLEN PIC 9(9) BINARY VALUE 128.
                02 FILLER PIC X(4).
                02 INSTBLK-ADDRESS POINTER.
                02 INSTBLK-USEDLEN PIC 9(9) BINARY.
                02 INSTBLK-MEMBER PIC X(8) VALUE ' '.
                02 INSTBLK-DDNAME PIC X(8) VALUE ' '.
                02 INSTBLK-SUBCOM PIC X(8) VALUE ' '.
                02 FILLER PIC X(4).
                02 INSTBLK-DSNLEN PIC 9(9) BINARY VALUE 0.
                02 INSTBLK-DSNAME PIC X(72) VALUE ' '.
        01 EVALBLOCK.
                02 EVALBLOCK-EVPAD1 PIC 9(9) BINARY VALUE 0.
                02 EVALBLOCK-EVSIZE PIC 9(9) BINARY VALUE 32.
```

```
            02 EVALBLOCK-EVLEN PIC 9(9) BINARY VALUE 0.
            02 EVALBLOCK-EVPAD2 PIC 9(9) BINARY VALUE 0.
            02 EVALBLOCK-EVDATA PIC X(240) VALUE ' '.
   01 ARGLIST.
            02 ARGLIST-ENTRY OCCURS 3.
               03 ARGSTRING-PTR POINTER.
               03 ARGSTRING-NULL REDEFINES ARGSTRING-PTR PIC 9(9) BINARY.
               03 ARGSTRING-LENGTH PIC 9(9) BINARY.
   01 INSTORE-VECTOR.
            02 INSTORE-ENTRY OCCURS 3.
               03 INSTORE-PTR POINTER.
               03 INSTORE-NULL REDEFINES INSTORE-PTR PIC 9(9) BINARY.
               03 INSTORE-LENGTH PIC 9(9) BINARY.
   *
   01 ARG1 PIC X(5) VALUE 'alpha'.
   01 ARG2 PIC X(4) VALUE 'beta'.
   01 STMT1 PIC X(15) VALUE 'PARSE ARG P1,P2'.
   01 STMT2 PIC X(17) VALUE 'RETURN (P1 || P2)'.
   *
   01 P1 POINTER.
   01 P2 POINTER.
   01 FLAGS PIC X(4) VALUE X'40000000'.
   01 P4 POINTER.
   01 P6 POINTER.
   01 P0 POINTER.
   01 P0-NULL REDEFINES P0 PIC 9(9) BINARY.
   PROCEDURE DIVISION.
            CALL 'SETPTR' USING ARG1 ARGSTRING-PTR(1)
            MOVE 5 TO ARGSTRING-LENGTH(1)
            CALL 'SETPTR' USING ARG2 ARGSTRING-PTR(2)
            MOVE 4 TO ARGSTRING-LENGTH(2)
            MOVE -1 TO ARGSTRING-NULL(3)
   *
            CALL 'SETPTR' USING STMT1 INSTORE-PTR(1)
            MOVE 15 TO INSTORE-LENGTH(1)
            CALL 'SETPTR' USING STMT2 INSTORE-PTR(2)
            MOVE 17 TO INSTORE-LENGTH(2)
            MOVE -1 TO INSTORE-NULL(3)
            CALL 'SETPTR' USING INSTORE-VECTOR INSTBLK-ADDRESS
            MOVE 24 TO INSTBLK-USEDLEN
   *
            CALL 'SETPTR' USING ARGLIST P2
            CALL 'SETPTR' USING INSTBLK P4
            CALL 'SETPTR' USING EVALBLOCK P6
```

```
            MOVE 0 TO PO-NULL
            CALL 'IRXEXEC' USING PO P2 FLAGS P4 PO P6 PO PO
 *
            DISPLAY RETURN-CODE
            DISPLAY EVALBLOCK-EVDATA
            STOP RUN.

 * Subprogram to set pointer
  IDENTIFICATION DIVISION.
  PROGRAM-ID. SETPTR.
  DATA DIVISION.
  LINKAGE SECTION.
  01 PARMDATA PIC X(8).
  01 PARMPTR POINTER.
  PROCEDURE DIVISION
            USING PARMDATA PARMPTR.
            SET PARMPTR TO ADDRESS OF PARMDATA
            GOBACK.
        END PROGRAM SETPTR.
  END PROGRAM BEXEXC.
```

14.5 PROGRAM ACCESS TO REXX VARIABLES (IRXEXCOM SERVICE)

Programs running in a REXX environment can use the IRXEXCOM service to access variables in the environment pool. Figure 14.4 illustrates the IRXEXCOM service. The sample function shown in Section 14.14 illustrates the use of the IRXEXCOM service.

The following functions are available:
· copy value;
· set variable;
· drop variable;
· retrieve symbolic name;
· set symbolic name;
· drop symbolic name;
· fetch next variable;
· fetch user data.

The function specifies the processing to be performed (SHVBLOCKs can be chained).

Assembler calling sequence:
```
    CALL IRXEXCOM,(irxexcom,DummyParm,DummyParm,shvblock[,AddrEnvBlk
    [,ReturnCode]]),VL
```

irxexcom

The 8-character string 'IRXEXCOM'.

DummyParm

Although the contents of the second and third parameters are not significant, they must be identical — 0 is valid.

shvblock

The first of a chain of Shared Variable (Request) Blocks (SHVBLOCK). The SHVBLOCK contains the information to perform the required service (function, variable name, address of data, etc.).

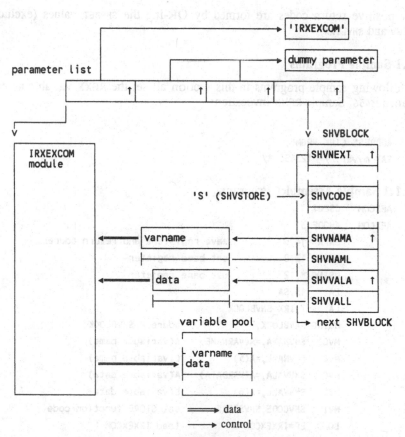

Figure 14.4 — IRXEXCOM service to store a variable

AddrEnvblock

A fullword containing the address of the Environment Block (ENVBLOCK). This entry is optional if specified it overrides register 0.

0 indicates that no ENVBLOCK is passed.

ReturnCode
>A fullword that IRXEXCOM sets to contain the return code, which is identical to that returned in register 15. This entry is optional.

Register 15 is returned with one of the following codes:

0	Complete chain successfully processed.
-1	At least one error condition detected (e.g. not invoked from a REXX exec).
-2	Insufficient main-storage available.
28	A language processor environment could not be located.
32	Invalid parameter list.

Other positive return codes are formed by OR-ing the SHVRET values (excluding SHVNEWV and SHVLVAR).

14.5.1 Sample Programs

The following sample programs in this section all set the REXX variable MYVAR to contain 123456. Sample REXX invocation:

```
ADDRESS LINK "PGM";
SAY myvar; /* 123456 */
```

14.5.1.1 Sample Assembler Program.

```
AEXCOM    CSECT
AEXCOM    AMODE 31
          BAKR  14,0              save registers and return address
          BASSM 12,0              set base register
          USING *,12              use base register
          LA    13,SA
          LA    7,IRX_SHVBLOCK
          USING SHVBLOCK,7        address SHVBLOCK
          MVC   SHVNAMA,=A(VARNAME)   A(variable name)
          MVC   SHVNAML,=A(5)      L(variable name)
          MVC   SHVVALA,=A(VARDATA)   A(variable data)
          MVC   SHVVALL,=A(6)      L(variable data)
          MVI   SHVCODE,SHVSTORE   set STORE function-code
          LOAD  EP=IRXEXCOM        load IRXEXCOM
          LTR   15,0               entry-point address
          BZ    EOJ                load error
          CALL  (15),(IRX_IRXEXCOM,0,0,IRX_SHVBLOCK),VL
EOJ       PR    ,                  return
SA        DS    18F                save area
VARNAME   DC    C'MYVAR'           variable name
VARDATA   DC    C'123456'          variable data
```

```
IRX_IRXEXCOM DC CL8'IRXEXCOM'        IRXEXCOM tag
IRX_SHVBLOCK DC (SHVBLEN)X'0'        SHVBLOCK data area
         IRXSHVB ,                   SHVBLOCK DSECT
         END
```

14.5.1.2 Sample C Program.

```c
#include <stdlib.h>
#include <stdio.h>
#include <string.h>

#pragma linkage (OSFUNC,OS)
typedef int OSFUNC();

main()
{
  OSFUNC * fptr;
  int rc;

  struct shvblock { /* Shared Variable Request Block */

     struct shvblock *shvnext; /* pointer to next shvblock */
     int shvuser; /* "fetch next": length of name buffer */
     char shvcode; /* function code - type of variable access request */
     unsigned int shvret :8; /* return codes */
     short shvrsv; /* reserved */
     int shvbufl; /* length of fetch value buffer */
     char *shvnama; /* address of variable name */
     int shvnaml; /* length of variable name */
     char *shvvala; /* address of value buffer */
     int shvvall; /* length of value buffer */
  } sb;
  char vn[9]; /* variable name */
  char vd[9]; /* variable data */
  char dummy_parm;

  /* execution code */
  fptr = (OSFUNC *)fetch("IRXEXCOM");
  if (fptr == NULL) {
    puts("fetch error");
    exit(4);
  }

  sb.shvnext = NULL; /* pointer to next shvblock */
  strcpy(vn,"MYVAR"); /* set variable name */
```

```
sb.shvnama = vn;
sb.shvnaml = strlen(vn); /* set name length */
strcpy(vd,"123456"); /* set variable data */
sb.shvvala = vd;
sb.shvvall = strlen(vd); /* set data length */
sb.shvcode = 'S'; /* function code */

rc = (*fptr)("IRXEXCOM",&dummy_parm,&dummy_parm,&sb);
if (rc != 0) {
  printf("SHVRET %d",(int)sb.shvret); /* return codes */
  printf(" %x",sb.shvret);
}
}
```

14.5.1.3 Sample COBOL Program.

```
IDENTIFICATION DIVISION.
PROGRAM-ID. BEXCOM.
DATA DIVISION.
WORKING-STORAGE SECTION.
01 VARNAME PIC X(8) VALUE 'MYVAR'.
01 VARDATA PIC X(8) VALUE '123456'.
01 DUMMY-PARM PIC X(4).
01 SHVBLOCK.
   02 SHVNEXT PIC S9(9) COMP VALUE 0.
   02 SHVUSER PIC S9(9) COMP.
   02 SHVCODE PIC X(1).
   02 SHVRET  PIC X(1).
   02        PIC X(2).
   02 SHVBUFL PIC S9(9) COMP.
   02 SHVNAMA POINTER.
   02 SHVNAML PIC S9(9) COMP.
   02 SHVVALA POINTER.
   02 SHVVALL PIC S9(9) COMP.
PROCEDURE DIVISION.
*    set REXX variable
     MOVE 'S' TO SHVCODE
     CALL 'SETPTR' USING VARNAME SHVNAMA
     MOVE 5 TO SHVNAML
     CALL 'SETPTR' USING VARDATA SHVVALA
     MOVE 6 TO SHVVALL
     CALL 'IRXEXCOM' USING BY CONTENT 'IRXEXCOM'
       BY REFERENCE DUMMY-PARM DUMMY-PARM SHVBLOCK
     STOP RUN.
```

```
* Subprogram to set pointer
  IDENTIFICATION DIVISION.
  PROGRAM-ID. SETPTR.
  DATA DIVISION.
  LINKAGE SECTION.
  01 PARMDATA PIC X(8).
  01 PARMPTR POINTER.
  PROCEDURE DIVISION
      USING PARMDATA PARMPTR.
      SET PARMPTR TO ADDRESS OF PARMDATA
      GOBACK.
    END PROGRAM SETPTR.
END PROGRAM BEXCOM.
```

14.5.1.4 Sample PL/I Program.

```
PEXCOM: PROC OPTIONS(MAIN);
/* declarations */
DCL IRXEXCOM EXTERNAL OPTIONS(RETCODE,INTER,ASSEMBLER);
DCL PLIRETV BUILTIN;
DCL 1 SHVBLOCK UNALIGNED,
    2 SHVNEXT FIXED BIN(31) INIT(0),
    2 SHVUSER FIXED BIN(31) INIT(0),
    2 SHVCODE CHAR(1),
    2 SHVRET CHAR(1),
    2 FILLER CHAR(2),
    2 SHVBUFL FIXED BIN(31),
    2 SHVNAMA PTR,
    2 SHVNAML FIXED BIN(31),
    2 SHVVALA PTR,
    2 SHVVALL FIXED BIN(31);
DCL 1 VARNAME CHAR(8) INIT('MYVAR');
DCL 1 VARVALUE CHAR(8) INIT('123456');
/* execution code */
SHVCODE = 'S';
SHVNAMA = ADDR(VARNAME);
SHVNAML = 5; /* length of name */
SHVVALA = ADDR(VARVALUE);
SHVVALL = 6; /* length of data */
FETCH IRXEXCOM; /* load address of entry point */
CALL IRXEXCOM('IRXEXCOM',DUMMY,DUMMY,SHVBLOCK);
IF PLIRETV > 0 THEN
  PUT SKIP LIST('PLIRETV',PLIRETV);
END;
```

14.5.2 Sample Retrieval Program

The following sample Assembler program displays the name and contents of all the current REXX variables. For simplicity, the TPUT service is used for display (TPUT is available only in TSO and can use only 24-bit addressing for its data areas).

```
AEXCOM2  CSECT
AEXCOM2  AMODE  31                               IRXEXCOM requirement
AEXCOM2  RMODE  24                               TPUT requirement
         BAKR   14,0                             save registers and return address
         BASSM  12,0                             set base register
         USING  *,12
         LA     13,SA                            define save-area
         LA     7,IRX_SHVBLOCK
         USING  SHVBLOCK,7                       address SHVBLOCK
         MVC    SHVNAMA,=A(VARNAME)    A(variable name)
         MVC    SHVUSER,=A(L'VARNAME) L(variable name)
         MVC    SHVVALA,=A(VARDATA)   A(variable data)
         MVC    SHVBUFL,=A(L'VARDATA) L(variable data buffer)
         MVI    SHVCODE,SHVNEXTV                 set NEXTV function-code
         LOAD   EP=IRXEXCOM                      load IRXEXCOM
         LTR    15,0                             entry-point address
         BZ     ERROR                            load error
         ST     15,IRXEXCOM                      save entry-point address
GETLOOP  L      15,IRXEXCOM
         CALL   (15),(IRX_IRXEXCOM,0,0,IRX_SHVBLOCK),VL
         CLI    SHVRET,SHVLVAR
         BE     LAST                             last variable was retrieved
         CLI    SHVRET,SHVTRUNC
         BE     OK                               truncated
         LTR    15,15                            test IRXEXCOM return code
         BNZ    ERROR                            IRXEXCOM error
* else CLEAN (ok)
OK       L      0,SHVNAML                        name length
         TPUT   VARNAME,(0)
         L      0,SHVVALL                        data length
         TPUT   VARDATA,(0)
         B      GETLOOP
LAST     LA     15,0                             normal return
EXIT     PR     ,                                terminate program
ERROR    LA     15,8                             error return condition
         B      EXIT
IRXEXCOM DS     A                                IRXEXCOM entry-point address
SA       DS     18F                              save-area
```

```
VARNAME DS    CL250              variable name
VARDATA DS    CL512              variable data
IRX_IRXEXCOM DC CL8'IRXEXCOM'    IRXEXCOM tag
IRX_SHVBLOCK DC (SHVBLEN)X'0'    SHVBLOCK data area
        IRXSHVB                  SHVBLOCK DSECT
        END
```

14.6 STACK PROCESSING (IRXSTK SERVICE)

Programs can use the IRXSTK service to perform processing on the current stack.
The operations:
- DELSTACK
- DROPBUF
- MAKEBUF
- NEWSTACK
- PULL
- PUSH
- QBUF
- QELEM
- QSTACK
- QUEUE
- QUEUED

have the same function as described in earlier chapters.

TSO and ISPF system routines use the following two operations to coordinate stack access:
- DROPTERM
- MAKETERM

These operations should not be used by application programs.

Assembler calling sequence:
```
CALL IRXSTK,(Function,DataPtr,DataLen,ReturnCode),VL
```

Function
> An 8-character string designating the function to be performed, DELSTACK, DROPBUF, etc.

DataPtr
> A pointer to the data element. *Note*: Data in the stack must not be changed. The data should be moved from the stack before any processing is performed that could alter the stack's contents.

DataLen
> A fullword containing the length of the data element.

ReturnCode

A fullword returned with the function return code. This field is meaningful only when the service return code (set in register 15) is zero. The values for the function return code can be obtained from the descriptions for the corresponding operation.

Register 15 is returned with one of the following codes:

0   Processing successfully completed.

4   The data stack is empty (PULL function).

Other codes indicate that an error has occurred.

14.6.1 Sample Programs

The sample programs in this section retrieve and display the next queue entry. Sample REXX invocation:

```
PUSH "line1";
ADDRESS LINK "PGM";
```

14.6.1.1 Sample Assembler Program. Note the allocation of storage to contain the retrieved queue entries.

```
AEXSTK   CSECT
AEXSTK   AMODE 31
         BAKR  14,0            save registers and return address
         BASSM 12,0            set base register
         USING *,12
         LA    13,SA
         LOAD  EP=IRXSTK
         LTR   15,15
         BNZ   EOJ             load error
         LR    2,0
         LR    15,0
         MVC   FC,=CL8'PUSH'
         LA    1,=C'internal stack element'
         ST    1,AELEM
         MVC   LELEM,=F'25'
         CALL  (15),(FC,AELEM,LELEM,FRC),VL
         MVC   FC,=CL8'PULL'
         LR    0,2
         LR    15,0
         CALL  (15),(FC,AELEM,LELEM,FRC),VL
         LTR   15,15
         BNZ   EOJ             IRXSTK error
         LM    2,3,AELEM       source field
*  allocate 24-bit (for TPUT) area
```

```
          STORAGE OBTAIN,LENGTH=(3),ADDR=(4),LOC=BELOW,SP=1
          LR    0,3            save length
          LR    1,4            save target address
          LR    5,3            length
          MVCL  4,2            move to 24-bit addressable area
          TPUT  (1),(0),R      display
          LA    15,0
EOJ       PR    ,              restore registers
SA        DS    18F
FC        DC    CL8'PULL'
FRC       DS    F
AELEM     DS    A ) contig-
LELEM     DS    L ) uous
          END
```

14.6.1.2 Sample C Program.

```c
#pragma linkage (OSFUNC,OS)
typedef int OSFUNC();

#include <stdio.h>
#include <stdlib.h>
#include <string.h>

main()
{
  int rc, frc;
  OSFUNC * fptr;

  char *pelem;
  char *pstring;
  int lelem;

  /* execution code */
  fptr = (OSFUNC *)fetch("IRXSTK");
  if (fptr == NULL) {
    puts("fetch error");
    exit(4);
  }
  rc = (*fptr) ("PULL    ",&pelem,&lelem,&frc);
  if (rc == 0) {
    /* allocate storage for the stack element */
    pstring = malloc(lelem+1);
```

```
            if (pstring == NULL) {
              puts("malloc error");
              exit(8);
            }
            memcpy(pstring,pelem,lelem);
            *(pstring+lelem) = 0x00; /* set string-end terminator */
            printf("element:%s",pstring); /* display */
          }
          else
            printf("IRXSTK error RC:%d FRC:%d",rc,frc);
        }
```

14.6.1.3 Sample COBOL Program. The sample COBOL program uses the CEEGTST (Get Storage) LE (Language Environment) function to allocate heap storage in the size of the retrieved data element; a subsequent call to the CEEFRST (Free Storage) function releases this allocated heap storage. To avoid over-complicating the code, the function return codes are not checked. Another, less satisfactory, approach would be to use a static data area.

```
        IDENTIFICATION DIVISION.
        PROGRAM-ID. BEXSTK.
        DATA DIVISION.
        WORKING-STORAGE SECTION.
        01 ALEM POINTER.
        01 LELEM PIC 9(9) COMP.
        01 FRC PIC 9(9) COMP.
        01 FUNCT PIC X(8) VALUE 'PULL'.
        01 HEAP-ID PIC 9(9) COMP VALUE 0.
        01 AHEAP POINTER.
        01 FC-COND.
           02 COND-ID PIC 9(9) COMP.
           02 FILLER PIC X(8).
        LINKAGE SECTION.
        01 STK-ELEMENT.
           02 STK-ELEMENT-TABLE OCCURS 1 TO 32767 DEPENDING ON LELEM.
              03 STK-ELEMENT-BYTE PIC X(1).
        01 HEAP-ELEMENT.
           02 HEAP-ELEMENT-TABLE OCCURS 1 TO 32767 DEPENDING ON LELEM.
              03 HEAP-ELEMENT-BYTE PIC X(1).
        PROCEDURE DIVISION.
            CALL 'IRXSTK' USING FUNCT ALEM LELEM FRC
            IF RETURN-CODE = 0
               THEN
```

```
               CALL 'CEEGTST' USING HEAP-ID LELEM AHEAP FC-COND
               SET ADDRESS OF STK-ELEMENT TO ALEM
               SET ADDRESS OF HEAP-ELEMENT TO AHEAP
               MOVE STK-ELEMENT TO HEAP-ELEMENT
               DISPLAY HEAP-ELEMENT
               CALL 'CEEFRST' USING AHEAP FC-COND
            ELSE DISPLAY RETURN-CODE ' ' FRC
         END-IF
         STOP RUN.
```

14.6.1.4 Sample PL/I Program.

```
         PEXSTK: PROC OPTIONS(MAIN);
         /* declarations */
         DCL IRXSTK EXTERNAL OPTIONS(RETCODE,INTER,ASSEMBLER);
         DCL PLIRETV BUILTIN;
         DCL 1 AELEM PTR;
         DCL 1 LELEM FIXED BIN(31);
         DCL 1 FRC FIXED BIN(31);
         DCL 1 HEAP_ELEM CHAR(LELEM) CONTROLLED;
         DCL 1 STACK_ELEM CHAR(1) BASED (AELEM);
         /* execution code */
         FETCH IRXSTK;
         CALL IRXSTK('PULL    ',AELEM,LELEM,FRC);
         IF PLIRETV = 0
           THEN DO;
             ALLOCATE HEAP_ELEM;
             HEAP_ELEM = SUBSTR(STACK_ELEM,1,LELEM);
             PUT SKIP LIST(HEAP_ELEM);
             FREE HEAP_ELEM;
           END;
           ELSE PUT SKIP LIST('IRXSTK:',PLIRETV,FRC);
         END;
```

14.7 COMMAND INTERFACE

Programs written in a conventional programming language (PL/I, COBOL, Assembler, etc.) can be assigned a command environment name, which the ADDRESS command is used to set. All commands (i.e. all non-REXX statements) are passed to the current environment.

14.7.1 Entry Conditions

Register 0
  The address of the current environment block.

Register 1
  The address of the parameter list.

Register 13
  The address of the higher-level register save area.

Register 14
  The return address.

Register 15
  The entry point address.

14.7.2 Parameter List

Register 1 points to a list of addresses. These addresses point to the individual parameters. Figure 14.5 shows the form of the parameter list passed to the command interface.

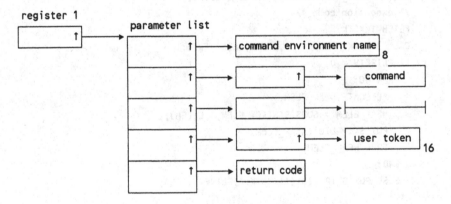

Figure 14.5 — Command interface

Parameter 1 (character 8)
  The name of the invoked host command.

Parameter 2 (address)
  The address of the passed command string.

Parameter 3 (fullword)
  The length of the passed command string.

Parameter 4 (address)
   The address of the user token.

Parameter 5 (fullword)
   The return code set returned by the host command processing program.

14.7.3 Exit Conditions

The host command processing program sets the return code in the fifth entry
parameter:

$<$-12	FAILURE condition
-12 to -1	ERROR condition
0	No error condition
1 to 12	ERROR condition
$>$12	FAILURE condition.

14.7.4 Examples

The sample command displays the environment name and the specified command,
and sets the command return to 0. The command processing program must be
registered; a subsequent ADDRESS statement with this environment name causes
commands to be passed to the associated processing program. Section 14.7.5
describes the command registration interface.

Sample invocation:

```
/* REXX */
ADDRESS USER "test command"
```

The command processing program displays: USER, and test command, respectively.

14.7.4.1 Assembler Command Processor. To simplify the code, the TPUT service
is used for display. Although TPUT can operate in 31-bit addressing mode, its
parameters must be located below the 16MB line.

```
ACMD     CSECT
ACMD     AMODE 31
ACMD     RMODE 24             TPUT requirement
* R0: A(ENVBLOCK) - Environment Block
* R1: A(parameter list)
         BAKR  14,0           save registers
         BASR  12,0           base register
         USING *,12
         LA    13,SA          A(save-area)
         LM    2,6,0(1)
* R2: A(command environment name)
* R3: A(A(command string))
```

```
* R4: A(L(command length))
* R5: A(A(user token))
* R6: A(return code)
          MVC    ENVNAME,0(2)
          TPUT   ENVNAME,8
          L      3,0(3)
          L      4,0(4)
          SH     4,=H'1'              LC(command string)
          EX     4,EXMOVE            move to AMODE(24) area
          LA     0,1(4)              true length
          TPUT   CMDPARM,(0)
          MVC    0(4,6),=F'0'        set command return code
          LA     15,0                set command processor return code (=0)
EXIT      PR     ,                   return
SA        DS     18A                 save-area
ENVNAME   DS     CL8
CMDPARM   DS     CL8
EXMOVE    MVC    CMDPARM,0(3)        EX-instruction
* DSECTs
          IRXENVB
          END
```

14.7.4.2 C Command Processor.

```c
#pragma environment(ccmd)
#include <stdlib.h>
#include <stdio.h>
#include <string.h>
#include <spc.h>

/* function prototype */
int setvar(char *vn, char *vd);

struct parm { /* parameter list */
  char *envname;
  char **cmdstring;
  int *cmdlen;
  char **usertoken;
  int *retcode;
} *pparm;

struct envblock { /* Environment Block */
  char envblock_id[8];
```

```
      char envblock_version[4];
      void *envblock_parmblock;
      void *envblock_userfield;
      void *envblock_workblok_ext;
      struct irxexte *envblock_irxexte;
   } *penvblock;

   struct irxexte { /* External Entry Points */
      int irxexte_entry_count;
      void *irxinit;
      void *irxload;
      void *irxexcom;
      void *irxexec;
      void *irxinout;
      void *irxjcl;
      void *irxrlt;
      void *irxstk;
   } *pirxexte;

   int ccmd()
   {
      char cmdparm[256];
      /* execution code */
      /* get registers on entry */
      penvblock = (void*)edcxregs(0); /* GPR 0 */
      pparm = (void*)edcxregs(1); /* GPR 1 */
      /* get VEEP */
      pirxexte = penvblock->envblock_irxexte;
      /* make C-processable command string */
      strncpy(cmdparm,pparm->cmdstring,pparm->cmdlen);
      cmdparm[pparm->cmdlen] = 0x00;
      /* list command string */
      printf("cmd:%s\n",cmdparm);
      /* set return */
      pparm->retcode = 0;
      return 0; /* command processor return code */
   }
```

14.7.4.3 COBOL Command Processor.

```
      IDENTIFICATION DIVISION.
      PROGRAM-ID. BCMD.
      DATA DIVISION.
```

```
WORKING-STORAGE SECTION.
LINKAGE SECTION.
01 ENVNAME PIC X(8).
01 PCMDSTRING POINTER.
01 CMDLEN PIC 9(9) BINARY.
01 PUSERTOKEN POINTER.
01 RETCODE PIC S9(9) BINARY.
*
01 CMDSTRING.
   02 CMDSTRING-ELEMENT OCCURS 1 TO 32767 DEPENDING ON CMDLEN.
      03 CMDSTRING-CHAR PIC X(1).
01 USERTOKEN PIC X(16).
PROCEDURE DIVISION
   USING ENVNAME PCMDSTRING CMDLEN PUSERTOKEN RETCODE.
   DISPLAY 'ENVNAME:' ENVNAME
   SET ADDRESS OF CMDSTRING TO PCMDSTRING
   DISPLAY 'CMDSTRING:' CMDSTRING
   MOVE 0 TO RETCODE
   STOP RUN.
```

14.7.4.4 PL/I Command Processor.

```
PCMD: PROC(DUMMY_ENVNAME,PCMDSTRING,CMDLEN,
  PUSERTOKEN,RETCODE) OPTIONS(MAIN,NOEXECOPS);
DCL 1 DUMMY_ENVNAME FIXED DEC(15);
DCL 1 ENVNAME CHAR(8) BASED(P);
DCL 1 PCMDSTRING PTR;
DCL 1 CMDSTRING CHAR(256) BASED(PCMDSTRING);
DCL 1 CMDLEN FIXED BIN(31);
DCL 1 PUSERTOKEN PTR;
DCL 1 RETCODE FIXED BIN(31);
DCL 1 P PTR;
/* execution code */
PUT SKIP LIST ('CMD:',SUBSTR(CMDSTRING,1,CMDLEN));
/* process first argument as CHAR(8) */
P = ADDR(DUMMY_ENVNAME);
PUT SKIP LIST ('ENVNAME:',ENVNAME);
RETCODE = 0;
END;
```

14.7.5 Command Registration Interface (IRXSUBCM)

A host command environment routine is invoked to process the host commands for the associated environment name; this is a so-called host command environment replaceable routine. The ADDRESS instruction is used to set the current environment. The Host Command Environment Table (SUBCOMTB table) contains the name of the associated processing routine. The IRXSUBCM service routine is used to maintain the SUBCOMTB table entries.

The IRXSUBCM service routine supports the following operations:
- ADD   Add a new entry
- DELETE   Delete an entry
- QUERY   Query
- UPDATE   Update an entry.

Entry conditions:

Register 0   The address of an Environment Block (optional).

Register 1   The address of the parameter list.

Assembler calling sequence:

```
CALL IRXSUBCM,(Function,AddrTableEntry,TableEntryLen,
    EnvName[,AddrEnvBlock[,ReturnCode]]),VL
```

Function

An 8-byte character field that contains the function to be performed:

ADD   Add a new entry. IRXSUBCM does not check for duplicate entries.

DELETE   Delete the last occurrence (e.g. duplicate) of the specified environment name.

QUERY   Return the entry values for the specified environment name.

UPDATE   Update the entry for the specified environment name.

AddrTableEntry

The address of a string that describes the table entry.

TableEntryLen

A fullword that contains the length of the table entry descriptor.

EnvName

An 8-byte character field that contains the host command environment name.

AddrEnvblock

A fullword containing the address of the Environment Block (ENVBLOCK). This entry is optional; if specified, it overrides register 0.
0 indicates that no ENVBLOCK is passed.

ReturnCode
A fullword that IRXSUBCB sets to contain the return code, which is identical to that returned in register 15. This entry is optional.

Register 15 is returned with one of the following codes:

0   Processing completed successfully.

8   The environment name could not be found.

20   An error occurred.

28   A language processor environment could not be located.

32   The parameter list is invalid.

Figure 14.6 shows the mapping of the Host Command Environment Entry fields.

Displ	Field name	Type	Description
0	NAME	CL8	The name of the host command environment
8	ROUTINE	CL8	The name of the host command environment processing routine
16	TOKEN	CL16	The user token that is passed to the processing routine

Figure 14.6 — Host Command Environment Table entry fields

14.7.5.1 Sample Registration Program. This sample program creates a SUBCOMTB table entry with the following contents:

· environment name: USER
· processing program: CMDPGM
· no user token (blank).

```
REXXENV   CSECT
REXXENV   AMODE 31
          BAKR   14,0 save registers and return address in hardware stack
          BASR   12,0 set base register
          USING  *,12
          LOAD   EP=IRXSUBCM
          LR     15,0 entry-point address
          CALL   (15),(P1,AP2,P3,P4),VL
          LA     15,0 program return code (=0)
          PR     , terminate program
P1        DC     CL8'ADD'
AP2       DC     A(P2)
P2        DC     CL8'USER' environment name
P2PGM     DC     CL8'CMDPGM' processing program
P2TOKEN   DC     CL16' ' user token
P2END     EQU    *
P3        DC     A(P2END-P2) length
```

```
P4        DC      CL8'USER'
          END
```

14.7.6 Command Router

If an installation has a relatively large number of command processors, it may be advantageous to write a single command processor as router, which then passes the specified command string to the appropriate processing program. This avoids having to register every processing program, and allows security checking, etc. One approach would be to specify the second-level environment name (or processing program) as the first argument in the command string.

Example:

```
    ADDRESS USER "MYENV ARG1 ARG2"
```

USER is the installation command router, MYENV is the application environment, and ARG1 and ARG2 are the actual command arguments.

14.8 FUNCTION INTERFACE

Programs written in a conventional programming language can be invoked as external REXX functions (or subroutines); the load module name or alias must be the function name. A function differs from a subroutine in that a function must return a value. Figure 14.7 depicts the function interface.

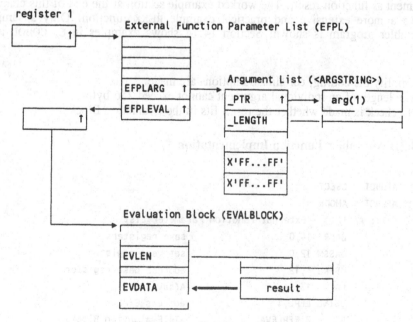

Figure 14.7 — Function interface

14.8.1 Entry Conditions

Register 0
  The address of the Environment Block.

Register 1
  The address of the External Function Parameter List (EFPL). The EFPL
  contains two addresses of direct interest for functions: EFPLARG (the address
  of the Argument List, which contains the pointers to the parsed arguments)
  and EFPLEVAL (the address of the pointer to the area which is to be set to
  contain the result).

14.8.2 Exit Conditions

Register 15
  Must contain 0, otherwise the message "IRX0043, Routine not found" will
  be displayed.

EVALBLOCK
  The evaluation block contains the function result.

14.8.3 Sample Function Program

The sample function RXFUNCT is a simple function that returns the (first) passed
argument as function result. The worked example section at the end of this chapter
shows a more extensive and practical example REXX function. Only a sample
Assembler program is shown; Section 14.14 shows examples in C, COBOL and
PL/I.

To simplify the coding, certain assumptions are made:
·   The length of an individual argument cannot exceed 256 bytes.
·   No check is made whether the result fits in the Evaluation Block.

14.8.3.1 Assembler Function Implementation.

```
AFUNCT   CSECT
AFUNCT   AMODE 31
* R1: A(EFPL) - External Function Parameter List
         BAKR  14,0              save registers
         BASSM 12,0              set base register
         USING *,12              address base register
         LA    13,SA             A(save-area)
         USING EFPL,1            address EFPL
         L     2,EFPLEVAL        PTR(Evaluation Block)
         L     11,0(2)           A(Evaluation Block)
```

```
          USING EVALBLOCK,11              address Evaluation Block
          L     10,EFPLARG                A(parsed Argument List)
          USING ARGTABLE_ENTRY,10         address Argument List
          LA    9,EVALBLOCK_EVDATA        A(result)
          LA    8,0                       L(result)
          L     7,EVALBLOCK_EVSIZE        L(EVALBLOCK in double-words)
          SLL   7,3                       length in bytes
          S     7,=A(EVALBLOCK_EVDATA-EVALBLOCK_EVPAD1) - header length
          LA    7,EVALBLOCK(7)            EVALBLOCK end address +1 (=limit)
          LA    15,4                      preset return code (if error)
NEXTPARM  LM    3,4,ARGTABLE_ARGSTRING_PTR
* R3: A(argument); R4: L(argument)
          LTR   4,4                       test length
          BM    LASTPARM                  negative length (=last parameter)
          LA    1,0(4,9)                  end address after move
          CR    1,7                       test against limit
          BH    EXIT                      result does not fit
          SH    4,=H'1'                   LengthCode(argument)
          EX    4,EXMOVE                  move argument
          LA    10,ARGTABLE_NEXT-ARGTABLE_ENTRY(10) next argument
          B     NEXTPARM                  get next argument
LASTPARM  ST    8,EVALBLOCK_EVLEN         entry size
          LA    15,0                      set function return code (=0)
EXIT      PR    ,                         return
SA        DS    18A                       save-area
EXMOVE    MVC   0(0,9),0(3)               EX-instruction
* DSECTs
          IRXEFPL
          IRXEVALB
          IRXARGTB
          END
```

14.8.3.2 Assembler Function With Test of Result Length.

The following sample function shows how the IRXRLT GETBLOCK function can be used to allocate a larger Environment Block if the result is too large. This sample function has been simplified to process a single argument.

```
BFUNCT    CSECT
BFUNCT    AMODE 31
* R0: A(Environment Block)
* R1: A(EFPL) - External Function Parameter List
          BAKR  14,0                      save registers
          BASSM 12,0                      base register
```

```
              USING *,12
              LA   13,SA                A(save-area)
              USING EFPL,1              address EFPL
              L    2,EFPLEVAL           PTR(Evaluation Block)
              L    11,0(2)              A(Evaluation Block)
              USING EVALBLOCK,11        address Evaluation Block
              L    10,EFPLARG           A(parsed Argument List)
              USING ARGTABLE_ENTRY,10   address Argument List
              LA   9,EVALBLOCK_EVDATA   A(result)
              LR   1,0                  A(Environment Block)
              USING ENVBLOCK,1
              L    8,ENVBLOCK_IRXEXTE   A(VEEP)
              USING IRXEXTE,8
              L    7,EVALBLOCK_EVSIZE   L(EVALBLOCK in double-words)
              SLL  7,3                  length in bytes
              S    7,=A(EVALBLOCK_EVDATA-EVALBLOCK_EVPAD1) - hdr length
              LM   3,4,ARGTABLE_ARGSTRING_PTR
* R3: A(argument); R4: L(argument)
              CR   4,7                  test against limit
              BNH  OK                   result fits into EvalBlock
* else allocate new evaluation block
              ST   4,SIZE               required size
              L    15,IRXRLT
              CALL (15),(GETBLOCK,AEVALBLK,SIZE),VL
              LTR  15,15
              BNZ  EXIT                 EVALBLOCK allocation error
              L    11,AEVALBLK
              LA   9,EVALBLOCK_EVDATA   A(result)
OK            ST   4,EVALBLOCK_EVLEN    entry size
              SH   4,=H'1'              LengthCode(argument)
              EX   4,EXMOVE             move argument
              LA   15,0                 set function return code (=0)
EXIT     PR   ,                        return
SA       DS   18A                      save-area
EXMOVE   MVC  0(0,9),0(3)              EX-instruction
SIZE     DS   F                        L(EVALBLOCK)
AEVALBLK DS   A                        A(EVALBLOCK)
GETBLOCK DC   CL8'GETBLOCK'
```

```
* DSECTs
        IRXEFPL
        IRXEVALB
        IRXENVB
        IRXARGTB
        IRXEXTE
        END
```

14.9 FUNCTION PACKAGE

For reasons of efficiency, functions can be grouped together as a **function package** — function packages are searched before the other libraries. Three classes of function package can be defined:
· user function package;
· local function package;
· system function package.

The system support personnel will usually be responsible for the local and system function packages, and so they will not be discussed in this book, although the general logic is the same as for the user function package.

A function package consists of a **function package directory** and functions, as described in the previous section. The function package directory is a load module contained in the load library — IRXFUSER is the standard name for the load module defining the user function package. This name can be changed in the Function Package Table. Figure 14.8 shows the diagrammatic representation of a function package.

The function package directory contains the names of the functions (subroutines) as invoked from a REXX exec and a pointer to the appropriate load module. This pointer can have one of two forms:
· The address of a load module which has been linkage edited together with the function package directory — such load modules must be serially reusable, as they are loaded only once.
· The name of a load module which will be loaded from the specified load library.

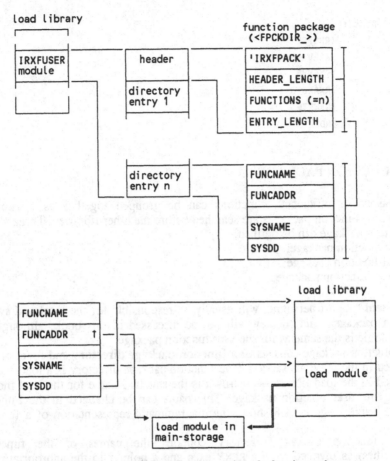

Figure 14.8 — Diagrammatic representation of a function package

14.9.1 Function Directory

The Function Directory defines the functions contained in a function package. The Function Directory consists of a header and one entry for each function contained in the Function Directory. Figure 14.9 shows the mapping of the Function Directory fields. The IRXFPDIR macro maps the Function Directory.

Displ	Field name	Type	Description
-	FPCKDIR_HEADER	DSECT	REXX Function Package Directory Header
0	FPCKDIR_ID	CL8	'IRXFPACK' character id
8	FPCKDIR_HEADER_LENGTH	F	Length of directory header
12	FPCKDIR_FUNCTIONS	F	Number of functions
16	-	F	Reserved
20	FPCKDIR_ENTRY_LENGTH	F	Length of directory entry
	FPCKDIR_ENTRY	DSECT	REXX Function Package Directory Entry
+0	FPCKDIR_FUNCNAME	CL8	Name of function or subroutine
+8	FPCKDIR_FUNCADDR	A	Address of the routine entry point
+12	-	F	Reserved
+16	FPCKDIR_SYSNAME	CL8	Name of the entry point
+24	FPCKDIR_SYSDD	CL8	DD name of load file
	FPCKDIR_NEXT		Next FPCKDIR entry

Figure 14.9 — Function Package Directory fields

14.9.1.1 Function Package Directory Header.

FPCKDIR_ID
> 'IRXFPACK' character identifier.

FPCKDIR_HEADER_LENGTH
> The length of the directory header (24 bytes).

FPCKDIR_FUNCTIONS
> The number of functions in the package.

FPCKDIR_ENTRY_LENGTH
> The length of a directory entry (32 bytes).

14.9.1.2 Function Package Directory Entry.

FPCKDIR_FUNCNAME
> The name of function or subroutine as invoked.
> Blank = ignore entry.

FPCKDIR_FUNCADDR
> The address of the entry point of the routine.
> 0 = load module from the load library specified by FPCKDIR_SYSDD.

FPCKDIR_SYSNAME
> The name of the entry point (module name in the load library).

14.9.1.3 Sample Function Package Directory.
This sample Function Package Directory contains two functions:
- FDIGIT   Linkage edit (bind) with the Function Package Directory.
- FGEDATE   Load from the ISPLLIB library.

```
IRXFUSER CSECT
         DC    CL8'IRXFPACK'       identifier
         DC    AL4(SOD-IRXFUSER)   length of header
         DC    AL4(ND)             no. of entries in directory
         DC    FL4'0'              zero
         DC    AL4(LDE)            entry length
SOD      EQU   *                   start of directory (first entry)
         DC    CL8'FDIGIT'         function name
         DC    VL4(FDIGIT)         address
         DC    FL4'0'              reserved
         DC    CL8' '              name of entry point
         DC    CL8' '              DD-name of load library
LDE      EQU   *-SOD               length of directory entry
* next entry
         DC    CL8'FGEDATE'        function name
         DC    AL4(0)              address, 0 = load from library
         DC    FL4'0'              reserved
         DC    CL8'FGEDATE'        name of entry point
         DC    CL8'ISPLLIB'        DD-name of load library
EOD      EQU   *                   end of directory
ND       EQU   (EOD-SOD)/LDE       no. of directory entries
         END
```

14.10 LOAD ROUTINE (IRXLOAD SERVICE)

The load routine (IRXLOAD) can be used in several ways:
· Load an exec into main-storage — this creates the In-storage Control Block for the exec.
· Check whether an exec is currently loaded in main-storage.
· Free an exec.
· Close the file from which execs have been loaded.

IRXLOAD is also used when the language processor environment is initialised and terminated. This book describes only the load function. Figure 14.10 illustrates the IRXLOAD service; - - indicates implicit linkage.

Entry conditions:
Register 0   The address of an Environment Block (optional).

Register 1   The address of the parameter list.

Assembler calling sequence:
```
CALL IRXLOAD,(Function,AddrExecBlock,AddrInstorageControlBlock
     [,AddrEnvBlock[,ReturnCode]]),VL
```

Function

An 8-byte character field containing the function to be performed: 'LOAD

AddrExecBlock

The address of the Exec Block (EXECBLK). The EXECBLK describes the exec to be loaded.

AddrInstorageControlBlock

The address of the allocated (and filled) In-storage Control Block (INSTBLK) is set into this address word.

AddrEnvblock

A fullword containing the address of the Environment Block (ENVBLOCK). This entry is optional; if specified it overrides register 0.
0 indicates that no ENVBLOCK is passed.

ReturnCode

A fullword that IRXLOAD sets to contain the return code, which is identical to that returned in register 15. This entry is optional.

Register 15 is returned with one of the following codes:
    0   Processing completed successfully.
  -3   The exec could not be located.
Other codes indicate a processing error.

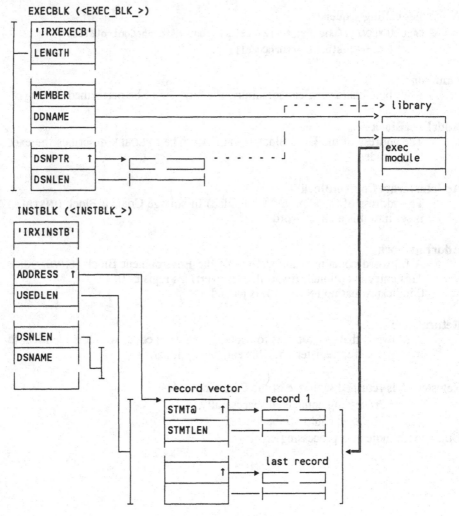

Figure 14.10 — IRXLOAD interface

14.11 INITIALISATION ROUTINE (IRXINIT SERVICE)

The initialisation routine (IRXINIT) can be used in two ways:
- Initialise a new environment.
- Obtain the address of the current Environment Block.

The first function is only used by system specialists, and so is not discussed in this book. The second function is used principally to access an error message which has been set by a service routine.

Entry conditions:
Register 0   The address of an Environment Block (optional).

Register 1   The address of the parameter list.

Return conditions:

Register 0   The address of the Environment Block; 0 indicates that the
               Environment Block could not be located.

Register 15   Return code; 0 or 4 indicates successful completion.

Assembler calling sequence:

```
CALL IRXINIT,(Function,BlankName,0,0,0,AddrEnvblock,
      ReasonCode[,AddrExtParmlist[,ReturnCode]]),VL
```

Function

The character string 'FINDENVB' indicates that the address of the current
Environment Block is to be returned.

BlankName

The string of 8 blanks indicates that no Parameter Module is to be used.

AddrEnvblock

The fullword is returned with the address of the Environment Block; the
address is also returned in register 0.

ReasonCode

The fullword is returned with the reason code for an unsuccessful
completion.

AddrExtParmlist

The address of an extended parameter list that contains the address and
length of the storage work-area. This entry is optional, if omitted or zero,
the system reserves a default work-area.

The extended parameter list consists of two paired fields. The first pair
contains the address and length, respectively, of the storage work-area.
Each field of the second pair contains -1 (X'FFFFFFFF').

ReturnCode

A fullword that IRXINIT sets to contain the return code, which is identical to
that returned in register 15. This entry is optional.

14.11.1 Sample Initialisation Program

The example (PL/I) coding retrieves the current Environment Block and displays
the error message.

```
/* Function: Display message from Environment Block */
DCL IRXINIT EXTERNAL OPTIONS(RETCODE,ASSEMBLER,INTER);
```

```
DCL 1 ENVBLOCK BASED(ADDR_ENVB),   /* REXX Environment Block */
       2 ENVBLOCK_ID CHAR(8),         /* identifier 'ENVBLOCK'*/
       2 ENVBLOCK_VERSION CHAR(4),   /* version number */
       2 ENVBLOCK_LENGTH FIXED BIN(31), /* length of ENVBLOCK */
       2 ENVBLOCK_PARMBLOCK PTR,      /* address of the PARMBLOCK */
       2 ENVBLOCK_USERFIELD PTR,     /* address of the user field */
       2 ENVBLOCK_WORKBLOK_EXT PTR, /* addr. of current WORKBLOK_EXT */
       2 ENVBLOCK_IRXEXTE PTR,        /* address of IRXEXTE */
       2 ENVBLOCK_ERROR,              /* error information */
         3 ERROR_CALL@ PTR,           /* address of the first caller */
         3 RSVR FIXED BIN(31),        /* reserved */
         3 ERROR_MSGID CHAR(8),      /* message id used by the 1st caller */
         3 PRIMARY_ERROR_MESSAGE CHAR(80), /* primary error message */
         3 ALTERNATE_ERROR_MSG CHAR(160); /* supplementary error msg */
DCL 1 ADDR_ENVB PTR;
DCL 1 RC FIXED BIN(31);
CALL IRXINIT('FINDENVB','          ',0,0,0,ADDR_ENVB,RC);
PUT SKIP LIST ('MESSAGE',PRIMARY_ERROR_MESSAGE);
```

14.12 GET RESULT (IRXRLT SERVICE)

The get result routine (IRXRLT) can be used in two ways:
· Fetch the result set by an exec invoked with the IRXEXEC service;
· Allocate an Evaluation Block of the specified size.

Entry conditions:
Register 0   The address of an Environment Block (optional).

Register 1   The address of the parameter list.

Return conditions:
Register 15   Return code.
      0   Successful completion, although the GETRLT result may have been
           truncated (if EVLEN is negative).
Other codes indicate that an error has occurred.

Assembler calling sequence:
```
CALL
IRXRLT,(Function,AddrEvalblock,DataLength[,AddrEnvblock[,RetCode]]),VL
```

Function
      The 8-character string which indicates the function to be performed.
      'GETRLT '. Obtain the result from the last exec invoked in this environment.
      This function is only valid when no exec is currently executing.

EVALBLOCK_EVLEN is set to the negative length of the result if it does not fit in the Environment Block (the return code is set to 0).

'GETRLTE '. This function is the same as GETRLT, except that nested REXX execs are supported.

'GETBLOCK'. Obtain an Evaluation Block for the current external function or subroutine. This function may only be invoked from an external function or subroutine. The current Evaluation Block is freed.

'GETEVAL '. Obtain an Evaluation Block to handle the result of a compiled exec. This function is valid only when a compiled exec is running.

AddrEvalblock

The address of the Evaluation Block to be used (for GETRLT) or returned (for GETBLOCK).

DataLength

A fullword containing the length (in bytes) of the data area in the new Evaluation Block which is to be allocated. This parameter is not used for the GETRLT and GETRLTE functions.

AddrEnvblock

The address of the Environment Block to be used. This entry is optional; if specified, it overrides register 0.

ReturnCode

A fullword in which the IRXRLT return code is placed. This entry is optional; if specified, its contents are the same as register 15.

14.12.1 Sample IRXRLT Program

This example PL/I program allocates a new Evaluation Block having a maximum data length of 800 bytes. The total length of the allocated Evaluation Block is displayed.

```
RXPPGM5: PROC OPTIONS(MAIN);
DCL IRXRLT EXTERNAL OPTIONS(RETCODE,ASSEMBLER,INTER);
DCL 1 EVALBLOCK BASED(ADDR_EVALBLOCK),
      2 EVPAD1 FIXED BIN(31),
      2 EVSIZE FIXED BIN(31),
      2 EVLEN  FIXED BIN(31),
      2 EVPAD2 FIXED BIN(31),
      2 EVDATA CHAR(1);
DCL 1 ADDR_EVALBLOCK PTR;
DCL 1 LEN FIXED BIN(31) INIT(800);
FETCH IRXRLT; /* load address of entry point */
CALL IRXRLT('GETBLOCK',ADDR_EVALBLOCK,LEN);
PUT SKIP LIST ('EVSIZE:',EVSIZE*8+16);
END;
```

14.13 CONTROL BLOCKS

This section describes the most important control blocks used by the REXX interfaces described in this chapter.

The control blocks are listed in alphabetic sequence:
· Argument List
· External Function Parameter List
· Environment Block
· Evaluation Block
· Exec Block
· In-storage Control Block
· Shared Variable (Request) Block
· Vector of External Entry Points.

14.13.1 Argument List

The Argument List describes the input arguments passed to a function. Each argument passed to the function has one Argument List entry (consisting of two words) in the Argument List. The Argument List is terminated with two words each containing binary -1 (X'F...F'). Figure 14.11 shows the mapping of the Argument List fields. The IRXARGTB macro maps the Argument List.

Displ	Field name	Type	Description
-	ARGTABLE_ENTRY	DSECT	REXX Argument Table Entry (ARGTABLE)
+0 +4	ARGTABLE_ARGSTRING_PTR ARGTABLE_ARGSTRING_LENGTH	A F	Address of the argument Length of the argument
+8	ARGTABLE_NEXT	-	Next ARGTABLE entry

Figure 14.11 — Argument List fields

ARGTABLE_ARGSTRING_PTR
   The address of the argument.

ARGTABLE_ARGSTRING_LENGTH
   The length of the argument.

14.13.2 EFPL — External Function Parameter List

The EFPL describes the external arguments for a function; the pointer to the input arguments and to the result field. The input arguments are defined in the Argument List. The result is defined in the EVALBLOCK (Evaluation Block). Figure 14.12 shows the mapping of the EFPL fields. The IRXEFPL macro maps the EFPL.

Displ	Field name	Type	Description
-	EFPL	DSECT	External Function Parameter List (EFPL)
0	EFPLCOM	A	Reserved
4	EFPLBARG	A	Reserved
8	EFPLEARG	A	Reserved
12	EFPLFB	A	Reserved
16	EFPLARG	A	Address of the Argument List
20	EFPLEVAL	A	Pointer to address of EVALBLOCK

Figure 14.12 — EFPL fields

EFPLARG

The address of the Argument List. The Argument List is a table containing the address and length of each parsed argument passed to the function.

EFPLEVAL

A pointer to a fullword containing the address of the EVALBLOCK. The EVALBLOCK contains the result returned by the function.

14.13.3 ENVBLOCK — Environment Block

The ENVBLOCK describes the REXX operating environment. An ENVBLOCK is automatically created when the REXX environment is initiated. The ENVBLOCK is principally used by the application developer to obtain error messages. Figure 14.13 shows the mapping of the ENVBLOCK. The IRXENVB macro maps the ENVBLOCK.

Displ	Field name	Type	Description
-	ENVBLOCK	DSECT	REXX Environment Block
0	ENVBLOCK_ID	CL8	'ENVBLOCK' character id
8	ENVBLOCK_VERSION	CL4	Version number
12	ENVBLOCK_LENGTH	F	Length of ENVBLOCK
16	ENVBLOCK_PARMBLOCK	A	Address of the PARMBLOCK
20	ENVBLOCK_USERFIELD	A	Address of the user field
24	ENVBLOCK_WORKBLOK_EXT	A	Address of current work-block extension
28	ENVBLOCK_IRXEXTE	A	Address of IRXEXTE
32	ENVBLOCK_ERROR	-	Error information
32	ERROR_CALL@	A	Address of error routine
36	-	F	Reserved
40	ERROR_MSGID	CL8	Message identifier (first message)
48	PRIMARY_ERROR_MESSAGE	CL80	First error message
128	ALTERNATE_ERROR_MSG	CL160	Supplementary error message
288	COMPGM	A	Address of compiler programming table
292	ATTNRTN	A	Address of attention handling routine
296	ECTPTR	A	Pointer to ECT
300	INFO	A	Bit 0 = 1 (abnormal termination)

Figure 14.13 — ENVBLOCK fields

ENVBLOCK_ID

The block identifier 'ENVBLOCK'.

ENVBLOCK_VERSION
The version number.

ENVBLOCK_LENGTH
The length of the ENVBLOCK (288 bytes).

ENVBLOCK_PARMBLOCK
The address of the PARMBLOCK.

ENVBLOCK_USERFIELD
The address of the user field.

ENVBLOCK_WORKBLOK_EXT
The address of the current WORKBLOK_EXT (Work Block extension).

ENVBLOCK_IRXEXTE
The address of IRXEXTE, the vector of external subroutine addresses.

ENVBLOCK_ERROR
The start of the error information.

ERROR_CALL@
The address of the routine that caused the error.

ERROR_MSGID
The message identifier of the first message.

PRIMARY_ERROR_MESSAGE
The first error message.

ALTERNATE_ERROR_MSG
The supplementary error message.

14.13.4 EVALBLOCK — Evaluation Block

The EVALBLOCK describes the result passed back from a function. Figure 14.14 shows the mapping of the EVALBLOCK fields. The IRXEVALB macro maps the EVALBLOCK.

EVALBLOCK_EVPAD1
Reserved — set to binary zero.

EVALBLOCK_EVSIZE
The size of EVALBLOCK (in double words, 8-byte units).

EVALBLOCK_EVLEN

The length of the data. This value is set to the negative length if the data do not fit in the Evaluation Block. The maximum length of the data which can be stored in the EVALBLOCK is EVALBLOCK_EVSIZE*8-16 bytes.

EVALBLOCK_EVPAD2

Reserved — set to binary zero.

EVALBLOCK_EVDATA

The start of the data. The IRXRLT (Get Result) routine can be used to retrieve the complete result, even if it cannot be stored in the EVALBLOCK, or to allocate a new Evaluation Block of the required size.

Displ	Field name	Type	Description
-	EVALBLOCK	DSECT	REXX Evaluation Block (EVALBLOCK)
0	EVALBLOCK_EVPAD1	F	Reserved - set to binary zero
4	EVALBLOCK_EVSIZE	F	Size of EVALBLOCK (in double words)
8	EVALBLOCK_EVLEN	F	Length of data
12	EVALBLOCK_EVPAD2	F	Reserved - set to binary zero
16	EVALBLOCK_EVDATA	0C	Start of data

Figure 14.14 — EVALBLOCK fields

14.13.5 EXECBLK — Exec Block

The EXECBLK describes an external exec. Figure 14.15 shows the mapping of the EXECBLK fields. The IRXEXECB macro maps the EXECBLK.

Displ	Field name	Type	Description
-	EXECBLK	DSECT	REXX EXEC Block (EXECBLK)
0	EXEC_BLK_ACRYN	CL8	Block identifier 'IRXEXECB'
8	EXEC_BLK_LENGTH	F	Length of EXECBLK
12	-	F	Reserved
16	EXEC_MEMBER	CL8	Member name of exec.
24	EXEC_DDNAME	CL8	DD name for the dataset
32	EXEC_SUBCOM	CL8	Initial subcommand environment name
40	EXEC_DSNPTR	A	Address of PARSE SOURCE dataset name
44	EXEC_DSNLEN	F	Length of EXEC_DSNPTR dataset name
-	EXECBLEN	EQU	Length of EXECBLK

Figure 14.15 — EXECBLK fields

EXEC_BLK_ACRYN

The block identifier 'IRXEXECB'.

EXEC_BLK_LENGTH

The length of EXECBLK (48 bytes).

EXEC_MEMBER
The member name of the exec, if partitioned dataset; blank if sequential dataset.

EXEC_DDNAME
The DD name for the dataset from which the exec is to be loaded ('LOAD') or to be closed ('CLOSEDD'). This entry is not used if an INSTBLK has been defined.

Blank means that the exec is loaded from the file defined by the LOADDD entry in the Module Name table — default is SYSEXEC.

EXEC_SUBCOM
The name of the initial subcommand environment.

EXEC_DSNPTR
The address of the dataset name to be returned by the PARSE SOURCE instruction; the dataset name may specify a member name within parentheses.

0 = no entry.

EXEC_DSNLEN
The normalised length of dataset name pointed to by EXEC_DSNPTR.

0 = no entry.

14.13.6 INSTBLK — In-Storage Control Block

The INSTBLK describes (address and length) the individual records (lines) of a REXX exec contained in main-storage. The IRXLOAD service can be used to build the INSTBLK. Figure 14.16 shows the mapping of the INSTBLK fields. The IRXINSTB macro maps the INSTBLK.

INSTBLK_HEADER (In-storage Block Header):

INSTBLK_ACRONYM
The block identifier 'IRXINSTB'

INSTBLK_HDRLEN
The length of the INSTBLK header (128 bytes).

INSTBLK_ADDRESS
The address of the first INSTBLK entry.

INSTBLK_USEDLEN
The total length of the INSTBLK entries. The number of entries (rows in the REXX exec) can be determined by dividing this total length by the size of each entry (= 8).

INSTBLK_MEMBER

The name of member of the partitioned dataset from which the exec was loaded — blank if loaded from a sequential dataset.

INSTBLK_DDNAME

The name of the DD statement which identifies the dataset from which the exec was loaded.

Displ	Field name	Type	Description
-	INSTBLK	DSECT	REXX In-storage Control Block
0	INSTBLK_HEADER	-	In-storage Block Header
0	INSTBLK_ACRONYM	CL8	Block identifier 'IRXINSTB'
8	INSTBLK_HDRLEN	F	Length of INSTBLK header
12	-	F	Reserved
16	INSTBLK_ADDRESS	A	Address of first INSTBLK_ENTRY
20	INSTBLK_USEDLEN	F	Total length of INSTBLK_ENTRYs
24	INSTBLK_MEMBER	CL8	Member name of loaded exec
32	INSTBLK_DDNAME	CL8	DD-name of dataset of loaded exec
40	INSTBLK_SUBCOM	CL8	Name of subcommand environment
48	-	F	Reserved
52	INSTBLK_DSNLEN	F	Length of dataset name
56	INSTBLK_DSNAME	CL54	Dataset name
-	INSTBLK_ENTRY	DSECT	REXX In-storage Block Entry
+0	INSTBLK_STMT@	A	Address of REXX statement
+4	INSTBLK_STMTLEN	F	Length of REXX statement

Figure 14.16 — INSTBLK fields

INSTBLK_SUBCOM

The name of the initial subcommand environment under which exec is run.

INSTBLK_DSNLEN

The normalised length of the dataset name (INSTBLK_DSNAME). The normalised length is the length excluding blanks.

INSTBLK_DSNAME

The dataset name from which the exec was loaded.

INSTBLK_ENTRIES

The start of the array of INSTBLK (data) entries. The INSTBLK_ENTRY DSECT maps each INSTBLK entry.

INSTBLK_STMT@

The address of the REXX statement in main-storage.

INSTBLK_STMTLEN

The length of the REXX statement.

14.13.7 SHVBLOCK — Shared Variable (Request) Block

The SHVBLOCK describes the variable to be accessed from the variable pool. SHVBLOCKs can be chained together. Figure 14.17 shows the mapping of the SHVBLOCK fields. The IRXSHVB macro maps the SHVBLOCK.

Displ	Field name	Type	Description
-	SHVBLOCK	DSECT	REXX Shared Variable Request Block
0	SHVNEXT	A	Address of next SHVBLOCK in chain.
4	SHVUSER	F	Used during "FIND NEXT" processing
8	SHVCODE	CL1	Function type
9	SHVRET	XL1	Return code flags
10	-	H	Reserved
12	SHVBUFL	F	Length of the fetch value buffer
16	SHVNAMA	A	Address of the variable name
20	SHVNAML	F	Length of the variable name
24	SHVVALA	A	Address of the data value
28	SHVVALL	F	Length of the data value

Figure 14.17 — SHVBLOCK fields

SHVNEXT

The address of the next SHVBLOCK in the chain. 0 = end of chain.

SHVUSER

This entry is used during "FIND NEXT" processing to contain the length of the buffer pointed to by SHVNAMA. The actual length of the fetched name is returned in SHVNAML.

SHVCODE

The function type:

'D' (SHVDROPV)	Drop variable
'd' (SHVSYDRO)	Drop symbolic name
'F' (SHVFETCH)	Copy value of shared variable
'f' (SHVSYFET)	Retrieve symbolic name
'N' (SHVNEXTV)	Fetch "next" variable (the repetitive use of this function retrieves successive variables)
'P' (SHVPRIV)	Fetch private information (see Note)
's' (SHVSTORE)	Store value for variable
's' (SHVSYSET)	Set symbolic name.

The parenthesised name is the EQU-name defined by the IRXSHVB macro.

Note: The variable name is interpreted as being a symbol for lowercase function codes. The usual REXX rules apply for symbolic names, i.e. the contents of the symbolic name to which SHVNAMA points are used as the variable name, or the symbolic name itself, if the named variable does not exist.

For example, if the REXX variable VN contains USERVAR, the following PL/I program statements will set USERVAR to ALPHA.

```
DCL VARNAME CHAR(8) INIT('VN');
DCL VARDATA CHAR(5) INIT('ALPHA');
SHVNAMA = ADDR(VARNAME);
SHVNAML = 2;
SHVVALA = ADDR(VARDATA);
SHVVALL = 5;
SHVSTORE = 's';
```

SHVRET
Return code flags:

X'00' (SHVCLEAN)   Execution completed successfully.
X'01' (SHVNEWV)   Variable did not exist.
X'02' (SHVLVAR)   Last variable transferred ("N" processing):
   X'04' (SHVTRUNC) — truncation occurred ("F" processing);
   X'08' (SHVBADN) — invalid variable name;
   X'10' (SHVBADV) — invalid value specified;
   X'80' (SHVBADF) — invalid function code (SHVCODE).

The parenthesised name is the EQU-name defined by the IRXSHVB macro.

SHVBUFL
The length of the value buffer (SHVVALA) used for fetch processing. The actual length of the fetched data is returned in SHVVALL.

SHVNAMA
The address of the variable name.

SHVNAML
The normalised length (without blanks) of the left-justified variable name.

SHVVALA
The address of the data value. The data are usually in character format.

SHVVALL
The length of the data value.

Note: Certain REXX internal data areas can be returned as private information. The following names can be used to obtain private information (which corresponds to some entries that can be obtained with the PARSE instruction):

ARG   The argument passed to the invoking exec
SOURCE   The current program source
VERSION   The current REXX version.

14.13.8 VEEP — Vector of External Entry Points

The VEEP contains the addresses of the external REXX service routines — both standard and replaceable routines. Figure 14.18 shows the mapping of the standard VEEP fields; the addresses of the replaceable routines have been omitted. The IRXEXTE macro maps the VEEP.

Displ	Field name	Type	Description
-	IRXEXTE	DSECT	REXX Vector of External Entry Points (VEEP)
0	IRXEXTE_ENTRY_COUNT	F	Number of entry points in the VEEP (=20)
4	IRXINIT	A	IRXINIT - initialisation routine
12	IRXLOAD	A	IRXLOAD - load exec routine
16	IRXEXCOM	A	IRXEXCOM - variable access routine
20	IRXEXEC	A	IRXEXEC - run exec routine
28	IRXINOUT	A	IRXINOUT - Input/Output routine
32	IRXJCL	A	IRXJCL - run JCL routine
36	IRXRLT	A	IRXRLT - get result routine
44	IRXSTK	A	IRXSTK - data stack processing routine
48	IRXSUBCM	A	IRXSUBCM - subcommand service routine
52	IRXTERM	A	IRXTERM - termination routine
56	IRXIC	A	IRXIC - immediate commands routine
64	IRXMSGID	A	IRXMSGID - message routine
72	IRXUID	A	IRXUID - userid routine
76	IRXTERMA	A	IRXTERMA - abnormal termination routine

Figure 14.18 - Vector of External Entry Points fields

IRXEXTE_ENTRY_COUNT
> The number of entry points in the VEEP (=20).

IRXINIT
> The address of the IRXINIT initialisation routine.

IRXLOAD
> The address of the IRXLOAD load exec routine.

IRXEXCOM
> The address of the IRXEXCOM variable access routine.

IRXEXEC
> The address of the IRXEXEC run exec routine.

IRXJCL
> The address of the IRXJCL run JCL routine.

IRXRLT
> The address of the IRXRLT get result routine.

IRXSTK
> The address of the IRXSTK data stack processing routine.

IRXSUBCM
The address of the IRXSUBCM subcommand service routine.

14.14 EXAMPLES

The sample FCONCAT function concatenates the passed arguments. The number of arguments is variable. The result is returned both as function result and as variable CONCAT.

For example

```
frv = FCONCAT(1,234);
SAY frv 'CONCAT:'CONCAT; /* 1234 CONCAT:1234 */
```

Coding for this sample function is shown in Assembler, C, COBOL and PL/I. These sample programs make certain assumptions in order to simplify the coding:
·   For Assembler, the length of an individual argument cannot exceed 256 bytes.
·   The maximum number of arguments for COBOL and PL/I is 10. Because the address of the argument list is used, this limit is arbitrary and has no affect on the overall program size.
·   No check is made as to whether the result fits in the EVALBLOCK.

14.14.1 Assembler Implementation

```
AFUNCT   CSECT
AFUNCT   AMODE 31
AFUNCT   RMODE 24
         BAKR  14,0                      save registers and return address
         BASR  12,0                      set base register
         USING *,12
         LA    13,SA
         USING EFPL,1
         L     2,EFPLEVAL                PTR(Evaluation Block)
         L     11,0(2)                   A(Evaluation Block)
         USING EVALBLOCK,11
         L     10,EFPLARG                A(parsed Argument List)
         USING ARGTABLE_ENTRY,10
         LA    9,EVALBLOCK_EVDATA        A(result)
         LA    8,0                       L(result)
NEXTPARM LM    3,4,ARGTABLE_ARGSTRING_PTR
* R3: A(argument)
* R4: L(argument)
         LTR   4,4
         BM    LASTPARM                  negative length (=last parameter)
         SH    4,=H'1'                   LengthCode(argument)
         EX    4,EXMOVE                  move argument
```

```
              LA    8,1(4,8)                    update length accumulator
              LA    9,1(4,9)                    update pointer
              LA    10,ARGTABLE_NEXT-ARGTABLE_ENTRY(10) next argument
              B     NEXTPARM                    get next argument
LASTPARM ST         8,EVALBLOCK_EVLEN           entry size
* set data into REXX variable
              LA    7,IRX_SHVBLOCK
              USING SHVBLOCK,7                   address SHVBLOCK
              MVC   SHVNAMA,=A(VARNAME)          A(variable name)
              MVC   SHVNAML,=A(6)               L(variable name)
              LA    9,EVALBLOCK_EVDATA          A(result)
              ST    9,SHVVALA
              ST    8,SHVVALL
              MVI   SHVCODE,SHVSTORE            set STORE function-code
              LOAD  EP=IRXEXCOM                  load IRXEXCOM
              LTR   15,0                         entry-point address
              BZ    EOJ                          load error
              CALL  (15),(IRX_IRXEXCOM,0,0,IRX_SHVBLOCK),VL
              LA    15,0                         set zero return code
EOJ      PR   ,                                  return
SA       DS   18F                                save-area
EXMOVE   MVC  0(0,9),0(3)
* data areas
VARNAME  DC   CL8'CONCAT'                        variable name
IRX_IRXEXCOM DC CL8'IRXEXCOM'
         DS   0A                                 align
IRX_SHVBLOCK DC (SHVBLEN)X'0'
* DSECTs
         IRXEFPL
         IRXEVALB
         IRXARGTB
         IRXSHVB
         END
```

14.14.2 C Implementation

```c
#pragma environment(cfunct)
#include <stdlib.h>
#include <stdio.h>
#include <string.h>
#include <spc.h>


/* function prototype */
int setvar(char *vn, char *vd);
```

```
struct arglist { /* Argument List */
  char *argstring_ptr;
  int argstring_length;
} *parglist;

struct evalblock { /* Evaluation Block */
  int evpad1;
  int evsize;
  int evlen;
  int evpad2;
  char evdata[1];
} *pevalblock, **ppevalblock;

struct parm { /* External Function Parameter List */
  char *efplcom;
  char *efplbarg;
  char *efplearg;
  char *efplfb;
  struct arglist *efplarg;
  struct evalblock **efpleval;
} *pparm;

struct envblock { /* Environment Block */
  char envblock_id[8];
  char envblock_version[4];
  int envblock_length;
  void *envblock_parmblock;
  void *envblock_userfield;
  void *envblock_workblok_ext;
  struct irxexte *envblock_irxexte;
  /* + additional fields */
} *penvblock;

struct irxexte { /* External Entry Points */
  int irxexte_entry_count;
  void *irxinit;
  void *load_routine;
  void *irxload;
  void *irxexcom;
  void *irxexec;
  void *io_routine;
  void *irxinout;
  void *irxjcl;
```

```
  void *irxrlt;
  void *stack_routine;
  void *irxstk;
  /* + additional infrequently-used routines */
} *pirxexte;

int cfunct()
{
  /* execution code */
  /* get registers on entry */
  penvblock = (void*)edcxregs(0); /* GPR 0 */
  pparm = (void*)edcxregs(1); /* GPR 1 */
  /* get VEEP */
  pirxexte = penvblock->envblock_irxexte;
  /* get Argument List */
  parglist = (void*)pparm->efplarg;
  /* get Evaluation Block */
  ppevalblock = pparm->efpleval;
  pevalblock = *ppevalblock;
  /* initialise result */
  memset(pevalblock->evdata,0x00,1);
  /* process arguments */
  for (;;parglist++) {
    int len;
    len = parglist->argstring_length;
    if (len < 0) break; /* end of argument list */
    strncat(pevalblock->evdata,parglist->argstring_ptr,len);
  }
  /* set variable */
  setvar("CONCAT",pevalblock->evdata);
  /* return result length */
  pevalblock->evlen = strlen(pevalblock->evdata);
  return 0; /* function return code */
}

#pragma linkage (OSFUNC,OS)
#pragma linkage (RXLOAD,OS)
typedef int OSFUNC();

int setvar(char *vn, char *vd)
{
  OSFUNC * fptr;
  int rc;
```

```
struct shvblock { /* Shared Variable Request Block */
struct shvblock *shvnext; /* pointer to next shvblock */
int shvuser; /* "fetch next": length of the name buffer */
char shvcode; /* function code - type of variable access request */
unsigned int shvret :8; /* return codes */
short shvrsv; /* reserved */
int shvbufl; /* length of fetch value buffer */
char *shvnama; /* address of variable name */
int shvnaml; /* length of variable name */
char *shvvala; /* address of value buffer */
int shvvall; /* length of value buffer */
} sb;

char dummy_parm;

/* execution code */
fptr = (OSFUNC *)pirxexte->irxexcom;
if (fptr == NULL) {
  puts("fetch error");
  exit(4);
}
sb.shvnext = NULL; /* pointer to next shvblock */
sb.shvnama = vn;
sb.shvnaml = strlen(vn); /* set name length */
sb.shvvala = vd;
sb.shvvall = strlen(vd); /* set data length */
sb.shvcode = 'S'; /* function code */
rc = (*fptr)("IRXEXCOM",&dummy_parm,&dummy_parm,&sb);
if (rc != 0)
  printf(" %x",sb.shvret); /* return code */
return rc;
}
```

Note: If a user-specific PGMLOAD function were used, the following statement
```
fptr = (OSFUNC *)PGMLOAD("IRXEXCOM");
```
would replace
```
fptr = (OSFUNC *)pirxexte->irxexcom;
```

14.14.2.1 PGMLOAD Program. For programs where the IRXEXTE control block is not available, a user-written C-callable function (e.g. PGMLOAD) can be invoked to load the specified program function. PGMLOAD returns the address of the loaded function; zero indicates that the function could not be loaded.

```
PGMLOAD   CSECT
PGMLOAD   AMODE 31
          EDCPRLG USRDSAL=8     prologue
          USING WKDSECT,13
* Entry conditions:
* R1: A(program name pointer)
* Exit conditions:
* R15: program entry point (with AMODE); 0 = program not loaded.
          L     1,0(1)          address of the program name
          MVC   PROGNAME,0(1)   move program name from stack
          LA    0,PROGNAME
          LOAD  EPLOC=(0)       load program
          LR    15,0            entry-point address
          EDCEPIL ,             epilogue
WKDSECT   EDCDSAD ,             working-storage
PROGNAME  DS    CL8
          END
```

14.14.3 COBOL Implementation

```
IDENTIFICATION DIVISION.
PROGRAM-ID. BFUNCT.
DATA DIVISION.
WORKING-STORAGE SECTION.
01 I PIC S9(9) COMP.
01 J PIC S9(9) COMP.
01 K PIC S9(9) COMP VALUE 1.
*
01 VARNAME PIC X(8) VALUE 'CONCAT'.
01 DUMMY-PARM PIC X(4).
*
01 SHVBLOCK.
   02 SHVNEXT PIC S9(9) COMP VALUE 0.
   02 SHVUSER PIC S9(9) COMP.
   02 SHVCODE PIC X(1).
   02 SHVRET  PIC X(1).
   02         PIC X(2).
   02 SHVBUFL PIC S9(9) COMP.
   02 SHVNAMA POINTER.
```

```
        02 SHVNAML PIC S9(9) COMP.
        02 SHVVALA POINTER.
        02 SHVVALL PIC S9(9) COMP.
    LINKAGE SECTION.
    01 EFPLCOM  PIC X(4).
    01 EFPLBARG PIC X(4).
    01 EFPLEARG PIC X(4).
    01 EFPLFB   PIC X(4).
    01 EFPLARG.
        02  ARGTABLE-ENTRY OCCURS 10.
          03 ARGSTRING-PTR POINTER.
          03 ARGSTRING-LENGTH PIC S9(9) COMP.
    01 EFPLEVAL POINTER.
    01 ARGSTRING.
        02 ARGSTRING-CHAR OCCURS 256.
          03 ARGSTRING-SINGLE-CHAR PIC X(1).
    01 EVALBLOCK.
        02 EVALBLOCK-EVPAD1 PIC X(4).
        02 EVALBLOCK-EVSIZE PIC S9(9) COMP.
        02 EVALBLOCK-EVLEN  PIC S9(9) COMP.
        02 EVALBLOCK-EVPAD2 PIC X(4).
        02 EVALBLOCK-EVDATA.
          03 RESULT-ENTRY OCCURS 256.
            04 RESULT-CHAR PIC X(1).
    PROCEDURE DIVISION
        USING
          EFPLCOM EFPLBARG EFPLEARG EFPLFB EFPLARG EFPLEVAL.
*       Get next Argument List entry
        DISPLAY 'BFUNCT'
        SET ADDRESS OF EVALBLOCK TO EFPLEVAL
        PERFORM
        VARYING I FROM 1 BY 1
        UNTIL ARGSTRING-LENGTH(I) = -1
          SET ADDRESS OF ARGSTRING TO ARGSTRING-PTR(I)
*         Concatenate result
          PERFORM
            VARYING J FROM 1 BY 1
            UNTIL J > ARGSTRING-LENGTH(I)
              MOVE ARGSTRING-SINGLE-CHAR(J) TO RESULT-CHAR(K)
              ADD 1 TO K
          END-PERFORM
        END-PERFORM
        MOVE K TO EVALBLOCK-EVLEN
*       Set REXX variable
```

```
            MOVE 'S' TO SHVCODE
            CALL 'SETPTR' USING VARNAME SHVNAMA
            MOVE 6 TO SHVNAML
            CALL 'SETPTR' USING EVALBLOCK-EVDATA SHVVALA
            MOVE K TO SHVVALL
            CALL 'IRXEXCOM' USING BY CONTENT 'IRXEXCOM'
              BY REFERENCE DUMMY-PARM DUMMY-PARM SHVBLOCK
            STOP RUN.
    * Subprogram to set pointer
     IDENTIFICATION DIVISION.
     PROGRAM-ID. SETPTR.
     DATA DIVISION.
     LINKAGE SECTION.
     01 PARMDATA PIC X(8).
     01 PARMPTR POINTER.
     PROCEDURE DIVISION
         USING PARMDATA PARMPTR.
         SET  PARMPTR TO  ADDRESS OF PARMDATA
         GOBACK.
       END PROGRAM SETPTR.
     END PROGRAM BFUNCT.
```

14.14.4 PL/I Implementation

```
PFUNCT: PROC(EFPLCOM,EFPLBARG,EFPLEARG,
 EFPLFB,EFPLARG,EFPLEVAL) OPTIONS(MAIN,NOEXECOPS);
DCL IRXEXCOM EXTERNAL OPTIONS(RETCODE,INTER,ASSEMBLER);
DCL PLIRETV BUILTIN;
/* declarations */
DCL 1 EFPLCOM FIXED BIN(31); /* reserved */
DCL 1 EFPLBARG FIXED BIN(31); /* reserved */
DCL 1 EFPLEARG FIXED BIN(31); /* reserved */
DCL 1 EFPLFB FIXED BIN(31);   /* reserved */
DCL 1 ARGTABLE BASED(P),
      2 ARGTABLE_ENTRY(10),
        3 ARGSTRING_PTR PTR, /* address of argument */
        3 ARGSTRING_LENGTH FIXED BIN(31); /* length of argument */
DCL 1 EFPLEVAL PTR; /* pointer to address of EVALBLOCK */
DCL 1 EVALBLOCK BASED(EFPLEVAL),
      2 EVALBLOCK_EVPAD1 FIXED BIN(31),
      2 EVALBLOCK_EVSIZE FIXED BIN(31),
      2 EVALBLOCK_EVLEN FIXED BIN(31),
      2 EVALBLOCK_EVPAD2 FIXED BIN(31),
      2 EVALBLOCK_EVDATA CHAR(256);
```

```
      DCL 1 SHVBLOCK UNALIGNED,
           2 SHVNEXT FIXED BIN(31) INIT(0),
           2 SHVUSER FIXED BIN(31) INIT(0),
           2 SHVCODE CHAR(1),
           2 SHVRET CHAR(1),
           2 FILLER CHAR(2),
           2 SHVBUFL FIXED BIN(31),
           2 SHVNAMA PTR,
           2 SHVNAML FIXED BIN(31),
           2 SHVVALA PTR,
           2 SHVVALL FIXED BIN(31);
      DCL 1 ARGSTRING CHAR(256) BASED(ARGSTRING_PTR(I));
      DCL 1 RESULT CHAR(256) BASED(ADDR_EVDATA); /* result data */
      DCL 1 P PTR;
      DCL 1 ADDR_EVDATA PTR;
      DCL 1 I FIXED BIN(31);
      DCL 1 J FIXED BIN(31);
      DCL 1 K FIXED BIN(31) INIT(1);
      DCL 1 VARNAME CHAR(8) INIT('CONCAT');
      /* execution code */
      ADDR_EVDATA = ADDR(EVALBLOCK_EVDATA);
      P = ADDR(EFPLARG);
      DO I = 1 BY 1 WHILE(ARGSTRING_LENGTH(I) > 0);
        J = ARGSTRING_LENGTH(I);
        SUBSTR(RESULT,K,J) = SUBSTR(ARGSTRING,1,J);
        K = K + J;
      END;
      PUT SKIP LIST ('RESULT',SUBSTR(RESULT,1,K));
      EVALBLOCK_EVLEN = K;
      /* set CONCAT variable */
      SHVCODE = 'S';
      SHVNAMA = ADDR(VARNAME);
      SHVNAML = 6; /* length of name */
      SHVVALA = ADDR(EVALBLOCK_EVDATA);
      SHVVALL = K; /* length of data */
      FETCH IRXEXCOM; /* load address of entry point */
      CALL IRXEXCOM('IRXEXCOM',DUMMY,DUMMY,SHVBLOCK);
      IF PLIRETV > 0 THEN
        PUT SKIP LIST('IRXEXCOM:',PLIRETV);
      END;
```

15

Worked Examples
So on we worked, and waited for the light,
And went without meat, and cursed the bread;

Richard Cory

Edwin Arlington Robison

15.1 INTRODUCTION

This chapter contains five worked examples:
- The first example uses components belonging to the standard REXX implementation.
- The second example uses standard REXX components to implement a simple VSAM interface.
- The third example uses extensions from the TSO implementation, although equivalent features are available in most implementations.
- The fourth example is a user-written command processor. This command processor program illustrates most of the techniques used in programs that utilise REXX services.
- The fifth example is a programmed version of the REXX function shown in Section 10.3.2.

These worked examples can be used in two ways:
- as an exercise with which the reader can test his knowledge and understanding of REXX;
- as annotated examples showing the use of REXX in different environments.

Each example is introduced by a specification explaining the exercise to be solved.

15.2 WORKED EXAMPLE 1

This example uses components belonging to the standard REXX implementation. Few non-trivial REXX execs make use of components belonging only to the standard implementation, components from the host environment normally will also be required.

Example 1 uses a subset of REXX to implement additional features. Although this would not be done in practice, the implemented features are themselves part of the standard implementation, it serves as a good example of how the various components fit together.

15.2.1 Specification

Aim: Positive integer multiplication or division of two numbers input on the terminal is to be performed using repeated addition or subtraction, as appropriate.

Multiplication is done by repeated addition; the multiplicand (first operand) is added to itself the number of times specified by the multiplicator (second operand).

Division is done by repeated subtraction; the divisor (second operand) is repeatedly subtracted from the dividend (first operand), which then yields the new dividend, until this new dividend is less than the divisor - the integer quotient is the number of iterations performed. The individual steps follow.

· Display the message: `"enter operand operator (* or /) operand"`.

· The first operand is to be processed using the second operand according to the specified operation (* represents multiplication, / represents division).
For example, 7 / 2 would divide 7 by 2 and yield the result 3.

· The non-rounded integer result is to be displayed. The result of a division is to be prefixed with the word "quotient".

· The operator is to be checked for validity, i.e. the message `"invalid operator"` is displayed if the operator is neither "*" nor "/".

· The operands are to be checked for validity, i.e. the message `"invalid operand"` (together with the operand in error) is displayed if an operand is non-numeric or the divisor is zero.

· Processing is terminated if an error is encountered.

· Procedures are to be used for the multiplication and division operations. Subroutines are to be used where possible.

15.2.2 Implementation

REXX exec:

```
1       /* REXX */
2       SAY "enter operand operator (* or /) operand";
```

```
3       PARSE PULL operand1 operator operand2

4        CALL CheckOperands;

5       SELECT

6         WHEN operator = '*'

            THEN CALL Multiplication;

7         WHEN operator = '/'

             THEN CALL Division;

8         OTHERWISE

            SAY "invalid operator";

9       END;

10      EXIT;

11      CheckOperands:

12        IF \DATATYPE(operand1,'N') THEN CALL ErrorExit 1;

13        IF \DATATYPE(operand2,'N') THEN CALL ErrorExit 2;

14        RETURN;

15      ErrorExit:

16        SAY "invalid operand" ARG(1);

17        EXIT;

18      Multiplication: PROCEDURE EXPOSE operand1 operand2

19        result = 0;

20        DO i = 1 TO operand2;

21          result = result+operand1;

22        END;

23        SAY result;

24        RETURN;

25      Division: PROCEDURE EXPOSE operand1 operand2

26        IF operand2 <= 0 THEN CALL ErrorExit "divisor";

27        n = 0;

28        result = operand1;

29        DO WHILE result >= operand2;

30          n = n + 1;

31          result = result-operand2;

32        END;

33        SAY "quotient" n;

34        RETURN;
```

Explanation:

1   Comment containing the word REXX must be the first statement of a REXX exec.

2   Display prompting message to enter input.

3   Obtain the two operands and the operator from the terminal. The operands are assigned to the variables operand1 and operand2, respectively. The operator is assigned to the variable operator.

4   The subroutine CheckOperands is called to validate the operands.

5   Introduce a SELECT-block to validate the operator and to pass control to the appropriate procedure, if the operator is valid.

6   Pass control to the Multiplication procedure if the operator is "*".

7   Pass control to the Division procedure if the operator is "/".

8   Introduce the processing to be performed if the operator is neither "*" nor "/" - the "invalid operator" message is displayed.

9   Terminate the SELECT-block and the OTHERWISE clause.

10   Terminate the exec.

11   Introduce the CheckOperands subroutine.

12   Call ErrorExit with parameter 1 if operand1 is not numeric. The DATATYPE function with parameter 'N' returns 0 if the specified variable is numeric. The result is negated, i.e. the returned value changed from 0 to 1, and vice versa, i.e. the value is now either 1 (true) or 0 (false).

13   Call ErrorExit with parameter 2 if OPERAND2 is not numeric.

14   Return to point of invocation if the operand validity checks are satisfied.

15   Introduce the ErrorExit subroutine.

16   Display the "invalid operand" message with the corresponding operand number (1 or 2), respectively.

17   Terminate the exec.

18   Introduce the Multiplication procedure; OPERAND1 and OPERAND2 are exposed, i.e. global variables.

19   Initialise the RESULT work-field.

20   Introduce the DO-loop which performs the number of iterations specified by OPERAND2.

21   Each iteration adds OPERAND1 to a running-counter (RESULT).

22   Terminate the DO-loop. OPERAND1 has been added to itself OPERAND2 times, this accumulation product is in the variable RESULT.

23   Display the result (equivalent to the multiplication of OPERAND1 by OPERAND2).

24   Return to the point of invocation.

25   Introduce the Division procedure.

26   Call ErrorExit with parameter "divisor" if OPERAND2 is either zero or negative.

27   Initialise the N work-field.

28   Initialise the RESULT work-field with OPERAND1.

29   Perform a DO-loop which is terminated when RESULT (the remainder) is smaller than the divisor (OPERAND2); the WHILE condition must be used so that the condition can be checked before each cycle.

30   Increment N (the quotient) for each iteration.

31   Subtract the divisor (OPERAND2) from the remainder (RESULT).

32   Terminate the DO-loop.

33   Display the text "quotient" with the calculated quotient (N).

34   Return to the point of invocation.

15.3 WORKED EXAMPLE 2

This example uses standard TSO components to implement a simple VSAM interface. Although standard REXX cannot process VSAM datasets, a simple VSAM interface can be implemented by using the IDCAMS utility to write VSAM records to a QSAM dataset that the REXX EXECIO host command can process.

A selection from a keyed VSAM dataset is written to a temporary sequential file, the records of which are subsequently read into REXX stem variables, i.e. the original VSAM records are made available as REXX variables.

This example shows how standard components can be used to extend the REXX facilities. In addition, run-time error checking is included to detect processing errors.

Note: Example 4 shows a REXX VSAM interface written in COBOL.

15.3.1 Specification

The name of a keyed VSAM dataset and the access key are specified as parameters. Because the REPRO service does not allow selection operations (for example, EQUAL), an equivalent key range (from-key, to-key) must be created. For simplicity, the VSAM records are read into REXX stem variables and listed.

Sample invocation:

```
CALL EX142 "TEST.VSAM", "alpha";
```
The records with generic key alpha are to be listed from the user's TEST.VSAM dataset.

15.3.2 Implementation

REXX exec:

```
1       /* REXX */
2       IF ARG() <> 2 THEN DO;
          SAY "Invalid parameters";
          EXIT;
        END;
3       PARSE ARG dsn, key;
4       ADDRESS TSO;
5       SIGNAL ON ERROR; /* enable ERROR trapping */
6       "ALLOC F(SYSPRINT) DUMMY REUS";
        "ALLOC F(VSAMFILE) DA("dsn") SHR REUS";
        "ALLOC F(TEMPFILE) NEW REUS RECFM(V) BLKSIZE(32760)";
7       SIGNAL OFF ERROR; /* disable ERROR trapping */
8       hexkey = C2X(key);
        fkey = "X'"hexkey"'"; /* from-key */
        tkey = LEFT(key,255,'FF'X);
        hexkey = C2X(tkey);
        tkey = "X'"hexkey"'"; /* to-key */
9       CALL OUTTRAP 'msg.','*','NOCONCAT'; /* trap messages */
10      "REPRO INFILE(VSAMFILE)",
            "OUTFILE(TEMPFILE)",
            "FROMKEY("fkey")",
            "TOKEY("tkey")";
11      IF RC > 0
          THEN DO i = 1 TO msg.0; /* error */
            SAY msg.i; /* display error messages */
          END;
          ELSE DO; /* REPRO OK */
12        "EXECIO * DISKR TEMPFILE (STEM record. FINIS";
13          IF RC = 0 THEN DO;
              SAY record.0 'record(s) processed';
              DO  i = 1 TO record.0;
                SAY i record.i; /* display the records */
              END;
```

```
            END;
          END;
14        CALL OUTTRAP 'OFF'; /* disable message trapping */
          EXIT;
15        ERROR:
          SAY "Allocation error" SOURCELINE(SIGL)
          EXIT;
```

Explanation:

1   Comment containing the word REXX must be the first statement of a REXX exec, if the exec is not in an exclusive REXX library.

2   Validate that only two invocation arguments have been specified.

3   Accept the dataset name and selection key as invocation arguments.

4   Set TSO as the default command environment. In this example, it is not necessary to explicitly set the command environment, as the exec can only run in TSO.

5   Enable error trapping in case a command error occurs.

6   Allocate the files that REPRO (and EXECIO) require. ALLOC is a TSO command.

7   Disable error trapping.

8   Convert the specified key to its equivalent hexadecimal value. The from-key (FKEY) has the specified value. The to-key (TKEY) is formed by suffixing 'FF'X's to the from-key. This conversion to hexadecimal stops the TSO REPRO service from its automatic translation of lowercase arguments into uppercase.

9   Trap any command messages. The asterisk (*) specifies that there is no limit to the number of messages that will be trapped. NOCONCAT specifies that any previously trapped messages will be discarded, i.e. any trapped messages apply only to the subsequent commands.

10 Invoke the REPRO IDCAMS service to copy the input VSAM dataset onto a temporary output (sequential) file.

11 Display the trapped error messages if REPRO signals an error.

12 If REPRO processed correctly, invoke the EXECIO host command to read the REPRO output file into the RECORD. stem variables.

13 Display the number of read records and the individual records.

14 Disable message trapping.

15 The error processing routine is invoked if an allocation error occurs. The "Allocation error" text is prefixed to the command that caused the error condition.

15.4 WORKED EXAMPLE 3

This is a more advanced example that makes use of REXX commands (EXECIO - read a dataset), TSO commands (ALLOC - allocate a dataset), and ISPF Dialog Manager services (DISPLAY - display a panel).

15.4.1 Specification

Aim: The contents of a dataset are to be displayed using panel RXPAN. Marked words in the display are to be converted from lowercase to uppercase, and vice versa. A word (in this context) is a series of characters delimited by one or more non-alphanumeric characters. A word is marked by placing the cursor somewhere in the word. The conversion function is selected by pressing either the PF5 key (convert to lowercase) or PF6 (convert to uppercase). The solution is simplified by not allowing vertical scrolling.

The name of the dataset to be processed is passed as parameter to the REXX exec. If the dataset name is not fully qualified (not specified within quotes), the current user's TSO prefix is appended at the start of the dataset name.

The data lines in the panel are named: L.1 through L.9. These data lines are filled with the first nine records read from the dataset.

For readers not familiar with TSO commands and ISPF Dialog Manager, the salient points needed for this example are described in the following section.

The TSO ALLOC command allocates a dataset. Allocation here means associate a dataset name with a file name, which can then be used in the REXX EXECIO command. The following TSO ALLOC command is needed in this example:

```
ALLOC FILE(FILEIN) DSN(datasetname) SHR
```

- The FILE keyword specifies the file name, in this case FILEIN. This file name is used by the EXECIO command to access the dataset.

- The DSN keyword specifies the dataset name.

- The SHR keyword specifies that the dataset already exists and can be shared by more than one user. The OLD keyword is required if the dataset cannot be shared by more than one user.

The ISPEXEC (ISPF Dialog Manager) DISPLAY command displays a panel. ISPF and REXX share a common pool of variables, i.e. variables having the same names are available to both environments. However, ISPEXEC variable names have a maximum length of eight characters. The variable is the variable name prefixed with an ampersand (&).

```
DISPLAY PANEL(panelname)
```

- The PANEL keyword specifies the name of the panel to be displayed.

The panel definition for RXPAN is not an essential part of example, this book is primarily concerned with REXX and not with the usage of ISPF Dialog Manager.

This example requires that the two PF keys (PF5 and PF6) are to be processed by the REXX exec. This is done by altering the standard definition for the corresponding system variables for these two keys (ZPF05 and ZPF06, respectively), and by storing these new definitions in the ISPF profile pool, which is done with the VPUT (ZPF05 ZPF06) PROFILE statement. This example assigns the character strings PF05 and PF06 to ZPF05 and ZPF06, respectively.

After the panel has been displayed, pressing either the PF5, PF6 or the END key will return control to the point of invocation. The panel processing section has set the two variables: &CSRPOS, &CURSOR, to contain the position of the cursor within a line and the name of the line, respectively, i.e. &CSRPOS will contain a number and &CURSOR will contain L.n (n is the line number). The character string (PF05 or PF06) which has been assigned to the pressed PF key is stored in the ZCMD system variable. Pressing the END key (usually PF3) sets the display return code to 8.

15.4.2 Implementation

REXX exec:

```
1       /* REXX - argument: datasetname */
2       PARSE UPPER ARG dsn;
3       IF SUBSTR(dsn,1,1) \= "'"
          THEN dsn = "'""SYSVAR(SYSPREF)"."dsn"'";
        /* allocate dataset */
4       "ALLOC F(FILEIN) DA("dsn") SHR REUS";
        /* read dataset */
5       "EXECIO * DISKR FILEIN (STEM d. FINIS)"
6       ADDRESS ISPEXEC;
7       nrec = d.0; /* number of records read */
        /* initialisation */
8       alphal = "abcdefghijklmnopqrstuvwxyz";
9       alphau = "ABCDEFGHIJKLMNOPQRSTUVWXYZ";
10      allcase = alphal||alphau||'0123456789';
11      lowercase = alphal||alphal||'0123456789';
12      uppercase = alphau||alphau||'0123456789';
        /* display loop */
13      DisplayRC = 0;
14      DO WHILE DisplayRC < 8;
15         CALL SetDisplay;
16         IF DisplayRC /= 8 THEN DO;
```

```
17          SELECT;
18            WHEN ZCMD = "PF05" THEN CALL MakeLowerCase;
19            WHEN ZCMD = "PF06" THEN CALL MakeUpperCase;
20            OTHERWISE NOP;
21          END;
22        END;
23      END;
        /* rewrite dataset */
24      ADDRESS MVS "EXECIO" nrec "DISKW FILEIN (STEM d. FINIS)";
25      EXIT; /* terminate exec */
26      MakeLowerCase:
27        newcase = lowercase;
28        CALL ChangeCase;
29        RETURN;
30      MakeUpperCase:
31        newcase = uppercase;
32        CALL ChangeCase;
33        RETURN;
34      ChangeCase:
        /* change case */
35        PARSE VALUE cursor WITH d '.' lno;
36        ix = csrpos;
37        exp = "line = "cursor;
38        INTERPRET exp; /* extract selected line */
39        wk = TRANSLATE(line,,allcase,'0')||' '; /* alphanumeric -> 0 */
40        wk = TRANSLATE(wk,'0','0'XRANGE(),' '); /* remainder -> ' ' */
        /* <wk> now contains either 0 or ' ' */
        /* locate previous delimiter */
41        iy = LASTPOS(' ',wk,ix);
42        IF iy = ix THEN RETURN; /* cursor not in a word */
        /* locate following delimiter */
43        iz = POS(' ',wk,iy+1);
44        wd = SUBSTR(line,iy+1,iz-iy-1); /* extract selected word */
45        wd = TRANSLATE(wd,newcase,allcase,' ');
46        exp = "d."lno "= OVERLAY(wd,"cursor",iy+1,iz-iy-1)";
```

```
47        INTERPRET exp;

48        RETURN;

49     SetDisplay:

50        j = 1; /* line index */

51        l. = ''; /* clear panel lines */

52        DO i = 1 TO 10 WHILE j < nrec;
              /* set panel lines from buffer */

53           l.i = d.j;

54           j = j+1;

55        END;

56        "DISPLAY PANEL(RXPAN)";

57        DisplayRC = RC; /* save display return code */

58        RETURN;
```

Panel definition:

```
┌ RXPAN ──────────────────────────────────────────────────────────────┐
│ )ATTR                                                                 │
│ $ TYPE(TEXT) INTENS(HIGH)                                             │
│ # TYPE(TEXT) INTENS(LOW)                                              │
│   TYPE(INPUT) CAPS(ON)                                                │
│ ] TYPE(OUTPUT) INTENS(LOW) JUST(ASIS) CAPS(OFF)                       │
│ )BODY EXPAND(//)                                                      │
│ %/-/ Dataset Display /-/+                                             │
│ %COMMAND ===>_ZCMD                                  #SCROLL%===>_SAMT+ │
│ %                                                                     │
│ )L.1                                                                  │
│ )L.2                                                                  │
│ )L.3                                                                  │
│ )L.4                                                                  │
│ )L.5                                                                  │
│ )L.6                                                                  │
│ )L.7                                                                  │
│ )L.8                                                                  │
│ )L.9                                                                  │
│ %                                                                     │
│ %PF5 make lowercase  PF6 make uppercase                               │
│ )INIT                                                                 │
│ &ZCMD = ''                                                            │
│ IF (&SAMT = &Z) &SAMT = 'HALF'                                        │
│ /* pre-assign function key definitions                               │
│ &ZPF05 = 'PF05'                                                       │
│ &ZPF06 = 'PF06'                                                       │
│ VPUT (ZPF05 ZPF06) PROFILE                                            │
│ )REINIT                                                               │
│ &ZCMD = ''                                                            │
│ REFRESH (ZCMD)                                                        │
│ )PROC                                                                 │
│ &CSRPOS = .CSRPOS                                                     │
│ &CURSOR = .CURSOR                                                     │
│ )END                                                                  │
└──────────────────────────────────────────────────────────────────────┘
```

Explanation:

1   Comment containing the word REXX must be the first statement of a REXX exec.

2   Fetch parameter (dataset name) passed to exec, store in DSN variable. The UPPER keyword converts any lowercase input to uppercase.

3   Check whether first character of DSN (dataset name) is "'". If not, prefix with the user's TSO prefix.

4   Use the TSO ALLOC command to allocate the dataset. The allocated dataset is assigned the FILEIN file name.

5   The complete dataset is read into the D. stem variables. The number of records read is stored in the D.0 variable.

6   The environment is set for ISPF Dialog Manager (ISPEXEC). This means that all subsequent REXX commands are passed to ISPEXEC.

7   The number of records read is stored in the NREC variable.

8   Define the variable ALPHAL to contain the full set of lowercase alphabetic characters (a through z).

9   Define the variable ALPHAU to contain the full set of uppercase alphabetic characters (A through Z).

10   Define the variable ALLCASE to contain the full set of alphanumeric characters (lowercase alphabetic, uppercase alphabetic and numerics).

11   Define the variable LOWERCASE to contain the full set of lowercase alphanumeric characters (a through z and 0 through 9).

12   Define the variable UPPERCASE to contain the full set of uppercase alphanumeric characters (A through Z and 0 through 9).

13   Initialise the DisplayRC variable to zero. DisplayRC is used to contain the return code from the panel display. Panel return code 8 means that the END key has been pressed, which, by convention, indicates that processing is to be terminated.

14   Introduce a DO-loop which is to be performed until the END key is pressed.

15   Invoke the SetDisplay subroutine.

16   Introduce a DO-group to be performed provided that the variable DisplayRC has not been set to 8.

17   Introduce a SELECT-block.

18   Invoke the MakeLowerCase subroutine if the PF5 key has been pressed.

19   Invoke the MakeUpperCase subroutine if the PF6 key has been pressed.

20   If neither key has been pressed, perform no particular processing. The pseudo-instruction NOP is not strictly necessary in the OTHERWISE clause, but it can be used to emphasise that no processing is to be done.

21   Terminate the SELECT-block introduced by statement 17.

22   Terminate the DO-group introduced by statement 16.

23   Terminate the DO-loop introduced by statement 14. This is the end of the display processing, the END key has been pressed.

24   Rewrite the dataset. The ADDRESS MVS clause is required to reset the environment because the current environment has been set to ISPEXEC.

25   Terminate the exec with code 0.

26   Introduce the MakeLowerCase subroutine.

27   Assign the lowercase definitions to the NEWCASE variable.

28   Invoke the ChangeCase subroutine to convert the marked word using the translation table contained in NEWCASE.

29   Return to the point of invocation. This is the logical end of the subroutine.

30   Introduce the MakeUpperCase subroutine.

31   Assign the uppercase definitions to the NEWCASE variable.

32   Invoke the ChangeCase subroutine to convert the marked word using the translation table contained in NEWCASE.

33   Return to the point of invocation.

34   Introduce the ChangeCase subroutine. The translation table to be used is contained in NEWCASE.

35   Analyse the contents of the CURSOR variable, which contains the name of the marked line. The variable CURSOR contains an entry of the form: L.n, n being the line number. This line number is assigned with the PARSE instruction to the LNO variable. The first operand (.) following the WITH keyword is a placeholder. The second operand ('.') is the delimiter.

36   Set the cursor position (within the line) to the IX line index.

37   Build a statement in EXP, which will assign the contents of cursor (line) to the LINE variable.

38   Perform the statement built in the EXP variable. This moves the selected display line into the LINE variable.

39   Translate all alphanumeric characters (a-z, A-Z, 0-9) to '0', and append a single blank character at the end of the transformed data, which is then assigned to WK.

40   Translate all other characters in the transformed data to blank. The WK variable contains only 0's (representing alphanumeric characters) and blanks (representing all other characters, i.e. word delimiters).

41   The first delimiter before the current cursor position (in IX) is determined by searching backwards. This is the position of the delimiter immediately in front of the marked word, it is assigned to IY.

42   If the contents of IX and IY are identical, the cursor has not been positioned within a word, and no further processing is performed.

43   The position of the next delimiter working forwards is determined and assigned to IZ. This is the position of the delimiter immediately following the marked word.

44   The limits (IY+1,IZ-1) of the marked word have now been determined. It is assigned to the WD variable.

45   The contents of WD are translated using the NEWCASE as transformation table.

46   Build a statement in EXP, which will overlay the marked line (CURSOR contains its name) with the transformed marked word.

47   Perform the statement built in the EXP variable. This overlays the selected display line with the transformed marked word.

48   Return to point of invocation.

49   Introduce the SetDisplay subroutine.

50   Initialise the line index (J).

51   Initialise L. stem variables. Non-initialised REXX variables are not valid when used in the ISPF environment.

52   Introduce a DO-loop which is performed nine times (the number of panel display lines) provided that the last buffer record (NREC) has not been reached. The control variable (i, the panel display line number) is incremented by one for each iteration through the DO-loop.

53   Move the buffer record line to the corresponding panel display line.

54   Increment the buffer line number.

55   Terminate the DO-loop initiated in statement 52. The control variable (I) is not strictly necessary. It is used to improve the robustness of the exec, i.e. facilitate the detection of misplaced END statements.

56   Display the ISPF Dialog Manager panel RXPAN. The ISPEXEC environment has been set in statement 6.

57   Assign the return code resulting from the panel display in the variable DisplayRC. The RC special variable is set by the invoked command, in this case ISPEXEC DISPLAY PANEL.

58   Return to the point of invocation.

15.5 WORKED EXAMPLE 4

This example shows a REXX command processor. Although it is written in COBOL, other conventional programming languages (e.g. Assembler) could also be used. This example illustrates most of the programming techniques that are used with the REXX service routines (process parameters passed to the program, invoke REXX from a program (here an in-store exec), use shared variable services). Chapter 14 contains a detailed description of the REXX programming interfaces.

15.5.1 Specification

The COBOL program (BCMDX) is a command processor. The command string contains two words: the keyword VARNAME and the name of the variable that contains the data to be written to a VSAM-ESDS dataset (filename: VSAMFILE).

BCMDX passes the command string to an in-store exec (function) that parses the string into the VARNAME keyword and the variable name. This in-store exec returns the variable name as function result. The IRXEXCOM service is called to fetch the data for this variable name. The fetched data are written as a single record in the VSAM dataset.

To avoid over-complicating the program, it can process only a single record. No new interfacing techniques are required to extend the program to write a set of stem variables (stem.1, stem.2, etc.) or to process the contents of the queue. The reader is invited to make these changes, and so extend REXX to process VSAM datasets. The command string could be expanded to provide the necessary parameters (queue or stem processing, read or write, file name, etc.).

15.5.2 Implementation

Program code:

```
IDENTIFICATION DIVISION.
PROGRAM-ID. BCMDX.
ENVIRONMENT DIVISION.
INPUT-OUTPUT SECTION.
FILE-CONTROL.
     SELECT VSAM-FILE    ASSIGN TO AS-VSAMFILE
               ORGANIZATION SEQUENTIAL
               ACCESS MODE  SEQUENTIAL
               FILE STATUS  FILE-STATUS,
                            VSAM-STATUS.
DATA DIVISION.
FILE SECTION.
FD VSAM-FILE
     RECORD IS VARYING IN SIZE
     FROM 1 TO 256 CHARACTERS
     DEPENDING ON VARDATA-LEN.
01  VSAM-REC.
   02 VARDATA PIC X(256).
WORKING-STORAGE SECTION.
01 VARNAME PIC X(250).
```

```
          01 VARNAME-LEN PIC 9(9) BINARY.

          01 VARDATA-LEN PIC 9(9) BINARY.

          01 REC-LEN PIC 9(9) BINARY.

          01 RETURN-STATUS.

            02 FILE-STATUS        PIC X(2).

              88 FILE-OK          VALUE '00' '04' '97'.

            02 VSAM-STATUS.

              03 VSAM-RETURN      PIC 9(2) COMP.

              03 VSAM-FUNCTION    PIC 9(1) COMP.

              03 VSAM-FEEDBACK    PIC 9(3) COMP.

          LINKAGE SECTION.

          01 ENVNAME PIC X(8).

          01 PCMDSTRING POINTER.

          01 CMDLEN PIC 9(9) BINARY.

          01 PUSERTOKEN POINTER.

          01 RETCODE PIC S9(9) BINARY.

          01 CMDSTRING.

            02 CMDSTRING-ELEMENT OCCURS 1 TO 32767 DEPENDING ON CMDLEN.

              03 CMDSTRING-CHAR PIC X(1).

1         PROCEDURE DIVISION

              USING ENVNAME PCMDSTRING CMDLEN PUSERTOKEN RETCODE.

              SET ADDRESS OF CMDSTRING TO PCMDSTRING

        * Analyze command string

2             CALL 'GETPARM' USING CMDLEN CMDSTRING VARNAME VARNAME-LEN

3             CALL 'GETVAR' USING VARNAME VARNAME-LEN VARDATA VARDATA-LEN

              OPEN OUTPUT VSAM-FILE

              IF NOT FILE-OK

                DISPLAY 'VSAM OPEN ERROR:' FILE-STATUS

4               MOVE 4 TO RETCODE

                STOP RUN

              END-IF

              WRITE VSAM-REC

              CLOSE VSAM-FILE

5             MOVE 0 TO RETCODE

              STOP RUN.
```

```
            * Parse parameter string

6             IDENTIFICATION DIVISION.

              PROGRAM-ID. GETPARM.

              DATA DIVISION.

              WORKING-STORAGE SECTION.

7             01 INSTBLK.

                  02 INSTBLK-ACRONYM PIC X(8) VALUE 'IRXINSTB'.

                  02 INSTBLK-HDRLEN PIC 9(9) BINARY VALUE 128.

                  02 FILLER PIC X(4).

                  02 INSTBLK-ADDRESS POINTER.

                  02 INSTBLK-USEDLEN PIC 9(9) BINARY.

                  02 INSTBLK-MEMBER PIC X(8) VALUE ' '.

                  02 INSTBLK-DDNAME PIC X(8) VALUE ' '.

                  02 INSTBLK-SUBCOM PIC X(8) VALUE ' '.

                  02 FILLER PIC X(4).

                  02 INSTBLK-DSNLEN PIC 9(9) BINARY VALUE 0.

                  02 INSTBLK-DSNAME PIC X(72) VALUE ' '.

8             01 EVALBLOCK.

                  02 EVALBLOCK-EVPAD1 PIC 9(9) BINARY VALUE 0.

                  02 EVALBLOCK-EVSIZE PIC 9(9) BINARY VALUE 34.

                  02 EVALBLOCK-EVLEN PIC 9(9) BINARY VALUE 0.

                  02 EVALBLOCK-EVPAD2 PIC 9(9) BINARY VALUE 0.

                  02 EVALBLOCK-EVDATA PIC X(250) VALUE ' '.

9             01 ARGLIST.

                  02 ARGLIST-ENTRY OCCURS 2.

                      03 ARGSTRING-PTR POINTER.

                      03 ARGSTRING-NULL REDEFINES ARGSTRING-PTR PIC 9(9) BINARY.

                      03 ARGSTRING-LENGTH PIC 9(9) BINARY.

10            01 INSTORE-VECTOR.

                  02 INSTORE-ENTRY OCCURS 3.

                      03 INSTORE-PTR POINTER.

                      03 INSTORE-NULL REDEFINES INSTORE-PTR PIC 9(9) BINARY.

                      03 INSTORE-LENGTH PIC 9(9) BINARY.

              01 STMT1 PIC X(31) VALUE 'PARSE ARG . "VARNAME" varname .'.

              01 STMT2 PIC X(14) VALUE 'RETURN varname'.
```

```
        01 P1 POINTER.

        01 P2 POINTER.

        01 FLAGS PIC X(4) VALUE X'40000000'.

        01 P4 POINTER.

        01 P6 POINTER.

        01 P0 POINTER.

        01 P0-NULL REDEFINES P0 PIC 9(9) BINARY.

        LINKAGE SECTION.

        01 CMDLEN PIC 9(9) BINARY.

        01 CMDSTRING.

           02 CMDSTRING-ELEMENT OCCURS 1 TO 32767 DEPENDING ON CMDLEN.

              03 CMDSTRING-CHAR PIC X(1).

        01 NAME-LEN PIC 9(9) BINARY.

        01 VARNAME PIC X(250).

        PROCEDURE DIVISION

             USING CMDLEN CMDSTRING VARNAME NAME-LEN.
11           CALL 'SETPTR' USING STMT1 INSTORE-PTR(1)

             MOVE 31 TO INSTORE-LENGTH(1)

             CALL 'SETPTR' USING STMT2 INSTORE-PTR(2)

             MOVE 14 TO INSTORE-LENGTH(2)

             MOVE -1 TO INSTORE-NULL(3)

             CALL 'SETPTR' USING INSTORE-VECTOR INSTBLK-ADDRESS

             MOVE 24 TO INSTBLK-USEDLEN

             SET ARGSTRING-PTR(1) TO ADDRESS OF CMDSTRING

             MOVE CMDLEN TO ARGSTRING-LENGTH(1)

             MOVE -1 TO ARGSTRING-NULL(2)

             CALL 'SETPTR' USING ARGLIST P2

             CALL 'SETPTR' USING INSTBLK P4

             CALL 'SETPTR' USING EVALBLOCK P6

             MOVE 0 TO P0-NULL
12           CALL 'IRXEXEC' USING P0 P2 FLAGS P4 P0 P6 P0 P0
13           MOVE EVALBLOCK-EVDATA TO VARNAME

             MOVE EVALBLOCK-EVLEN TO NAME-LEN

             GOBACK.

        * Subprogram to set pointer
```

```
         IDENTIFICATION DIVISION.
14       PROGRAM-ID. SETPTR.
         DATA DIVISION.
         LINKAGE SECTION.
         01 PARMDATA PIC X(8).
         01 PARMPTR POINTER.
         PROCEDURE DIVISION
             USING PARMDATA PARMPTR.
             SET PARMPTR TO ADDRESS OF PARMDATA
             GOBACK.
           END PROGRAM SETPTR.
          END PROGRAM GETPARM.
        * Get variable
         IDENTIFICATION DIVISION.
15       PROGRAM-ID. GETVAR.
         DATA DIVISION.
         WORKING-STORAGE SECTION.
         01 DUMMY-PARM PIC X(4).
16       01 SHVBLOCK.
             02 SHVNEXT PIC S9(9) BINARY VALUE 0.
             02 SHVUSER PIC S9(9) BINARY.
             02 SHVCODE PIC X(1) VALUE 'F'.
             02 SHVRET  PIC X(1).
             02        PIC X(2).
             02 SHVBUFL PIC S9(9) BINARY VALUE 250.
             02 SHVNAMA POINTER.
             02 SHVNAML PIC S9(9) BINARY.
             02 SHVVALA POINTER.
             02 SHVVALL PIC S9(9) BINARY.
         LINKAGE SECTION.
         01 VARNAME PIC X(250).
         01 VARDATA PIC X(250).
         01 LNAME PIC 9(9) BINARY.
         01 LDATA PIC 9(9) BINARY.
         PROCEDURE DIVISION
```

```
                    USING VARNAME LNAME VARDATA LDATA.
                    SET SHVNAMA TO ADDRESS OF VARNAME
                    MOVE LNAME TO SHVNAML
                    SET SHVVALA TO ADDRESS OF VARDATA
          17        CALL 'IRXEXCOM' USING BY CONTENT 'IRXEXCOM'
                    BY REFERENCE DUMMY-PARM DUMMY-PARM SHVBLOCK
                    MOVE SHVVALL TO LDATA
                    GOBACK.
                END PROGRAM GETVAR.
              END PROGRAM BCMDX.
```

Explanation (for the REXX-relevant coding):

1   Five parameters are passed to the command processor: ENVNAME (the environment name), PCMDSTRING (a pointer to the command string), CMDLEN (the length of the command string), PUSERTOKEN (a pointer to the user token; not used in this example), and RETCODE (the return code set by the command processor).

2   Call the GETPARM subprogram to obtain the variable name from the command string. The variable name and its length are returned in VARNAME and VARNAME-LEN, respectively.

3   Call the GETVAR subprogram to obtain the contents of the specified variable name.

4   Abort the command processor if the VSAM file cannot be opened.

5   Terminate the command processor.

6   The GETPARM subprogram returns the variable name from the command string. The GETPARM subprogram uses the powerful REXX facilities to parse the command string; the command string parameter is passed to an in-store exec, which returns the specified variable name.

7   The INSTBLK contains information pertaining to the in-store exec statements.

8   The EVALBLOCK contains the result returned from the exec.

9   The ARGLIST defines the arguments to be passed to the exec. The command string is the first argument. The address of the second argument is set to -1 to indicate the end of the argument list.

10   The INSTORE-VECTOR defines the in-store statements (address and length). The address of the last entry is set to -1 to indicate the end of the list.

11   Call the SETPTR subprogram to obtain the address of the specified first parameter. *Note*: Because the ADDRESS OF clause can be used only for LINKAGE SECTION entries, a subprogram is required to meet these conditions.

12   Call the REXX IRXEXEC service function (the REXX interpreter) to process a REXX exec; depending on the parameters, the exec can be either in-store or external. The FLAGS parameter specifies the form of the exec (command, function or subroutine), which in turn determines the form of the result. The X'40000000' setting specifies a function call.

13   Set the returned name (EVALBLOCK-EVDATA) and its length (EVALBLOCK-EVLEN) into the appropriate invocation parameters.

14   The SETPTR subprogram returns the address of the specified data area.

15   The GETVAR subprogram returns the contents of the REXX variable whose name is passed as parameter.

16   The SHVBLOCK contains the parameters that the IRXEXCOM REXX service function requires.

17   Call the REXX IRXEXCOM service function to access the REXX variable pool. SHVCODE specifies the operation to be performed; 'F' = fetch.

Invocation exec:

```
1      /* REXX - BCMDX test */
2      ADDRESS TSO "ALLOC F(VSAMFILE) DA(VSAM.ESDS) SHR";
3      rec = 'alpha beta gamma';
4      ADDRESS USER " VARNAME REC ";
```

Note: This invocation exec assumes that BCMDX has been registered as command processor for the USER environment.

Explanation:

1   Comment containing the word REXX must be the first statement of a REXX exec.

2   Allocate the VSAM file.

3   Set the record data to the REC variable.

4   Pass the command to the processor for the USER environment.

15.6 WORKED EXAMPLE 5

This example serves two purposes: it is a programmed REXX function, and it illustrates how a REXX exec can be reprogrammed in a conventional programming language (here Assembler, although other programming languages could have been used).
   This example is functionally the same as the D2P function in Section 10.3.1 that was coded in REXX. Such reprogramming can be desirable for frequently-used routines where performance is critical.

15.6.1 Implementation

Program code:

```
        D2P     CSECT
        D2P     AMODE 31
                BAKR  14,0      save regs and return addr
                BASSM 12,0      set base register
                USING *,12
                LA    13,SA     set internal save-area
1               USING EFPL,1
                L     11,EFPLEVAL  PTR(Evaluation Block)
                L     11,0(11)     A(Evaluation Block)
                USING EVALBLOCK,11
                L     10,EFPLARG    PTR(Argument List)
                USING ARGTABLE_ENTRY,10
                LA    15,4     preload ReturnCode
2               LM    3,4,ARGTABLE_ARGSTRING_PTR
                LTR   4,4       test parameter length
                BM    EXIT      parameter missing
                CH    4,=H'16'  maximum length
                BH    EXIT      parameter too long
* test whether negative
                SH    4,=H'1'   LengthCode(source)
                MVI   SIGN,0    set default sign
                CLI   0(3),C'-'
                BNE   NOTNEG    non-negative
                MVI   SIGN,#NEG negative field
                SH    4,=H'1'   correct length
                LA    3,1(3)    data address
                BM    EXIT      parameter error
        NOTNEG  LA    5,1(4)    determine number
                SRL   5,1        of byte-pairs
                SLL   5,4       LC -> 1st half-byte
                OR    4,5       OR the two lengths
                EX    4,EXPACK  PACK
                SRL   5,4       restore true LC(target)
```

```
                    CLI    SIGN,#NEG   test whether negative
                    BNE    POSITIVE
                    IC     0,VAR(5)    last character
                    N      0,=X'000000F0'   clear sign
                    O      0,=X'0000000D'   set negative
                    STC    0,VAR(5)    last character
3       POSITIVE EX 5,EXMOVE    move to result
                    LA     5,1(5)      L(result)
                    ST     5,EVALBLOCK_EVLEN entry size
                    LA     15,0        normal function return
4       EXIT    PR    ,             program end
* execute instructions
EXPACK    PACK  VAR(0),0(0,3)
EXMOVE    MVC   EVALBLOCK_EVDATA(0),VAR
* data areas
SA        DS    18F           save-area
VAR       DS    CL16          result work-area
SIGN      DS    X
#NEG      EQU   X'01'
* DSECTs
                    IRXEFPL     External Function Parm List
                    IRXEVALB    Evaluation Block
                    IRXARGTB    Argument List
                    END
```

Explanation:

1 Register 1 points to the function invocation parameter list. The actual function argument (the value to be processed) is obtained from the Argument List.

2 Get the first argument: register 3 has the address of the argument, and register 4 its length. This function expects a single parameter (it ignores any additional parameters).

3 Move the result and its length into the Evaluation Block that was passed as invocation parameter.

4 Terminate the function. The function return code set into register 15 is not the function return value but an indicator as to whether the function processing was successful.

16

REXX Compiler

All the makers of dictionaries, all compilers who do nothing else than repeat backwards and forwards the opinions, the errors, ...

A Philosophical Dictionary: Plagiarism

Voltaire

16.1 INTRODUCTION

The REXX compiler is a separate program product that can be leased to produce an executable load module from a standard REXX exec. The compiler provides three major benefits:
- improved performance compared with interpreted code
- improved syntax checking
- improved source code security (the source code can be neither read nor changed).

The term compiler, however, is somewhat of a misnomer; in effect an intermediate code is produced that requires the run-time component (supplied with the compiler) to execute.

There are two general forms of output depending on from where the compiled exec is to be run:
- from a procedure library (precompiled exec)
- from a load library (object exec).

When the REXX compiler is available, the benefits of the ease and speed of development using the interpreter can be combined with the robustness and execution speed of compiled code. Because of the extra overhead in using the compiler, it will normally only be used at the end of the development phase to produce the final productive code.

16.2 JCL PROCEDURES

IBM supplies a number of JCL procedures for the REXX compiler, the most useful of which are:
- REXXC   Compile-only (object and precompiled output)
- REXXCG   Compile and go (precompiled output)
- REXXCL   Compile and link
- REXXL   Link-only (of object).

The compiler output destination depends on which of the CEXEC and OUTPUT options are set. CEXEC and OUTPUT output is written to SYSCEXEC and SYSPUNCH, respectively. The procedures with link write the output to SYSLMOD. Because these standard procedures define all these outputs as files, the invoker must override them if the output is to be retained. The OBJECT-option requires that a stub be specified (EFPL is used as default). The predefined stubs call the compiled exec appropriately for the environment (for example, prepare the parameters). Table 16.1 summarises the procedures.

Example:
These procedures use the following symbolic parameters (when appropriate):
- OPTIONS   Compiler options
- STUB   The name of the stub to be included.

Table 16.1 - REXX compiler procedure summary

Procedure	Stepname	Symbolic Parameters	DD-Names
REXXC	REXX	OPTIONS	SYSCEXEC SYSPUNCH (SYSIN)
REXXCL	REXX	OPTIONS STUB	SYSPUNCH (SYSIN)
	PLKED LKED		SYSLMOD
REXXCLG	REXX	OPTIONS STUB	SYSPUNCH (SYSIN)
	PLKED LKED GO		SYSLMOD
REXXL	PLKED LKED	STUB	(SYSIN) SYSLMOD

The DD-name in parentheses is not defined in the procedure but must be specified.

16.2.1 REXXC Procedure

The REXXC procedure produces a compiled REXX exec. Two outputs are produced:
- SYSCEXEC CEXEC output
- SYSPUNCH OBJECT output.

Default symbolic parameters:
- OPTIONS XREF OBJECT

Example:

```
//S1 EXEC REXXC,OPTIONS='XREF OBJECT'
//REXX.SYSIN DD *
 /* REXX */
 MYFUNCT:
  PARSE ARG p
  SAY 'ARG:' p
  RETURN 0
//REXX.SYSPUNCH DD DSN=TUSER01.SYSEXEC.EXEC(MYFUNCT),DISP=SHR
```

16.2.2 REXXCL Procedure

The REXXCL procedure produces a compiled REXX exec that is linked to produce a load module. Two outputs are produced:
- SYSPUNCH OBJECT output
- SYSLMOD load module.

REXXCL combines the REXXC and REXXL procedures. A stub appropriate for the execution environment must be specified.

Default symbolic parameters:
- OPTIONS XREF OBJECT NOCEXEC
- STUB   EFPL

Example:

```
//S1 EXEC REXXCL,STUB=EFPL,OPTIONS='OBJECT NOCEXEC DLINK'
//REXX.SYSIN DD *
 /* REXX */
 MYFUNCT:
  PARSE ARG p
  SAY 'ARG:' p
  RETURN 0
//LKED.SYSLMOD DD DSN=TUSER01.TEST.LOAD(MYFUNCT),DISP=SHR
```

16.2.3 REXXCLG Procedure

The REXXCLG procedure produces a compiled REXX exec that is linked to produce a load module. The resulting load module is executed (as batch job). Two outputs are produced:
- SYSPUNCH OBJECT output
- SYSLMOD   load module.

REXXCLG adds a GO-step to the REXXCL procedure. A stub appropriate for the execution environment must be specified.

Default symbolic parameters:
- OPTIONS   XREF.OBJECT NOCEXEC
- STUB   MVS

Example:

```
//S1 EXEC REXXCLG,PARM.REXX='SL NOCEXEC XREF OBJ'
//REXX.SYSIN DD *
 /* REXX */
 SAY 'Message from REXX'
//LKED.SYSLMOD DD DSN=TUSER01.TEST.LOAD(RXHI),DISP=SHR
```

16.2.4 REXXL Procedure

The REXXL procedure links a compiled REXX object to produce an executable program. One output is produced:
- SYSLMOD   load module.

Default symbolic parameter:
- STUB   EFPL

Example:

```
//S1 EXEC REXXL,STUB=MVS
//PLKED.SYSIN  DD DSN=TUSER01.SYSEXEC.EXEC(MYCALL),DISP=SHR
//LKED.SYSLMOD DD DSN=TUSER01.TEST.LOAD(MYCALL),DISP=SHR
```

16.3 COMPILER OPTIONS

Various options can be specified for the REXX compiler. The most important are discussed briefly:
- CEXEC   Produce a precompiled exec (written to SYSCEXEC)
- DLINK   Produce object output with external references
- OBJECT   Produce an object (written to SYSPUNCH)
- PRINT   Produce a compiler listing (written to SYSPRINT)

- SLINE   The compiled output contains the source code (this option is required
             to support the SOURCELINE built-in function)
- TESTHALT   Support the HI command
- TRACE   Support the TRACE command
- XREF   Produce a cross-reference.

All these options can be negated (e.g. NOEXEC).

16.4 COMBINING COMPILED OBJECTS

The demands of modular programming and reusable components mean that an installation will have a library of (compiled) object components. Such components (modules) can be fetched in two ways: implicitly or explicitly.

Modules fetched implicitly are stored on an appropriate library (exec or load, depending on the form of the compiled output) and are loaded when required (dynamic loading). This has two advantages: the invoking program is smaller and the loaded module is always up-to-date. This method, however, has the disadvantage of the extra overhead in finding and loading the module. Although this can be mitigated by using function packages, this may not be warranted for applications that are not used widely.

Explicitly loaded modules (static loading) are included in the executable program. This overcomes the disadvantage of implicit loading but without the advantages provided by implicit loading.

16.4.1 Produce a Statically Loaded Program

Each of the components must be present as a load module with the appropriate stub. These individual components are then linked together to form the executable program.

16.4.1.1 Create MYFUNCT as load module.
```
//S1 EXEC REXXC,OPTIONS='OBJECT DLINK'
//REXX.SYSIN DD *
/* REXX */
MYFUNCT:
 PARSE ARG p
 SAY 'ARG:' p
 RETURN 0
//REXX.SYSPUNCH DD DSN=TUSER01.SYSEXEC.EXEC(MYFUNCT),DISP=SHR

//S2 EXEC REXXL,STUB=EFPL
//PLKED.SYSIN  DD DSN=TUSER01.SYSEXEC.EXEC(MYFUNCT),DISP=SHR
//LKED.SYSLMOD DD DSN=TUSER01.TEST.LOAD(MYFUNCT),DISP=SHR
```

These two jobs could be combined using the REXXCL procedure.

16.4.1.2 Create MYCALL as load module.

```
//S1 EXEC REXXC,OPTIONS='OBJECT DLINK'
//REXX.SYSIN DD *
 /* REXX */
 PARSE ARG goparm
 PARSE PULL inparm
 SAY 'precall'
 CALL MYFUNCT 'args:' goparm inparm
 SAY 'postcall'
//REXX.SYSPUNCH DD DSN=TUSER01.SYSEXEC.EXEC(MYCALL),DISP=SHR


//S1 EXEC REXXL,STUB=MVS
//PLKED.SYSIN  DD DSN=TUSER01.SYSEXEC.EXEC(MYCALL),DISP=SHR
//LKED.SYSLMOD DD DSN=TUSER01.TEST.LOAD(MYCALL),DISP=SHR
//S1 EXEC REXXCL,STUB=MVS,OPTIONS='OBJECT NOCEXEC'
//REXX.SYSIN DD *
 /* REXX */
 SAY 'pre-call'
 CALL MYFUNCT 'myarg'
 SAY 'post-call'
//LKED.SYSLMOD DD DSN=TUSER01.TEST.LOAD(MYCALL),DISP=SHR
```

16.4.1.3 Create MYPROG as executable program. MYPROG combines MYCALL and MYFUNCT.

```
//S2       EXEC PGM=IEWL,PARM='XREF,REUS,MAP,LIST'
//SYSLMOD  DD  DSN=TUSER01.TEST.LOAD,DISP=SHR
//SYSUT1   DD  UNIT=WORK
//SYSPRINT DD  SYSOUT=*
//SYSLIN   DD  *
 INCLUDE USERLIB(MYCALL)
 INCLUDE USERLIB(MYFUNCT)
 NAME MYPROG(R)
//USERLIB DD DSN=TUSER01.TEST.LOAD,DISP=SHR
```

16.4.1.4 Sample execution.

```
//GO EXEC PGM=MYPROG,PARM='alpha beta'
//STEPLIB DD DSN=TUSER01.TEST.LOAD,DISP=SHR
//SYSTSPRT DD SYSOUT=*
//SYSTSIN  DD *
gamma
```

Sample output:

```
precall
ARG: args: alpha beta gamma
postcall
```

16.5 STUBS

A compiler stub is required to provide the appropriate invocation environment (place invocation parameters into the appropriate form, invoke the compiled exec, place the returned values into the appropriate form). The following predefined stubs are available:

- CALLCMD   TSO CALL
- CPPL   TSO command
- EFPL   External REXX routine (default)
- CPPLEFPL   TSO command or external REXX routine
- MVS   MVS program (JCL).

16.5.1 CALLCMD Stub

The CALLCMD stub provides the linkage for the invocation of a compiled REXX exec as a TSO CALL.

Example:

```
//S1 EXEC REXXCL,STUB=CALLCMD
//REXX.SYSIN DD *
 /* REXX */
 SAY 'PLEASE ENTER YOUR NAME'
 PARSE PULL NAME
 SAY 'YOUR NAME:' NAME
//LKED.SYSLMOD  DD DSN=TSUSE01.USER.LOAD(HI2),DISP=SHR
```

Invocation:

```
PROC 0
 CALL SEWB(HI2)
```

Execution:

```
PLEASE ENTER YOUR NAME
Jones
YOUR NAME: Jones
```

16.5.2 CPPL Stub

The CPPL stub provides the linkage for the invocation of a compiled REXX exec as a TSO command.

Example:
```
//S1 EXEC REXXCL,STUB=CPPL
//REXX.SYSIN DD *
 /* REXX */
 ADDRESS ISPEXEC
 "DISPLAY PANEL(PN)"
//LKED.SYSLMOD  DD DSN=TUSER01.SEWB.LOAD(HIPN),DISP=SHR
```

Invocation (as ISPF command)
```
 /* REXX */
 ADDRESS ISPEXEC
   "SELECT CMD(HIPN) LANG(CREX)"
```

16.5.3 EFPL Stub

The EFPL stub provides the linkage for the invocation of a compiled REXX exec as a REXX CALL.

Example:
```
//S1 EXEC REXXCL,STUB=EFPL
//REXX.SYSIN DD *
 /* REXX */
 SAY "Please enter your name"
 PARSE PULL name
 SAY "Your name:" name
//LKED.SYSLMOD  DD DSN=TSUSE01.USER.LOAD(HIRX),DISP=SHR
```

Invocation:
```
 /* REXX */
 CALL HIRX
```

16.5.4 CPPLEFPL Stub

The CPPLEFPL stub provides the functionality of both the CPPL stub and the EFPL stub, i.e. the resulting program can be executed as either a TSO command or a REXX CALL.

16.5.5 MVS Stub

The MVS stub provides the linkage for the invocation of a compiled REXX exec as a normal (batch) executed program.

Example:
```
//S1 EXEC REXXCL,STUB=MVS
//REXX.SYSIN DD *
```

```
/* REXX */
SAY 'Please enter your name'
PARSE PULL name
SAY 'Your name:' name
//LKED.SYSLMOD   DD DSN=TSUSE01.USER.LOAD(RX1),DISP=SHR
```

Invocation:

```
//S2 EXEC PGM=RX1
//STEPLIB DD DSN=TSUSE01.USER.LOAD,DISP=SHR
//SYSTSPRT DD SYSOUT=*
//SYSTSIN DD *
Smith
```

Execution:

```
Please enter your name
Your name: Smith
```

16.6 PERFORMANCE

The performance gains that the REXX compiler makes depend on the form of the
code. A REXX exec that contains only native REXX code (only REXX instructions
and functions) will show the greatest improvements over interpreted code. On the
other hand, a compiled REXX exec that makes extensive use of command
environment services (such as ISPEXEC, TSO) will show less improvement.

Example:
The following REXX exec that uses only native REXX facilities (the SYSVAR MVS
command functions are outside the timed section) was timed.

```
/* REXX - Run time measurement */
su1 = SYSVAR('SYSSRV') /* get current service units */

DO i = 1 TO 100000
  r = i//10000
  q = i%10000
  IF r = 0 THEN DO
    SAY q
  END
END

su2 = SYSVAR('SYSSRV')

SAY 'SU:' su2-su1
EXIT
```

Whereas the compiled version required only 20,000 service units (SUs), the interpreted version used 617,000 SUs, i.e. a 30-fold increase.

A service unit is a weighted measure of system loading (CPU time, main-memory, peripherals, etc.). As such it is not an absolute measure and will depend on installation settings, hardware, etc. However, it is usually a better basis to compare resource usage than just CPU time or elapsed time.

16.7 COMPATIBILTY

Compiled execs should run without change. The load library will need to be added to the execution job. The only direct change is the addition of the LANG(CREX) parameter for the execution of an ISPEXEC command.

I have personally converted a large REXX application with approximately 4000 lines. I had to change just one statement for it to compile correctly (there was a missing END in an exception processing routine in the original version). The compiled version ran without any problems.

Example:
```
    ADDRESS ISPEXEC
      "SELECT CMD(HIPN3) LANG(CREX)"
```
rather than
```
    ADDRESS ISPEXEC
      "SELECT CMD(HIPN3)"
```

16.7.1 Execution Sequence

When a REXX exec (with the same name) is present in both native mode and compiled form, the following sequence determines which version is used.

1. Internal function in the source (unless the name of the invoked module is specified as an explicit literal (e.g. CALL 'myfunct' or "myfunct"()), in which case sequence 2-4 applies (external module).

2. Function packages.

3. Load library concatenation.

4. Procedure library concatenation.

17

Other Environments

... We accept and welcome, therefore, as condition to which we must accommodate ourselves, great inequality of environment, the concentration of business, industrial and commercial, in the hands of a few, ...

Wealth, For the North American Review

Andrew Carnegie

17.1 INTRODUCTION

Although this book concentrates on the TSO environment, this chapter also provides a brief description of two other associated REXX environments:
· REXX for CICS
· REXX for UNIX Services.

Examples are provided to show the use of these environments.

17.2 REXX FOR CICS

"REXX for CICS" provides a hierarchically structured high-level file system, the REXX File System (RFS).

"REXX for CICS" provides several transactions to support REXX. The most important of these are:
· EDIT (or some installation-assigned transaction name), an editor to a REXX exec in the CICS environment. The name of the exec specified for EDIT must have .EXEC as qualifier, e.g. EDIT MYTRANS.EXEC. EDIT is a full-screen editor that stores execs in the RFS.

·   A REXX runtime component used to execute the REXX exec in the CICS
    environment from the user's RFS.
·   FLST (or some installation-assigned transaction name), file list utility as a full-
    screen interface to the RFS. Execs can be directly executed from FLST.

Example:

```
/* REXX */

message = "REXX/CICS Write/Read Queue";
i = LENGTH(message);

"CICS SEND TEXT ERASE FROM(message)";
"CICS RECEIVE INTO(reply) MAXLENGTH(72) LENGTH(i)";

/* write message to queue */
tqsname = 'myqueue';
outmsg = "write a message to a queue";
len = LENGTH(outmsg);
"CICS WRITEQ TS QUEUE(tsqname) FROM(outmsg) LENGTH(len)";

/* read back*/
"CICS READQ TS QUEUE(tsqname) INTO(inmsg)";

SAY "READ QUEUE:";
SAY "LENGTH:" LENGTH(inmsg);
SAY inmsg;

"CICS SEND TEXT ERASE FROM('REXX/CICS end')";
"CICS RECEIVE INTO(reply) MAXLENGTH(72) LENGTH(i)";

"CICS RETURN";
```

This simple example writes a message to a queue (named MYQUEUE), reads back this
queue and lists the contents. Both CICS and REXX instructions are used for the
input/output.

17.3 REXX FOR UNIX SERVICES

"REXX for UNIX Services" provides access to UNIX services from TSO. The SYSCALL
environment passes the commands to UNIX. The SYSCALLS('ON') function
establishes the SYSCALL environment (the corresponding SYSCALLS('OFF') removes
the environment). The ADDRESS SYSCALL instruction sets the current address
environment.

SYSCALL commands invoke the OS/390 UNIX callable service associated with the command verb.

Example 1:

```
/* REXX */
pfx = "/u/tuser01"
CALL SYSCALLS 'ON'
ADDRESS SYSCALL
'READDIR 'pfx' s. info.'
DO i=1 TO s.0
  IF info.i.ST_TYPE = S_ISDIR
    THEN fn.i = s.i '*' /* directory */
    ELSE fn.i = s.i    /* regular file, etc. */
END
DO i=1 TO s.0
  SAY fn.i
END
```

This example reads and lists tuser01's user directory. An asterisk identifies directory entries.

```
. *
.. *
.profile
.setup
.sh_history
bin *
chiworld.c
chiworld.o
cpp0.exe
cpp0.c
stderr
stdout
unaerx.class
unaerx.java
```

Example 2:

```
/* REXX */
RC = SYSCALLS('ON')
IF RC <> 0 THEN DO
  SAY 'RC:'RC '; SYSCALLS environment could not be established'
  EXIT 12
END
ADDRESS SYSCALL
"open /u/tuser01/cpp.c" o_rdonly
IF retval < 0 THEN error(retval)
fd = retval
"read (fd) buf 1000"
IF retval < 0 THEN error(retval)
SAY LEFT(buf,retval)
```

```
"close (fd)"
IF retval < 0 THEN error(retval)
EXIT
error:
  PARSE ARG rc
  SAY 'Retval:'rc
EXIT 8
```

This example reads and lists the contents of the `tuser01/cpp.c` file.

18

Program Development
Every vital development in language is a development of feeling as well.

Philip Massinger

T.S.Eliot

18.1 INTRODUCTION

Program development consists essentially of five phases:
· design
· coding
· testing
· commissioning
· maintenance.

Figure 18.1 illustrates these development phases. For simplicity, each phase returns to the design phase, although errors found in one phase may return to the previous phase (in particular, if testing detects coding errors, then the code will need to be corrected). The usual development diagram has been extended to include the use of standard components (**program reusability**).

The aim of program development should be to rationalise the development process. **Efficiency** should be one of the main considerations in the program development. Efficiency has many aspects and is to some extent subjective, but typically encompasses such aspects as **use of resources**, **readability**, **reliability**, and **maintainability** of a program. Resources are those used during development and operation. Resources in this context include both human and machine resources; ou should expend as little effort as possible during the development and running of a program (but without neglecting other important aspects).

The aspects of **performance** and **compatibility** can also be of importance for a program. A feature of the REXX language is its **expansibility**.

The programming practices discussed in this chapter are principally concerned with their use with REXX. A specialised text should be consulted for the more general aspects of 'good programming'.

The REXX language allows much flexibility; how this flexibility is used is up to the programmer. In many cases it is better not to use all the facilities which are available (for example, the use of self-defining terms rather than explicit literals).

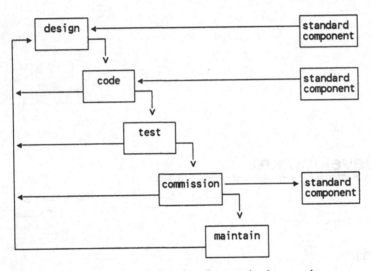

Figure 18.1 - Program development phases

18.2 REUSABILITY

Program reusability has several aims, the most important of which are the related topics of **productivity** and **standardisation**. Reusability primarily affects three phases: design, coding and commissioning. The design phase specifies which reusable components can be used. The coding phase makes use of reusable components. The commissioning phase makes available a new reusable component.

18.2.1 Productivity

The use of reusable components affects productivity in two ways:
·   The use of existing components obviously saves the effort of developing a
    program (with the associated effort for the coding, testing and maintenance)
    and so can positively affect the productivity. However, poor design of a
    reusable component can add to the development effort of the programs that use
    it. Similarly, a poorly implemented reusable component can have negative
    effects.
·   A reusable component will normally need more development effort compared
    with that required for a custom program. The need to determine potential users
    and their requirements can add to the complexity of designing the component.
    Similarly, a more general interface will increase the complexity of coding and
    so add to the testing effort. Reusable components must be publicised and may
    need to be adapted to changing requirements and conditions.

These two factors lead to a break-even point: the number of users that warrant the
development of a reusable component. This break-even point is typically around 4.
In other words, only when this break-even point is reached does it make economic
sense to write a reusable component, although there may be other aspects that
justify its use. This, of course, is a somewhat paradoxical situation: obviously, a
reusable component cannot be used unless it is available beforehand, but initially
there will probably not be sufficient users to justify its existence.

18.2.2 Standardisation

Standardisation, through the use of reusable components, can act positively in an
installation by improving the understandability of application code. When
application code uses standard (reusable) components, it is typically easier to be
understood by persons new to the project. This can improve the interchangeability
of team members.

18.3 READABILITY

Readability, as the word says, is the ease with which a program can be read, i.e. a
physical characteristic. A program which is not easy to read is not easy to
understand; however, the converse does not necessarily apply - a program which
is easy to read may not also be easy to understand.

Readability can be influenced in a number of ways:
·   Do not use uppercase exclusively. It is well known that text written in
    uppercase is more difficult to read than text written in mixed case. I use the
    convention: instructions, non-internal functions and keywords are written in
    uppercase, all other entries are written in lowercase. Similarly, I use double
    quotes (") for normal literals and single quotes (') to delimit parameterised
    operands - unless a quote-delimited operand is to be passed to some
    environment or the literal itself contains the delimiting quote, for example,
    "O'Brien".

· Format the program in a logical (structured) manner. Devise some consistent method to format structured constructions (Do-groups, Select-blocks, etc.). For example, indent at least two positions for each hierarchy in a Do-group, start related Then and Else clauses in the same column. My first recommendation to colleagues with a program which does not function correctly is to first structure the program - in many cases the errors resolve themselves. Table 18.1 shows that structuring a program is not just a visual nicety (this structuring exercise did not change the functionality).

· If possible, rather than having a large monolithic program, divide the program into manageable portions, for example, as internal (or external) functions and routines. Unfortunately, this may have an adverse effect on the performance; externally invoked routines have a very significant performance penalty. However, this can be countered by storing the individual components as modules and then use a standard utility (e.g. IEBGENER using concatenated input files, see example) to combine them as a single runable module, which then has internal calls without a performance penalty.

· The actual conventions adopted are not so significant, consistency is more important.

	original version	revised version
lines of code	299	241
GoTos	87	0
labels	44	0
errors	3	0

Table 18.1 - Example of the benefits of a structured program

Example:

```
//S1        EXEC PGM=IEBGENER
//SYSPRINT DD SYSOUT=*
//SYSUT1    DD DSN=TUSER01.REXX.EXEC(GOCPP),DISP=SHR
//          DD DSN=TUSER01.REXX.EXEC(GOHIST),DISP=SHR
//SYSUT2    DD DSN=TUSER01.REXX.EXEC(NEWVERS),DISP=SHR
//SYSIN     DD DUMMY
```

This example shows how the IEBGENER utility program can be used to combine individual routines (modules), here GOCPP and GOHIST, as a composite module, here NEWVERS.

18.4 RELIABILITY

A program can be regarded as being reliable (robust) when it behaves in a controlled fashion under both normal and abnormal (exception) conditions.

Certain features that make it easy to write REXX programs pose potential problems, because they conflict with the aims of reliability.

·   A non-initialised symbol has its name (in uppercase) as content, for example, the symbol Alpha has ALPHA as its initial content. Although this simplifies the writing of alphanumeric literals, there is the danger that the contents of the symbol are inadvertently altered in the program. This potential problem can be solved in one of two ways:
    · write alphanumeric literals explicitly, e.g. "ALPHA";
    · set the SIGNAL ON NOVALUE instruction to trap the use of non-initialised symbols.

·   A REXX program is normally interpreted. This means that the syntax is only checked when the statements are executed, and so latent syntax errors may be present in sections of the code which are not normally executed, for example, error processing routines. The TRACE SCAN instruction can be used to perform a syntax scan of the complete program, and should be used before a program is put into productive use. The TRACE SCAN instruction also detects such errors as missing or excessive END statements. *Note*: This is no longer an SAA instruction. The REXX compiler performs a more comprehensive syntax check and will detect many latent errors, and, so if it is available, should also be used for this reason and not just to improve performance.

·   Input data should be checked for validity if there is the possibility that they may be invalid, for example, numeric data entered from the keyboard. As a general rule, error messages should be displayed as near as possible to the source of error.

·   Terminate a program with an explicit EXIT instruction.

·   Terminate each statement (clause) with a ";" (semicolon). This can avoid unexpected continuations being made.

·   Use control variables on END statements. This can help in the detection of unbalanced blocks.

18.5 MAINTAINABILITY

Maintainability is the ease with which a program can be maintained. Maintenance is not restricted to removing errors but also includes extensions to include new functions and facilities. The observance of readability and reliability considerations is a necessary requirement for a maintainable program.

18.6 COMPATIBILITY

The major significance of compatibility is when a REXX program is to be used in various environments, for example, in MVS/TSO and CICS. Full compatibility is only possible for those applications which do not use components specific for the particular host environment - such components include input/output (other than simple terminal operations using the SAY and PULL instructions). The porting of applications can be simplified by isolating environment-specific features in subroutines.

Certain implementations demand a comment as the first line in a REXX program, in some cases this comment must also include the word REXX - this is necessary to be able to distinguish REXX execs from other procedures. It is in any case a good practice to begin every REXX exec with a comment briefly describing its function.

18.7 PERFORMANCE

REXX programs are typically interpreted, although a MVS compiler is available. An interpreted program has advantages such as flexibility, ease of debugging (errors can be corrected on the spot), speed of implementation (compilation, etc. is not required). However, the execution time of a REXX program will of necessity be longer than a compiled program. The size of this time-overhead is influenced by optimising measures built into the REXX interpreter (for example, certain REXX implementations can use preprocessed intermediate code as input, which saves the conversion of the source program to this code) and how the REXX program is written. Although modularity considerations dictate the use of external routines (modules), their invocation has a very significant performance penalty (Section 18.3 suggests a solution).

The best way to influence the speed of execution is not to execute unnecessary statements. Two examples: use a SELECT instruction rather than a series of IF statements, when not more than one condition can apply; if the result of a function is required more than once, set the result into an intermediate variable (see Example 1).

To improve performance use REXX instructions rather than built-in (REXX) functions. The powerful PARSE instruction can be used instead of some functions (see Example 2). The overhead to invoke built-in functions is less than that required to write user-written functions, although user-written functions can be optimised by including them in a function package.

The REXX compiler program product can be used for time-critical applications, although the speed benefits must be evaluated in regard to the compiler cost. It may be desirable to use a conventional programming language to recode frequently-used time-critical routines; Chapter 14 describes how to code such routines.

Example 1:
If a timestamp is to be created, use code such as (4 function invocations)

```
temp = TIME('Normal'); /* hh:mm:ss */
timestamp = SUBSTR(temp,1,2)SUBSTR(temp,4,2)SUBSTR(7,2);
```

rather than (6 function invocations)

```
hh = TIME('Normal');
timestamp = SUBSTR(hh,1,2);
mm = TIME('Normal');
timestamp = timestamp || SUBSET(mm,4,2);
ss = TIME('Normal');
timestamp = timestamp || SUBSET(ss,7,2);
```

Note: In this particular example, the TRANSLATE and SPACE functions could be used to reduce the number of function invocations to three; see Section 10.2.44.

Example 2:

The PARSE instruction used to extract a word from a list of words requires approximately half the time than that required by the WORD built-in function. The following two code fragments serve the same purpose.

```
str = "alpha beta gamma"
PARSE VAR str . w2 .
```

```
str = "alpha beta gamma"
w2 = WORD(str,2)
```

18.8 EXPANSIBILITY

An important feature of the REXX language is its expansibility. The proposed ANSI REXX specification envisages implementation-specific interfaces, for example, to access the REXX variable pool. The MVS REXX implementation offers a wide range of interfaces that can be used to create installation-specific or application-specific language extensions. Such extensions are usually functions and command processors written in a conventional programming language. These extensions can be used by execs in the same way as the standard components. An increasing number of products provide such REXX interfaces for execs.

Third-party DB2 interfaces are a typical example; such products normally allow an exec to formulate an SQL query, pass the query to the SQL processor, and to retrieve the query results as REXX variables that can be further processed using standard REXX instructions. Another example could be a site-specific data access routine. These can provide higher-level access to essentially low-level data, etc. Chapter 13 provides a detailed description and usage examples of the most commonly used service routines.

18.9 STEPWISE REFINEMENT

REXX is wellsuited to using the technique known as stepwise refinement. Stepwise refinement, which is related to prototyping, means that the application is successively extended to incorporate increased functionality, i.e. similar to top-down programming. In REXX, stepwise refinement is implemented by initially writing stub procedures, which are later filled with program code.

The concept of stepwise refinement is based on reducing the programming task to entities that are such a (small) size so as to be easily understandable.

18.10 PORTABILITY

REXX is becoming increasingly a portable language with most hardware and software environments now supporting REXX. With the ANSI standardisation, this process will probably increase. Despite the commonalty of the basic REXX language and functions, most implementations have their own extensions.

18.11 TESTING

REXX, being an interpretive language, is inherently easier and quicker to test than a compiled programming language; there are no compilation and link phases, and many of the errors can be corrected during the debugging process (although the source code must be updated to make the changes permanent). Furthermore, the type-free nature of REXX avoids many errors in the first place. Despite this, the testing phase should not be underestimated; the test phase is often longer that the programming phase. Even execs written for personal purposes need to be tested. Chapter 9 contains a detailed description of the REXX debugging facilities.

Compared with compiled complied programs, interpreted programs have a hidden danger; whereas a compiled program must be processed in its entirety, only those parts of an interpreted program that are executed are analysed (errors may be lurking in the non-executed parts). If possible, the testing process should exercise the whole program. *Hint*: Use interpretive trace to devise error situations, etc., to force all program paths to be executed.

18.12 RUN-TIME DEBUGGING

Despite extensive tests, it is quite possible that REXX applications do not perform as expected. This is particularly the case for large-scale applications that contain many thousands lines of code. The inherent nature of REXX as an interpretative language (even for compiled execs) can be used to advantage here by the REXX application providing a "trapdoor" to activate the trace facility (see Sections 9.5 (Interactive Debug) and 9.6 (Parametric Debug)). There are several possible ways of implementing such a run-time debug capability.

Method 1
In the simplest case, a parameter is passed to the initial procedure, which then activates the interactive trace and passes this invocation parameter to all invoked procedures. These procedures then also activate the interactive trace and pass this invocation parameter to the procedures they invoke, etc.

Example:

```
/* REXX */
PARSE ARG p1 p2 debug
IF debug = 'Y' THEN TRACE ?R
...
        CALL rout p3 p4 p5 debug /* invoke routine */
```

In this example, p1 and p2 are invocation parameters required by the procedure.
This method has the disadvantage that the debugging information can be too
extensive for large applications. Method 2 shows how the debugging can be better
tailored.

Method 2
The method I normally use involves defining a "global" variable that contains the
names of the procedures (routines) to be debugged. Every routine has a trace block
that imports this variable and tests whether its own name is contained in the list of
names. It activates the interactive trace when this is the case. Depending on the
form of the application, there are different ways of entering the names into this
list. In a Dialog Manager application, a good solution is to provide a simple dialog
in which the names can be entered (for example, as a command line). Another
possibility is to pass the names to the initial invoking exec, which then stores them
in a global variable. However, this has the disadvantage that the routine(s) to be
debugged must be known in advance.

Example:

```
/* REXX */
ADDRESS ISPEXEC
dbglist = "AADB2 AADB7"
"VPUT (dbglist)"
CALL AADB2

/* REXX */
AADB2:
INTERPRET RTTRX('AADB2') /* TRACE */
...
EXIT

/* REXX - RTTRX Run-time trace */
RTTRX:
PARSE ARG procname
ADDRESS ISPEXEC "VGET (dbglist trmode)"
IF (trmode = 1) THEN SAY 'PROC:'procname TIME('L')
IF WORDPOS(procname,dbglist) > 0 THEN DO
  SAY 'PROC:'procname
  RETURN "TRACE ?R"
END
RETURN '' /* no trace */
```

For simplicity, the initial exec sets the debug list (DBGLIST) statically. The RTTRX run-time trace routine shown in this example accepts a second parameter (TRMODE), which when set to 1 logs the names of all invoked routines with the time of invocation and so displays the calling sequence.

18.13 DEVELOPMENT WITH THE REXX COMPILER

When the REXX compiler is available, this provides the best of both worlds. An interpretive language is quicker to develop and test. The (final) compiler version provides an optimised production version.

Appendix A

Syntax Notation

A.1 SYNTAX DIAGRAM

This book makes use of syntax diagrams to describe the syntax of expressions. Syntax diagrams are read left to right, top to bottom.

▶▶— Start of statement.

—▶◀ End of statement.

—▶ Statement is continued.

▶— Statement continuation.

▶⊤ Junction (branch-point). The principal path is the horizontal.

· Mandatory items cannot be branched around.

Example:

```
▶—mandatory──────────▶
           └optional┘
```

"mandatory" must be selected - it is on the horizontal path and cannot be branched around. At the following junction either the horizontal path (containing no entries) or the branch containing the entry optional can be taken - as there is a choice of paths the entry is optional.

· If **one** of a number of mandatory items must be selected, then these items appear in a vertical stack.

Example:

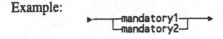

Either "mandatory1" or "mandatory2" must be selected. The first junction offers two paths - one path with mandatory1 and one path with mandatory2 - each path contains an entry, and so one of the entries is mandatory.

· Multiple options appear in a vertical stack, **one** of the specified options may be selected.

Example:

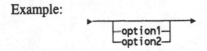

Either "option1" or "option2" may be selected. The first junction offers three paths: the horizontal path has no entry; the other two paths have the entries option1 or option2, respectively. Because the paths containing option1 and option2 need not be taken, these entries are optional.

· Repetition is indicated by the following construction:

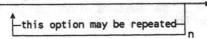

n at the right, if present, specifies the maximum number of times that the item **may** be repeated; the default value is unlimited.

Example:

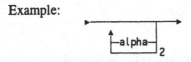

In this case the first junction is at the right-hand side of the diagram. This junction offers two paths, one horizontal to the end of the statement and one vertical. This vertical path has two subsequent paths, which contain either alpha or no entry. The value 2 indicates that up to two repetitions may be made. This means that either no entry, one alpha entry or two alpha entries may be specified.

· If the repeat path contains an item, then this item is mandatory for repetitions.

Example:

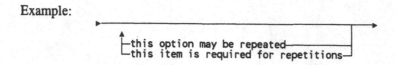

- An item written in upper case must be spelled exactly as shown, an item written in lower case is replaced by a valid entry (described in the text). An underlined entry is the default value.

Example:

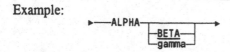

The first item is mandatory and must be ALPHA; the second item is optional, the default value is BETA. If an item is selected, then it must be a valid value for gamma.

- If an item is written italicised, then this is a parameter, the definition of which follows.

Example:

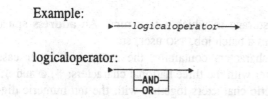

logicaloperator:

The "logicaloperator" parameter may be replaced by one of the optional values: AND or OR.

A syntax diagram is formed by combining the simple elements defined above.

A.2 FONT

The sans serif font is used to depict commands, keywords or dataset names.

Example:
The statement TSO DELETE is a command which invokes the TSO component DELETE.

Appendix B

Glossary

address space   The virtual storage in which a task runs. An **address space** accommodates a batch job, TSO user, etc.

alphabetic   The set of characters containing the lower and upper case letters together with the three national characters: #, @ and $.

alphanumeric   The **alphabetic** characters together with the ten numeric digits: 0 through 9.

ASCII   American Standard Code for Information Interchange. The data encoding used primarily on personal computers (PCs), workstations, etc.

batch   One or more programs (steps) that run as a unit (job) without user interaction.

Binder   The IBM program to combine one or more object modules into an executable load module. The Binder is the replacement for the Linkage Editor, although this still exists (the two terms are often used interchangeably). The Binder provides more advanced features when used in conjunction with PDSEs (mixed case names, etc.).

C++(TM)   C-Plus-Plus. Originally object-oriented extension to the C programming language, but now a programming language in its own right.

CICSTM   Customer Information Control System. IBM's most popular online transaction processing system.

clause   In the REXX sense, a subexpression.

CLIST Command List. Procedure consisting of TSO commands and subcommands and control statements. CLISTs are also known as **command procedures**. The more powerful and portable REXX has largely superseded the CLIST language.

CMS Conversational Monitor System. VM's user interface - functionally similar to TSO.

command procedure *see* CLIST.

compiler A software component which converts a source program into an object module. The REXX Compiler licensed product converts a REXX exec into an executable module, which, however, requires the REXX runtime component.

database A logically related set of named data elements. Database systems largely isolate users from the physical data storage.

DATABASE2™ IBM's relational database, usually known as DB2.

dataset Synonymous term for a file.

DBCS Double-Byte Character Set. A set of pairs of characters used to represent characters in Far-East languages (Chinese, Japanese, Korean, etc.).

DBMS Database Management System.

DB2™ DATABASE2. IBM relational database.

DD Data Definition. The JCL statement used to assign the physical data (dataset, printer output class, etc.) to the logical dataset defined in the program. The **ddname** links the logical dataset to the JCL DD statement.

Dialog Manager ISPF component which administers dialogue facilities. Dialog Manager is usually synonymous with ISPF.

dialogue Man-machine interaction using a terminal directly attached to a computer. Various levels of program systems (application program, terminal monitor program, etc.) control the dialogue.

DSORG Dataset organisation. The organisation of information in a dataset, for example, PS = physical sequential, PO = partitioned organisation (=PDS).

EBCDIC Extended Binary Coded-Decimal Interchange Code. The data encoding used primarily on IBM (and compatible) mainframe computers.

edit macro A procedure (REXX or CLIST) invoked from (or with) the ISPF/PDF Editor to perform a predefined series of operations on the current dataset. An edit macro combines the facilities offered by procedures and the Editor.

EXEC (Uppercase) Execute program or procedure. The JCL statement used to invoke a program or JCL procedure.

exec (Lowercase) Synonymous with a REXX procedure.

FIFO	First-in/First-out. Storage management concept where the elements are retrieved in the same order in which they were inserted - this is also known as **queue processing**.
file	A collection of data (= dataset). With regard to TSO it is equivalent to the JCL DD statement.
filename	The identifier of the **file**. In TSO it is equivalent to the **ddname**.
hexadecimal	Coding scheme which uses 16 as base. The decimal values 10, 11, 12, 13, 14 and 15 are represented by A, B, C, D, E and F, respectively. One byte (8 bits) in hexadecimal notation can be represented by 2 digits, 00 through FF. The prefix or suffix operator x is used to denote a hexadecimal value, for example, '10'x represents decimal 16.
IBM™	International Business Machines Corporation, supplier of ISPF, PDF, OS/390, etc., licensed products.
interpreter	A software component which directly executes a source program without producing an intermediate object module. An interpreter offers more flexibility than a compiler and usually has better diagnostics (the complete source code is available). However, this flexibility is bought at the cost of increased resource usage at run-time.
ISPEXEC	ISPF component which provides dialogue services for CLISTs and REXX procedures.
ISPF	Interactive System Productivity Facility, IBM programming system to provide dialogue facilities. ISPF runs under TSO.
ISPLINK	ISPF component which provides dialogue services for programs.
ISPSTART	ISPF component which initiates the ISPF environment.
ISREDIT	ISPF component which makes available ISPF/PDF Editor services. Such services can be used to implement so-called edit macros.
JCL	Job Control Language. The statements used to control the processing of a batch job. The principal JCL statements are: DD and EXEC.
library	A general term for a partitioned dataset. More correctly, this is a specialised term for a PDSE.
LIFO	Last-in/First-out. Storage management concept where the elements are retrieved in the reverse order as that with which they were inserted - this is also known as **push-down stack processing**.
Linkage Editor	The IBM program to combine one or more object modules into an executable load module. The **Binder** has largely superseded the linkage editor.

link list   System programs (e.g. compilers) which can be invoked without having to specify from which library they come.

load module   Machine-readable Linkage Editor output in a form suitable for loading into virtual storage for execution.

member   Independent part of a partitioned dataset. A member can be directly accessed and processed as if were a sequential dataset.

MVS™   Multiple Virtual Systems operating system, the predecessor to OS/390. For historical reasons, REXX uses the term MVS to refer to the host operating system environment.

object module   Machine-readable compiler output. Object modules are not directly executable but must be converted into an executable format (load module) with the Linkage Editor.

OS/390™   The successor to MVS. TSO REXX uses MVS to identify the host operating system. OS/390 consists of base elements (e.g. the Base Control Program, ISPF, TSO) and optional features, most of which are priced.

partitioned dataset A data set comprising of members. Each member can be accessed directly by means of its (member) name. A partitioned dataset is often called a **library**, although this term nowadays applies to a PDSE (extended partitioned dataset).

PDF   Program Development Facility, IBM dialogue utility package to assist the programmer in program development. PDF is an ISPF application.

PDS   *see* partitioned dataset.

PDSE   Extended partitioned dataset. A more modern library organisation. Although a PDSE has the same programming interface as a PDS, it provides several advantages over PDSes (e.g. self-reorganising, indexed directory access, the number of directory blocks is not predefined). Any one PDSE can contain either load (object) modules or source members, but not both.

phrase   In the REXX sense, one or more characters. A phrase is usually used as argument for a longer string.

PL/I   High-level structured programming language that combines many of the features of COBOL and FORTRAN.

QMF™   Query Management Facility. End-user interface to DB2.

RACF™   Resource Access Control Facility. RACF is an IBM security package.

REXX   Restructured Extended Executor. REXX is a high-level programming language functionally similar to CLIST. The REXX language is more powerful and efficient than the CLIST language.

SAA™   Systems Application Architecture™. SAA is an IBM concept designed to provide a standard interface to the user (application developer).

SBCS Single-Byte Character Set. The standard character set where one byte represents one character, see also **DBCS**.

session The dialogue environment for the current user. TSO is the lowest level session.

shared pool The pool of dialogue variables belonging to the current ISPF session.

source program Input to a compiler. A source program constitutes the "computer instructions" produced by the programmer. Source programs can exist in a number of levels of detail. **Low-level** languages (e.g. Assembler) require that the programmer has an intimate knowledge of the machine instructions available on the computer on which his program will run. **High-level** languages (e.g. PL/I) remove much of this burden from the programmer and enable him to be more concerned with the procedure required to solve his problem; such languages are often referred to as **procedure oriented** languages. So-called **4th generation** languages (REXX offers certain features) are **problem oriented**. Modern high-level languages offer structuring facilities.

string In the REXX sense, one or more characters.

TSO Time Sharing Option, programming system to provide users with on-line access to computing system. Despite the name, TSO is now a standard OS/390 component.

TSO/E Time Sharing Option Extended.

userid The unique code associated with the user when he logs onto the TSO system.

VM™ Virtual Machine. Mainframe operating system which supports the concurrent operation of multiple operating systems. CMS is VM's user interface.

word In the REXX sense, one or more non-blank characters that is separated from the previous and subsequent words by one or more blanks.

word-list In the REXX sense, one or more **words** separated by one or more blanks.

™ Registered trademark of International Business Machines.
(TM) Registered trademark of AT&T.

Index